HENRY SIDGWICK

HENRY SIDGWICK

&

Later Utilitarian Political Philosophy

WILLIAM C. HAVARD

UNIVERSITY OF FLORIDA PRESS
GAINESVILLE
1959

To Wilhelmenia, Sylvia & Deborah

A University of Florida Press Book
published with assistance from
The Ford Foundation

PRINTED BY FLORIDA GROWER PRESS
TAMPA, FLORIDA

Preface

HISTORIANS of political ideas have tended to close their
discussions of English utilitarianism with John Stuart
Mill, who died in 1873. Some commentators even treat
Mill's writings during the last twenty years of his life
as a sort of addendum to utilitarianism proper, indicating that the
inconsistency of Mill's later work demonstrates the untenability of
the basic doctrines of utilitarianism. There is a certain plausibility
in this procedure for several reasons. In the first place the practical
influence of Benthamic utilitarianism was greatest and most direct
before 1850, when the Philosophical Radicals (who were avowedly
Benthamic in their aims and methods) constituted a parliamentary
force that had to be reckoned with. Furthermore, the momentum
of this movement was sufficient to effect a broad consensus on the
efficacy of individualistic liberalism as the basis of public policy, at
least down to the Reform Act of 1867. After 1870, however, the
dominance of classical liberalism as a practical influence was increasingly challenged by legislation of a collectivistic nature, while
at the same time other philosophical schools, especially positivism
and idealism, rose to prominence in an intellectual sphere once
heavily dominated by the utilitarians.

Even if partly justified by these developments, such a break is
especially unfortunate in the history of utilitarian ideas because it

v

has resulted in a tendency to ignore both the influence of utilitarianism on other systems of thought and the persistence of utilitarian doctrines as the basis for the practice of politics in the later liberal (and collectivistic) state. These oversights might have been corrected if more attention had been paid to Henry Sidgwick, the last philosopher in the direct line of the utilitarian tradition.

Writing in the last quarter of the nineteenth century, Sidgwick was certainly the clearest and, considered solely as a *philosopher,* probably the ablest of the English utilitarians after Hume. Although his moral philosophy has continued to receive some of the recognition that it merits, particularly in the works of Professor C. D. Broad, and on occasion one or another of his books has been accorded sporadic attention by individuals in various disciplines, Sidgwick's philosophy as a whole has been somewhat obscured by the tendency to establish a definite (and premature) cutoff date for the history of utilitarian ideas. Even apart from the opportunity that a general review of Sidgwick's ideas affords for establishing the abiding influence of utilitarianism in the course of general opinion and political practice (whether for good or ill), Sidgwick himself deserves treatment as a chapter (perhaps the concluding one) in the history of utilitarianism as a system of political philosophy.

When the subtlety of his thought and the range of his interests are considered in relation to the academic specialization of our times, a number of hazards are involved in the attempt to establish some of the antecedents of Sidgwick's ideas and to relate the core of his philosophy to various aspects of his work. The risks are worth taking because errors of detail can always be corrected by criticism, but lack of perspective resulting from the neglect of certain areas of historical study require confrontation of the problem on a broad front.

Certain aspects of Sidgwick's work lighten the burden of the commentator. It is important, for example, to note that no major shifts took place in the focus of his ideas; he adopted the utilitarian position very early in his academic career, and all of his books turn on a criticism of the earlier doctrines of the school and the working out of correctives to the theoretical weaknesses of the system. This does not mean that there is no development in Sidgwick's thought; on the contrary, the chronology of his publications indicates a gradual broadening of the range of his inquiries into ever more generalized philosophical problems, culminating in the metaphysical speculations of the closing years of his life. In some respects the structure of his work may be compared with Bodin's—each book treats a special set of problems from the perspective of a general philosophy. The parallel cannot be taken too far, however, because the broadening of Sidgwick's philosophical horizon is always very closely related to what went before and does not involve the complex shifts in fundamentals apparent in Bodin. Because of this characteristic unity in diversity, the organizational problem involved in presenting Sidgwick's thought practically solves itself—each major work requires topical presentation. This does not mean, however, that the works may be treated in the order of their appearance. The reader of a study in the history of ideas should have the main conceptions about the nature of man and society of the writer before him at a fairly early stage, even though (as in the case of Sidgwick) these were only partly discernible in the early works and were worked out completely in the later periods of his life. For that reason the order of treatment of Sidgwick's thought proper, which begins in Chapter 3, has followed a logical rather than chronological structure.

For a closely related reason a rather long chapter on earlier utilitarianism has been included. The writer realizes that this chapter traverses ground that has already been covered many times. In fact, the real trouble is that it has been covered almost too well and from too many angles to serve present purposes. The numerous facets of the writings of the earlier utilitarians themselves and the quantity of secondary materials on them seemed to require some reduction and systematization of the main contributions of these early men, in order to provide a compact guide to the theoretical deficiencies of their thought. For it is from basic and omnipresent philosophical defects in his predecessors that the criticism and reconstruction effected by Sidgwick begins; and the appearance of these weaknesses in the methodology, the ethical ideas, the political theory, and the concept of economic policy of the Benthamites required Sidgwick to reformulate the main doctrines of each of these theoretical structures.

The completion of this work in its preliminary form was made possible by a grant from the Southern Fellowships Fund, and the kind assistance of that organization is hereby acknowledged. I also wish to express my gratitude to my acquaintances at the London School of Economics for the stimulating and rewarding experiences that were mine during my years of study there. A special note of appreciation goes to Professor K. B. Smellie, whose critical abilities were given ample scope for application during the preparation of various drafts of this study. His patient guidance and encouragement are warmly acknowledged.

Helpful suggestions were made on several key points by Professor Wilfrid Harrison of the University of Liverpool and by Allen Milne now at Queen's University, Belfast. The manuscript was also read in whole or in part (in various stages of preparation) by Robert J. Harris, Loren P. Beth, and Peter J. Fliess. Their individual acts of helpfulness over the years are too numerous to be fully acknowledged and must, therefore, be recorded as the unrecompensable rewards of friendship. Again, a very special debt is owed to Professor Eric Voegelin, not only for his perceptive suggestions for the improvement of this study, but for his tutorial guidance during my undergraduate and graduate studies, his unparalleled example as a scholar, and his continuing interest and counsel. I also wish to thank the Graduate School of Louisiana State University for furnishing very efficient typing services in the course of preparing the manuscript for publication.

All of these individuals and organizations have contributed in large part to whatever merits the book may possess. The responsibility for defects of fact or interpretation rests entirely with the author.

Contents

CHAPTER ONE

Educator & Philosopher

ENRY SIDGWICK was born in 1838, the year following Queen Victoria's accession; and he died in 1900, the year before the end of her reign. It is not merely by virtue of this chronological accident, however, that the term Victorian may be so suitably applied to Sidgwick, for much of the background and many of the events of his life are readily identifiable with values and patterns of behavior that are in the best sense characteristic of that period. In his middle-class origin, in the history of his education, and in the philosophical, political, and educational problems with which he struggled, certain dominant themes of Victorian life are clearly discernible. Above all, perhaps, there is a Victorian contrast between the quiet simplicity of his ordinary life and the heroic cast of his intellectual achievements.

Sidgwick was born at Skipton in the West Riding of Yorkshire, the fourth child of the Reverend William Sidgwick, who was at the time headmaster of the grammar school at Skipton. Henry Sidgwick's paternal grandfather had been a prosperous cotton spinner at Skipton; and his mother, who was orphaned early in life, had been brought up by an uncle who held the living at Bolton Abbey. Sidgwick's father died in 1841, and after moving several times in a vain attempt to provide a healthful location for her eldest daughter, Mrs. Sidgwick settled in Redland, on the outskirts of Bristol, in

1844. Sidgwick's schooling began here, first under a governess, later at a day school in Bristol, and later still at a boarding school in Blackheath.[1*]

Sidgwick's secondary education corresponded to his position in life; it was cut directly from the pattern of the middle class, whose particular mid-nineteenth-century virtues and aspirations found remarkably apt expression in the reformed public school. Sidgwick's father had been opposed to the public school system on moral grounds, undoubtedly with good reasons since his knowledge of these institutions was based on the period, before Thomas Arnold's tenure at Rugby, when the rule of the bully and deference to public opinion were characteristic.[2] However, acting on the advice of the future Archbishop Edward White Benson, a cousin of Sidgwick's father and later married to Sidgwick's sister, his mother sent young Henry to Rugby in 1852.[3] Arnold had then been dead only ten years, and the atmosphere at Rugby was permeated with the memory of his impact on the moral tone of Victorian life produced by his strong emphasis on the building of character based on the highest ideals of Christian gentlemanliness.

Benson went to Rugby as assistant master in the same year and he proved to be one of the early important influences on Sidgwick. Mrs. Sidgwick moved with her family to Rugby in 1853, and Benson came to live with them. Since Henry also lived at home during his last two years at school, his relations with Benson were far closer than those which normally subsist between a teacher and an exceptionally gifted pupil. Benson was a thorough scholar and a stimulating teacher. Sidgwick said that "the occasional lessons he gave the Sixth far surpassed any other teaching I had at Rugby or indeed afterwards."[4] Although Sidgwick noted that new influences in his second year at Cambridge eventually led to his enlistment as an "Academic Liberal" and thereby profoundly changed his relation to Benson, he never forgot the moral and intellectual example set for him by his cousin. It was his acceptance of Benson as an ideal that decided Sidgwick in favor of an academic career; and it was Benson's implicit preference that led him to choose Trinity College, Cambridge, rather than to take his headmaster's advice to compete for the Balliol Scholarship which was Rugby's most coveted scholarly prize.[5] At any rate, in 1855 Sidgwick went to Cambridge where he was to settle permanently.

*Notes to this chapter begin on page 173.

Sidgwick's whole life was centered in Cambridge. He was there forty-five years, from his entrance until his death, during which time he missed only one term of active work. This exception was the Lent term of 1883 which he spent traveling in Italy with his wife and, for part of the tour, James Bryce.[6]

As an undergraduate Sidgwick showed the intellectual promise that he was to fulfill later. He soon attracted attention; in his second term he divided one of the two Bell Scholarships with J. M. Wilson of St. John's. The scholarships were awarded annually to freshmen who were sons of clergymen. Arthur Holmes, also of St. John's, was awarded the full second scholarship, and with this award a keen competition began between Sidgwick and Holmes which added a stimulus to the traditional rivalry between Trinity and John's. Sidgwick continued to take prizes throughout his residence. In 1857 he won the most coveted classical scholarship, the Craven. Holmes, however, was out of the running, having been the recipient of the award the preceding year.

In his second year at Cambridge Sidgwick became a member of the "Apostles," and his participation in that organization meant more to him perhaps than any of his formal honors. The Apostles were a supposedly secret group who remained select through their policy of co-option of a new member only after every old member had become acquainted with and approved the—again supposedly—unaware candidate. In its earliest days the society had numbered among its membership persons who were, by the time of Sidgwick's admission, some of the most distinguished English men of letters. Tennyson, Hallam, Merivale, and Charles Buller had all been Apostles. It was the practice of the Society to meet every Saturday at eight-thirty in the room of the member who was to open the discussion. A traditional tea, with anchovy toast, was the first order of business, followed by the scheduled essay of the day. After the prepared paper was read, discussion was carried on with each member stating, in turn, his views on the subject. The "question was put" after the discussion, and the meeting was closed by the group's acceptance of one of four questions—three serious, one in jest—presented to them by the following week's host and essayist.

Although Sidgwick was to mingle in intellectual groups of more astute and diversified character than the Apostles, the influence of this exchange of ideas occupied the unique position of having had, in his own view, more effect upon his intellectual life than any single

3

later event. His biographers point out that Sidgwick's high estimation of the effect of these discussions on his development resulted not only from the particular advantages of the organization itself, but also from "the new influx of ideas, the activity of thought and discussion, the theological, scientific and political changes which marked the twenty years 1855-1875. It is enough to give the names of Mill, Comte, Spencer, Strauss, Renan, Carlyle, Matthew Arnold, George Eliot, and Darwin, to remind . . . readers how deep and wide and many-sided the intellectual movement was. The time was such that even sluggish minds were caught by the current and swept into new regions. It was not surprising that Sidgwick, with rapidly maturing powers, with new leisure, like-minded friends, and full opportunity of discussion, should feel at such a time an impulse which the tamer decades that followed could never again so powerfully supply."[7]

In 1858 Sidgwick won five prizes and shared with one of his closest friends, G. O. Trevelyan, the prize for Greek and Latin epigrams. He developed broad intellectual interests at Cambridge, which never left him. He was always attracted by imaginative literature, and though his publications in this line are slight,[8] they indicate a sensitivity that is in contrast with his intellectual forebears, Bentham and James Mill. His long friendship with Arthur Clough, his contacts with Tennyson, and his frequent references in correspondence and in his journal to the novels, belle-lettres, and poetry of his day attest to his continued interest in literature.

Sidgwick completed his degree in 1859. His honors represent a major triumph—he came out first in the Classical Tripos and took the first Chancellor's Medal. Holmes and John's finished a close second to Sidgwick and Trinity. In addition to his success in the classics, he surpassed his own expectations in the January examinations for the mathematical tripos by coming out thirty-third wrangler.[9] Thus he accomplished the difficult task of completing his degree with first class honors in both classics and mathematics.

In October, 1859, Sidgwick was elected to a Trinity fellowship. The transition from student to teacher was a natural one for him, and it was a good time to begin a faculty association with Cambridge. In the first half of the nineteenth century the University had not fully recovered from the long academic decline that it had experienced in the eighteenth century when academic duties had rested lightly on clergymen whose life and work—a mild occupation undertaken to relieve one from the tedium of his social activities—lay elsewhere.[10] In fact, the Knightbridge Professorship of Moral Philosophy, the chair that Sidgwick was later to occupy, is a good example of this lack of interest and endeavor in intellectual pursuits. From 1813 to 1838, for example, it was held as something of a sinecure by Francis Barnes. As late as 1853 Adam Sedgwick, himself a continued exception to the slothful pattern, warned the new Fellows against holding their fellowships into old age. He noted that "there was little to tempt a man of vigorous intellect to pass the whole of his life within the walls of a college, unless he was attracted by the opportunity of study and research, or had a reasonable chance of becoming a Tutor or Bursar."[11]

However, by the time Sidgwick became a Fellow and Assistant Tutor, the beginnings of reform were already well under way. Under the guiding hand of the Chancellor—Prince Albert—the Government and those people at Cambridge who were sincerely interested in the University's welfare were enlisted in support of the Royal and Statutory Commissions on the Universities.[12] The Royal Commission of 1850-1852 and the Acts of 1854 and 1856 "accelerated and consolidated" a process of internal reform which had already been undertaken by the Universities themselves. The Royal Commission recommended a fairly complete plan for the reorganization and expansion of the educational system at Cambridge. These recommendations included administrative changes aimed at tightening the relationship between the work of the colleges and that of the University as a whole, as well as suggestions for more effective overall supervision of the programs in the various degree subjects. In addition, it clearly defined the need for increasing the areas in which honors could be obtained, recommended a corresponding enlargement of the number of University professorships and lectureships, and expressed the necessity for redefining the statutory duties of professors to the University. The work of the Commission and the subsequent revision of the University statutes prepared the way for the Universities to adapt themselves to the changing needs of an industrial society without sacrificing their broader aims.

The object of the Commission was to clear away the constitutional obstructions to internal development and to make the Universities more accessible to the middle classes, more useful to the pass-man, and more serviceable to pure learning. But in principle the Universities affirmed their essence, against Germany and Scotland, as places not of professional but of liberal education in a world which still acknowledged that public life, in the Church, in Parliament, or on the County Bench, was not only a more distinguished, but a better life than the pursuit of wealth by industrial competition.[13]

Among changes at Cambridge which had been produced internally even before the recommendations of the Royal Commission and statutory revision were the establishment in 1848 of the Natural Science Tripos and the Moral Science Tripos. The conditions of both of these divisions were to interest Sidgwick in his capacity as an educational reformer; and the Moral Sciences were, of course, to become his main preoccupation both as a teacher and as a thinker. By the end of the nineteenth century a University member could look back with pride over the preceding forty years which, if ever a period deserved that well-worn adjective, was a golden age of University life at Cambridge. Adam Sedgwick's warning to prospective Fellows was certainly no longer applicable to late Victorian Cambridge; even the most demanding academician would have found the persons, ideas, and activity there sufficiently stimulating.

Sidgwick shared with his Cambridge colleagues the desire for good company, serious discussion, and travel. He first went abroad in the summer after taking his degree. It was at this time that he developed his love for Germany and admiration for the thoroughness of German scholarship. He made another trip in 1860, when he met Ranke and, of more importance to him, Ewald. Ewald attracted him greatly, and although he later found the professor somewhat narrow-minded, he continued to admire his abilities and to attend his lectures. Ewald apparently responded favorably to Sidgwick in return, for the latter wrote his mother in 1864 that Ewald had extended his lectures a half-hour solely for his sake.[14] The real appeal of German intellectual life for Sidgwick lay in its ascetic simplicity. He expressed himself on occasion to the effect that should he have to leave England, yet could fall back on Germany, the banishment would amount only to semi-exile.[15]

After his initiation to the continent, he returned regularly. His sensitive powers of observation enabled him to appreciate the most subtle differences in national modes of life, an understanding which is reflected in his work, especially in the later periods when, in *The Development of European Polity*, he makes extensive use of the historical method to show how political institutions came to be what they are.

In the vacations during the years immediately after taking his degree, Sidgwick began a thorough study of utilitarianism, the philosophy that became the basis of his own thinking. Since this time followed closely on the period in which John Stuart Mill was strongly influenced by Auguste Comte and had, in fact, assisted the spread of Comtian ideas in England through his own work, it was natural that Sidgwick should simultaneously have studied Comte. In the manner characteristic of him, Sidgwick undertook both studies with great care. Dr. John Venn says that he was the only man in Cambridge who had approached Comte "at first hand—that is, otherwise than through the medium of Mill's *Logic*."[16] As a result of these efforts Sidgwick seems to have undergone his only major intellectual metamorphosis. For a short while he was a direct intellectual disciple of Mill and was even "so far inclined towards dogma as to have adopted much of the Positive Philosophy."[17]

Late in life Sidgwick wrote that when he began to read him carefully, Mill was at the "full height of that remarkable influence which he exercised over youthful thought, and perhaps I may say the thought of the country generally, for a period of some years. No one thinker, so far as I know, has ever had anything like equal influence in the forty years or so that have elapsed since Mill's domination began to weaken."[18] The appeal that Mill and Comte had for youth was due to the apparent comprehensiveness of their systems and the thesis of revolutionary social reconstruction embodied in their ideas:

What we aimed at from a social point of view was a complete revision of human relations, political, moral and economic, in the light of science directed by comprehensive and impartial sympathy; and an unsparing reform of whatever, in the judgment of science, was pronounced to be not conducive to the general happiness. This social science must of course have historical knowledge as a basis: but, being science, it must regard the unscientific beliefs, moral or political, of past ages as altogether wrong—at least in respect of the method of their attainment, and the grounds on which they were accepted.[19]

Sidgwick's critical powers were too great and his mind of too independent a turn to permit a close permanent adherence to the system of thought which he found in John Stuart Mill and his utilitarian predecessors. Flaws began to appear in the great structure when carefully examined. Knowledge, method, and values might be derived from sources other than the natural and physical sciences. As early as 1863 in a letter to H. G. Dakyns he unconsciously predicted his future philosophical contribution to the history of utilitarian ideas by saying that "intuitions turn the scale. I shall probably fall away from Mill and Co. for a phase."[20] Three years later he was able to write to Roden Noel that he had "parted company with Mill I feel for ever." By that time he had studied Kant and, while not a Kantian, would "always look on him as one of his teachers."[21]

Philosophically, Henry Sidgwick remained a utilitarian all his life. But after his brief subservience to the doctrinaire form in which utilitarianism had been elaborated by Bentham and the Mills, he altered both the philosophical fundamentals and the practical conclusions of the school. As Lord Bryce puts it: "The system of utility takes in his hands a form so much more refined and delicate than was given to it by Bentham and James Mill, and is expounded with so many qualifications unknown to them, that it has become a very different thing, and is scarcely, if at all, assailable by the arguments which moralists of the idealistic type have brought against the older doctrine."[22]

In the meantime Sidgwick's ties with the intellectual life of Cambridge were growing stronger. He was apparently one of the original members of the Grote Club. This was a small discussion group named after the Reverend John Grote, Knightbridge Professor from 1855 until his death in 1866. For several years the members met at his home in Trumpington, and it was reputed to be the only really speculative society, other than the Apostles, in Cambridge. Although the club was only a small, informally organized discussion group, its meetings brought Sidgwick into direct contact with certain important contemporaries, including in later years Alfred Marshall and W. K. Clifford.

In 1864 Sidgwick's brother William founded the Ad Eundem Society, an inter-university organization which met each term, alternating between Oxford and Cambridge. By this means Sidgwick remained in personal communication with old and new friends at Oxford. Among other persons, this organization kept him in close contact with T. H. Green, whom he had known at Rugby. Green was his foremost intellectual opponent, and their friendly feud was undoubtedly carried on verbally at the Ad Eundem meetings in preparation for their written encounters in books and periodicals.

After his teaching and writing, Sidgwick's part in University reform ranks next in importance among his achievements. Trinity had already established a better record of internal reform than most of the colleges in the early nineteenth century. Even so, the infusion of new blood was necessary for the changes brought about later in the century; "and by a happy chance some of the junior Fellows of Trinity at this time were men who were politically wise as well as enlightened, and therefore not likely to indulge in extravagances. The names of Henry Sidgwick, Coutts Trotter and Henry Jackson, who were elected into fellowships between the years 1859 and 1864, are still remembered in their colleges, but what they and others did to promote its welfare and efficiency is forgotten. And this is regrettable, for it is not the least of their titles to remembrance."[23]

Despite the impetus that had been given to reform by the Commissions of the 1850's, the full implementation of the changes which their efforts involved was necessarily gradual and depended to a large extent on overcoming the prejudices which were displayed among influential Fellows of the various colleges. Apart from the antipathy felt by many conservatives toward any suggested revision of the religious tests, two biases were especially strong. The first was that classics and mathematics alone gave adequate mental training, and the second was that almost any increase in the activities of the University constituted a threat to the independence and prerogatives of the colleges. Both these conceptions stood in opposition to the need for enlargement of the University's educational function expressed by the Royal Commission. These attitudes narrowly circumscribed and formalized the honors curricula, divided college instruction from University instruction and examination to such an extent as to handicap both the ordinary and the honors degree men, and prevented the application of funds to their most efficient use.

The tendency to depreciate studies other than mathematics and the classics, for example, had left the Moral Science Tripos and the Natural Science Tripos in unfortunate positions. Until 1860 honors could be taken in these areas, but success in them did not admit the student to a degree. Both the Moral Science Tripos and the Natural Science Tripos covered too many subjects, they were not supported well enough to secure a sufficient number of outside examiners or to provide valuable honors or fellowships, and they attracted very few students. This failure to give the moral and natural sciences a proper opportunity to prove their worth was ironic because the poor showing of the subjects under such circumstances could be used as a charge against them. Even after their admission to degree status and the establishment of the Boards of Moral and Natural Sciences in 1860, it was necessary for those who were interested in expanding the functions of the University to work extremely hard in order to overcome the poor reputation of these fields.

Fear of interference with the independence of the colleges acted as a supplement to this conservative attitude towards the fields of study in some cases, and provided its own rationale of obstruction to other changes. Many of the colleges did not want to increase the charges of the University on their separate endowments in order to provide the additional University instruction necessary to carry out an expanded responsibility, nor did they concern themselves very much about the University's attempts at building such facilities as laboratories which were so necessary for effective teaching and research in the rapidly diversifying fields of natural science. The colleges also closely guarded what they looked upon as their exclusive right to instruct the undergraduate, thereby helping to perpetuate the old problem of the negligent attitude of the professor toward his University duties and contributing to the excessive use of private tutors in the preparation for examinations, especially by the passmen. Many of the changes necessary to correct this situation were worked out in the two decades 1860 to 1880, during which time practically all honors subjects and all degree subjects were reworked and the system of examinations was substantially overhauled.[24]

As an academic liberal Sidgwick was much concerned with these problems. He favored and worked for very broad expansion of degree subjects and for equalization of the status of these various subjects through the provision for them of adequate instructional staffs and facilities. He was anxious that the University and colleges between them should provide all the instruction required to enable the student to complete his degree without resort to private tutorship. He was strongly opposed to the "Idle Fellowships" and to the over-compartmentalization of instruction and funds by the colleges, and he was an unremitting opponent of the requirement that all entering students qualify in Greek and Latin. By his teaching and by his example as a scholar he did much to raise the prestige of the moral sciences at Cambridge; and because of his willingness to participate actively in the controversy which reform entailed, he contributed in a variety of ways to the broadening of the University's functions in the latter half of the nineteenth century.

Sidgwick's active part in reform comes to light about 1866 when he helped the Board of Moral Sciences make some revision of the reading lists for the Moral Science Tripos.[25] At the college meeting in the same year he brought forward a plan for the appointment of at least one praelector in natural science. Undaunted by the failure of this motion, he was instrumental in preparing and bringing up at the general college meeting of 1867 an extensive program of reform. The resolutions embodying these changes called for the establishment of scholarships and fellowships for students of natural science, for a redistribution of tuition money and a closer supervision of tutors, for a system of praelectors to teach and direct studies in different departments, and for an omission of the words on conformance to the Church of England in the Fellow's Oath. When voted on in December, 1868, the fellowship and tuition provisions carried in the main, but the religious proposal failed, leaving the matter of the oath much as it was until the Tests Act of 1871.[26]

Sidgwick had examined in the Moral Science Tripos since 1865, and in 1867 he shifted from the classics to philosophy by accepting a Moral Science lectureship in place of his position as a classical scholar. Thereafter he could give full time both in teaching and writing to contemporary philosophical problems which had now become his main interest.

In 1869 came the first, and for that matter the only, major crisis in his relations with Cambridge. In June of that year he resigned his assistant tutorship and fellowship in order to free himself from what he regarded as the dogmatic obligations imposed by the necessity of being a bona fide member of the Church of England in order to be a Fellow. At the same time he wrote to E. W. Benson that while he could not accept the Apostle's Creed, he did not intend to secede from the Church of England and that after consulting Joseph Lightfoot "as a sufficiently unconcerned reasonable orthodox clergyman," he assumed that the Creed was not dogmatically obligatory on laymen.[27] Although Bryce and F. W. H. Myers contend that Sidgwick's resignation struck an important blow for the abolition of the tests, Winstanley differs by holding that it was an act of great courage, born of genuine honesty, but that the test issue was already largely settled by 1869 and the resignation, therefore, had little ultimate effect on the matter.[28]

Despite his resignation, Sidgwick's relation with Cambridge was not severed. He "was already so eminent and so respected a figure that all Cambridge felt the absurdity of excluding such a man from its honours and emoluments,"[29] and he was appointed by his College to a lectureship in the Moral Sciences.

The year 1869 also witnessed the foundation of the Metaphysical Society, the most distinguished of all the intellectual organizations to which Sidgwick belonged. The Society grew out of a meeting between James Knowles and Tennyson, and its main purpose was an attempt to bridge by discussion the wide channels between faith and reason, science and revelation, intuition and empiricism. In the middle of the 1870's it could boast a more celebrated membership than any similar organization in England. Within its circles clergymen at the apex of the hierarchy argued with leading English scientists, and distinguished politicians contended against important literary figures. Cardinal Manning, James Martineau, Dr. W. G. Ward, T. H. Huxley, John Tyndall, Ruskin, Bagehot, Froude, Pollock, Frazer, and James and Leslie Stephen were but a random few of its participants.

Although he was not an original member, Sidgwick joined soon after the Society's foundation. He was regular in his attendance at the meetings, which were held monthly except during the summer at the Grosvenor Hotel in London. Sidgwick was a "joiner," but not an indiscriminate one. All the clubs in which he held membership had something to contribute to his intellectual growth, and he firmly believed in the idea that one received from an organization what one put into it. Consequently he was numbered among the most active participants in any society to which he belonged. His interest in the Metaphysical Society is proof positive of this statement. He read six papers to the group during its continuance, which was only one less than the seven papers each contributed by R. H. Hutton and Sir James Stephen, the most prolific members of the organization.[30]

The purpose and efforts of the Metaphysical Society are closely related to a basic religious struggle in Sidgwick—the tension between faith and reason which is so frequently found in the mid-Victorian intellectual. The development of science and the extension of Biblical criticism which had taken place in the middle of the nineteenth century led many people to reinvestigate the foundations of their belief. In the case of an inquiring and philosophical mind like Sidgwick's the investigation was one which continued throughout life.

In order to understand the full implications that this problem contained for Sidgwick, it is necessary to recall the pervasive influence that Anglican Christianity exercised on his day-to-day life during his formative years. Sidgwick was the son of a clergyman and had other clerical connections on both sides of his family. There was an atmosphere of Anglican dominance both in his school and University life, and he himself did not completely abandon the possibility of taking orders until his early twenties. The impact on him of the doubts created by the claims that science and historical criticism had destroyed the evidence for the New Testament miracles was tremendous. After reading Renan's *Etudes d'histoire religieuse* in 1862, he began the study of Hebrew and Arabic in preparation for a comparative historical investigation of religion. This project was carried out, as he explained in a letter written to A. C. Benson near the end of his life, in an attempt to examine the evidence for historical Christianity with "strict scientific impartiality." Naturally his demand for such completely satisfying evidence could never be fulfilled because "no religion which depended on the correctness of historical statements about mysterious events in a foreign country and a remote period could possibly reach the evidential standards which he demanded."[31] Still later he abandoned the idea of historical investigation and concluded that a comparative study of the mystical and ecstasy might be more fruitful, especially if major attention was given to the present rather than to the remote past. By his early forties, some ten years after the religious crisis which involved the resignation of his fellowship, he wrote that he had long since ceased to think of himself as a Christian in the orthodox sense, but he was not inclined to reject the miraculous as such, nor had he rejected theism.

Of his theism he said, "I don't know whether I *believe* or merely *hope* that there is a moral order in this universe that we know, a supreme principle of Wisdom and Benevolence, guiding all things to good ends, and to the happiness of the good. I certainly *hope* that this is so, but I do not think it capable of being *proved.* All I can say is that no opposed explanation of the origin of the cosmos—for instance, the atomistic explanation—seems to me even plausible, and that I cannot accept life on any other term, or construct a rational system of my own conduct except on the basis of this faith." But he recognized that the basic question is not whether one would *like* to believe in God, but whether such belief is *true*. To this he answered, "What criterion have you of the truth of any of the

13

fundamental beliefs of science except that they are consistent, harmonious with other beliefs that we find ourselves naturally impelled to hold. And this is precisely the relation that I find to exist between theism and the whole system of my moral beliefs. Duty is to me as real a thing as the physical world, though it is not apprehended in the same way; but all my apparent knowledge of duty falls into chaos if my belief in the moral government of the world is conceived to be withdrawn."[32]

Sidgwick's belief in the revealed truths of Christianity had been shattered because he could not find historical evidence (in that age of positivistic historiography) to convince him of their accuracy and uniqueness, but he was still compelled by his moral sensitivity to postulate a theistic order of the universe. C. D. Broad sums up this attitude of Sidgwick's as follows:

We cannot make an intellectually coherent system out of the data of sense-perception unless we interpret them in terms of certain general principles, such as the Uniformity of Nature and the Law of Universal Causation, which go beyond them and cannot be proved inductively from them. We cannot make an intellectually coherent system out of the data of our moral intuitions unless we interpret and supplement them in terms of theism, which also cannot be proved from them. Now the latter data are as indubitable as the former, the demand for intellectual coherence is the same in both cases, and the principles required are not self-evident or capable of proof in either case. Logically and epistemologically there is complete parallelism. Either we have no right to make the postulate in either case or we have an equal right to make it in both. The one position which cannot be defended is to make the postulates demanded by science, and then, in spite of or even because of this, to refuse to make the postulates demanded by morality.[33]

Sidgwick's interest in the Metaphysical Society follows naturally from such an intellectual position because "the intellectual battles of the seventies [reflected in the meetings of the Society] represent a struggle not merely between popular faith and popular science, but also between at least two major English philosophical positions, the intuitional or a priori and the empirical or experience schools."[34] Since he could not accept the claims of either science or Christianity without reservation, Sidgwick tried to occupy the middle ground on these counts, as his presentations to the group indicate. He was not concerned in these papers to defend one side of the controversy or the other, but through criticism and reconstruction of each on the basis of his own theism to effect a reconciliation. His contributions include "The Verification of Beliefs" (April, 1870), "Utilitarianism" (December, 1873), "The Theory of Evolution in its Application to Practice" (July, 1875), "The Relation of Psychogony to Metaphysics and Ethics" (January, 1878), "Incoherence of Empirical Philosophy" (January, 1879), and "The Scope of Metaphysics" (February, 1880).

The failure of the Society in 1880, resulting from an inability of the opposing groups to come to grips with one another once they reached their bedrock fundamentals, might be said to be mirrored in Sidgwick individually, for he, too, could never completely reconcile the absolute demands of the religious as opposed to the scientific urges of his spirit, and he remained to the end sceptical but hopeful.

The debts owed Sidgwick by Trinity and Cambridge pale somewhat in comparison with those owed him by women students. His hand may be discerned in almost every change in the status of women's education at Cambridge in the latter half of the nineteenth century. He was an advocate of the establishment of an examination for women; and when this preliminary hurdle was cleared and the first examination held in 1869, he was one of the examiners. That autumn his connection with the movement for higher education for women began in earnest. He then proposed that lectures be organized for women in order to prepare them for the examinations. He was enthusiastically supported in this move by Professor and Mrs. Henry Fawcett; and when a committee was formed to further this end, he was one of the honorary secretaries. This committee drew up a scheme for a series of lectures to be given in the Lent term of 1870. The lectures were attended by seventy or eighty women, and their success encouraged the group to try to obtain subscriptions for scholarships. Sufficient funds were raised so that two or three small scholarships were offered.[35]

The work of the committee did not completely absorb Sidgwick's zeal for the cause of women's education. By the end of 1870 he decided that some provision should be made for those who wanted to come to the lectures from places outside Cambridge. When he could not find a means of raising funds to provide for this venture, Sidgwick took a house on his own responsibility, furnished it, and persuaded Miss Anne Clough to supervise it. She and five students began residence there in 1871. Miss Clough paid her own board, and the students contributed certain fees to help meet the expense. This idea of a residential hall for women was eventually to result in the foundation of Newnham College.

The seventies saw an upswing, too, in the moral sciences at Cambridge, for which Sidgwick was partially responsible. He continually urged in articles and fly sheets—the usual method of carrying on debate over controversial issues—the necessity for stimulation of these studies. The moral sciences had attracted few good men because the examination standard was considered low and the remuneration in terms of fellowships and scholarships was too slight to be attractive. Between 1870 and 1880, however, William Cunningham, F. W. Maitland, James Ward, John Neville Keynes, and T. E. Scrutton took firsts in the Moral Science Tripos. Here was proof indeed that men capable of holding their own in any scholarly discipline were being attracted into philosophy and the social sciences.[36]

In 1872 the Eranus Society, a Cambridge discussion group, was formed with Clerk Maxwell, J. R. Seeley, Henry Jackson, F. J. A. Hort, B. F. Westcott, Joseph Lightfoot, and Sidgwick as original members. The paper-and-discussion method of the Apostles and the Metaphysical Society were used in this organization, too. Although the nucleus of the club was formed by theologians, it was not confined to the consideration of religious subjects. Later noteworthy members were Lord Acton, Clifford Allbutt, and George Darwin.[37]

About 1873 it is possible to pick up new threads of an old interest of Sidgwick's—psychical research. In an involved way the problems of psychical phenomena have a bearing on Sidgwick's personal religious dilemma. Although, as has been mentioned, Sidgwick no longer considered himself an orthodox Christian, he had the greatest respect for institutional Christianity and regarded it as "indispensable and irreplaceable—looking at it from a sociological point of view." Because of his concern about the scientific attack on its myths, however, he wanted to use the canons of science to put his "Natural Theism" on an unshakable empirical basis. His interest in psychical research was the main channel into which he poured his scientific curiosity, especially in the latter half of his life, in the hope that it might flow into the quiet pool of religious experience.

While an undergraduate he had joined the Ghost Society which E. W. Benson had helped found. After that time there are numerous remarks in his letters expressive of his interest in mental phenomena outside sense experience. He read widely and regularly on the subject; and his zeal for inquiry into any event that might lead to discoveries along these lines, along with his academic thoroughness, prevented his refusal to investigate even fairly obvious charlatans. In 1873 he began a more or less formal cooperation with his old friend F. W. H. Myers in delving into reported psychical occurrences. In 1874 Myers suggested that they organize an informal association with a common fund for carrying out systematized projects. Sidgwick readily assented, and their work continued and grew eventually into a more ambitious undertaking to which further reference is made below.

In December, 1874, Sidgwick's first and perhaps greatest book, *The Methods of Ethics,* was published. Professor C. D. Broad attests that this work seems to him "to be on the whole the best treatise on moral theory that has ever been written, and to be one of the English philosophical classics."[38] Although only thirty-six at the time of its publication, Sidgwick had already developed the philosophical maturity and even the basic point of view that was to be characteristic of all his writing. *Methods of Ethics* was in many respects in the direct line of utilitarian thought, but it was a new type of utilitarianism which drew extensively upon other and older traditions and philosophies. Its primary concern was to present the main methodological approaches to ethics and to demonstrate their interdependence. The book deservedly excited considerable controversy and was attacked and defended by partisans of contemporary schools of thought, including the utilitarians, the evolutionists, and the idealists.

As a writer Sidgwick had many shortcomings of a virtuous nature. He was one of the most thoroughgoing analysts in print. His mind was "of singular subtlety, fertility, and ingenuity, which applied to every topic an extremely minute and patient analysis. It discovered objections to every accepted doctrine, exceptions to every rule. It perceived minute distinctions and qualifications which had escaped the notice of previous writers."[39] While these qualities make each of his works an education in itself, they also make for laborious reading. His very impartiality, which caused Dicey to say that Sidgwick was the most disinterested thinker he had ever known,[40] means that his arguments are evenly balanced and the conclusions carefully qualified. Sidgwick is not easy for the reader; he never balks at slippery places, and he never leaves the student with the satisfaction of broad, easily derived generalizations. As lessons in analytical thinking, set in a framework of complete detachment, his books and articles are masterpieces.

In October of the year following the publication of *Methods of Ethics*, Sidgwick was appointed Praelector of Moral and Political Philosophy by his college. This promotion improved his income and put him in a permanent position, which was a good thing in view of his approaching marriage. His investigation of psychical occurrences had taken him frequently to séances at Arthur Balfour's home where he had met and become interested in Balfour's sister, Eleanor Mildred (Nora). They were engaged in December, 1875, and married the following April.[41]

The parties to this marriage complemented each other unusually well. Mrs. Sidgwick (1845-1936) was a competent administrator and research worker in her own right, as her later positions in Newnham College and in the Society for Psychical Research demonstrated. But even more, she was well adapted by her unassuming nature and extensive educational background to fit Sidgwick's pattern of life.

Sidgwick himself was still caught up in the process of University reform. Parliament constituted another University Commission in 1877. In anticipation of this move Cambridge had organized a Syndicate, of which Sidgwick was a member, to consider University needs. He devoted many hours to the preparation of statements for the Commission and in addition made a two-week tour of German universities to study arrangements that might prove useful to Cambridge. When the statutes resulting from the Commission's work were passed in 1882, he played a part in the reorganization which they entailed. He served from that time until 1899 as representative of the Special Board for Moral Science on the General Board of Studies, as well as on the Board for Indian Civil Service Studies. The General Board of Studies had the important responsibility of administering a University fund to be used for the increase of professorial salaries, establishment of new positions, and expansion of physical facilities.[42]

Women's education, too, was taking its place in the Cambridge sun. In 1873 the committee on women's lectures transformed itself into an Association for Promoting the Higher Education of Women in Cambridge. Sidgwick was still giving a great deal of time to the organization, lecturing to the women students and doing a large share of the secretarial work. The efforts were paying off splendidly.

Although admission of women to University examinations was on an informal basis, Miss Paley (Mrs. Alfred Marshall) and Miss Bully took honors in the Moral Science Tripos in 1874 and Miss Creak took double honors in mathematics and classics in 1875.[43] The house rented by Sidgwick had been quickly outgrown, and in 1875 Newnham Hall, built by subscriptions and shares on ground leased from St. John's, was opened for thirty students.

After their marriage the Sidgwicks carried on the work on women's education jointly, with Mrs. Sidgwick acting as treasurer for the Association. In 1879 a new hall was required to house the increasing number of women coming to the University. About the same time it was decided that the Association and Newnham Hall Company should be amalgamated. The two projects were carried out the following year, and the name Newnham College was given the Association and the buildings. Mrs. Sidgwick was made Vice-Principal (on a temporary acceptance), and she and her husband moved into the new hall which was eventually to acquire the name "Sidgwick Hall."

In the year of Newnham's establishment as a college a big step was taken toward securing recognition for women in the University. A syndicate on which Sidgwick served recommended formal admission of women to honors examinations and publication of results, provided that the requirements of residence and preliminary arrangements governing male students were met. In 1881 the Senate passed these provisions by a surprising vote of 331 for and 32 against.[44]

About this time there was a general upsurge of interest in psychical research. Professor W. F. Barrett of Dublin achieved some experimental success in thought transference, a phenomenon to which Myers later gave the name "mental telepathy."[45] Barrett was enthusiastically supported by Sidgwick and Myers when in January, 1882, he convened a conference to discuss the formation of a Society for Psychical Research. The Society was actually constituted only a month later, with Sidgwick becoming its first president. All the phases of psychical research were to be carried out under the direction of various committees. Extrasensory perception, hypnotism and mesmerism, apparitions, and spiritualism were included in the research plans of the organization.[46]

Sidgwick and his wife were among the most active workers in the Society. Sidgwick always felt that Mrs. Sidgwick was better qualified than he for this research. The importance that he attached to the Society's efforts are indicated by the fact that her acceptance of the Newnham principalship (1892) caused him to worry about the loss of time from psychical research that the position would involve. They labored prodigiously, but the results were for the most part discouraging. They traveled to all parts of the country and even went abroad on occasion to collect evidence. They obtained and classified literally thousands of cases of "phantasms of the living" and "phantasms of the dead." A substantial amount of this material was published by the Society, including the long *Report on the Census of Hallucinations.*[47] Mrs. Sidgwick also contributed an article on spiritualism to the ninth edition of the *Encyclopaedia Britannica.*[48] Although both orthodox science and his own meager gleanings were discouragingly pitted against him, Sidgwick never fully lost hope in certain divisions of the Society's research.

In 1883 Sidgwick was elected to the Knightbridge Professorship of Philosophy, a position for which he had applied and been rejected in favor of the Reverend T. R. Burks in 1872 on the death of Professor F. D. Maurice. Two years later Sidgwick was re-elected to his Trinity fellowship, a gesture which pleased him immensely.[49]

The moral sciences at this time included logic, psychology, ethics, metaphysics, political economy, and politics. At one time or another Sidgwick contributed something of importance to each of the subject-matter divisions. Perhaps his greatest contribution to all of them was the manner in which he handled them as a teacher. His ability was measured not so much by the size of his classes as by his method and by the type of student that he attracted. He remained predominantly a student and regarded himself as a fellow learner with those under his tutelage. Tributes from two of his most outstanding students sum up the experience of the good student under him.

F. W. Maitland says that he found in Sidgwick's lecture room "teaching the like of which had never come in my way before. There is very much else to be said of Sidgwick . . . but I should like to add this: I believe that he was a supremely great teacher. In the first place, I remember the admirable patience which could never be outworn by stupidity, and which nothing but pretentiousness could disturb. Then there was the sympathetic and kindly endeavour to overcome our shyness, to make us talk, and to make us think. Then there was that marked dislike for any mere reproduction of his own opinions, which made it impossible for Sidgwick to be in the bad sense the founder of a school."[50]

Arthur Balfour remembered most of all his ability to accord recognition and to give encouragement to those whose flagging spirits needed bolstering. "This form of conveying encouragement came naturally to Sidgwick. Of all the men I have ever known he was the readiest to consider every controversy and every controversialist on their own merits."[51]

Another and more naïve tribute took the fancy of Sidgwick. After a series of lectures delivered in the sixties, one of his students wanted to express his appreciation of the course. "They are the best I ever attended," he told Sidgwick, "except perhaps the lectures of Professor Kingsley; but then his are intended to improve the mind."[52]

In the same year that he was appointed Professor, Sidgwick published *The Principles of Political Economy*. Never very enthusiastic about his own work, Sidgwick apparently liked this book least of all. He had a great deal of trouble getting it into final shape. When the time came for a second edition, he wrote that he disliked the task of revising it. "I think there are some good things in it; but I regard it as on the whole a failure, and I don't think I can improve it much."[53] It is probable that part of this dissatisfaction was due to the general condition of economics at this time. The sweeping success which the analytical school of Ricardo had achieved both in the theoretical field and in the extent to which the doctrine of laissez faire had come to be accepted as a practical guide to economic policy was giving way to new methods of thinking about economic problems as a result of the dual critical attack of the rising historical school of economics and of groups concerned to advance reforms of a collectivist type.[54] Inevitably this change involved a struggle; in this case it was between the spokesmen of the middle class with their fixation on laissez faire and the socialist reformers with their emphasis on the need for amelioration of the conditions of large segments of the working class by wholesale governmental intervention. On the one hand, "the theory of Ricardo had become something like an institution" whose "underlying political philosophy" was so influential in practice and so difficult to alienate from his purely theoretical economics; and on the other, the egalitarianism of the reformers did not take the omnipresent factor of scarcity or the delicate balance among social institutions sufficiently into account. Both groups seemed ill informed about

21

the basic problems: the concentration of the proponents of laissez faire on the problems of production and of the reformers on the evils of the system of distribution seemed to prevent either from properly assessing the service that economic theory might render in the formation of a governmental economic policy designed to cope with the productive and distributive problems of large-scale industrialism. Sidgwick frequently complained about the lack of fundamental economic knowledge among the people who were leading in the formation of the opinions which were in conflict on these issues. Economic theory seemed somewhat moribund even in the Economic and Statistical Section of the British Association. In 1886 the Association met in Birmingham, and he indicates that there were few advantages from the sessions in economics, since the good papers were so limited in time and the rest were such bores.[55]

Only two items enliven his remarks on the Economics Sections. The year of his presidency (1885) the meeting was held in Aberdeen, and while there he stayed with Alexander Bain. He was able to get Bain to gossip considerably about Mill and Grote, which pleased him a great deal. In 1888 at Bath he had a noteworthy experience which is well worth relating in his own style:

The most interesting thing at my Section (Economic Science) was the field day on Socialism which we had yesterday. The Committee had invited a live Socialist, redhot "from the Streets," as he told us, who sketched in a really brilliant address the rapid series of steps by which modern society is to pass peacefully into a social democracy. The *node* of the transition was supplied by urban ground-rents (it is interesting to observe that the old picture of the agricultural land-lord-drone, battening on social prosperity to which he contributes nothing is withdrawn for the present as too ludicrously out of accordance with the facts). It is now urban ground-rent that the municipal governments have to seize, to meet the ever growing necessity of providing work and wages for the unemployed. How exactly this seizure of urban rents was to develop into a complete nationalization of industry I could not remember afterwards, but it seemed to go very naturally at the time. There was a peroration rhetorically effective as well as daring, in which he explained that the bliss of perfect socialism would only come by slow degrees with lingering steps and long delays, and claimed our sympathy for the noble-hearted men whose ardent philanthropy had led them to desire to cut these delays short by immediate revolution and spoliation. It was, indeed, a mistake on their part; the laws of social development did not admit of it; but if we were not quite lost in complacent selfishness we should join him in regretting that this shorter way with property was impossible.

Altogether a noteworthy performance:—the man's name is *Bernard Shaw*: Myers says he has written books worth reading.[56]

Sidgwick published again in 1886, this time it was *Outlines of the History of Ethics for English Readers,* which was enlarged from an article on ethics done in 1878 for the *Encyclopaedia Britannica.* This was also the year in which Newnham College Council decided to build a third hall involving an expenditure of £20,000. In spite of the rashness of the plan, he and his wife "concluded that it was a case for *audace.*"[57] Although Sidgwick did not live to see the granting of degrees to women, he did see success for Newnham beyond anything he had hoped for, when in 1899 the College obtained a freehold on its property through a gift from Mr. and Mrs. Bertrand Russell. The Sidgwicks themselves had played no small part in the achievement of this financial freedom. They gave at various times a total of £10,000.[58]

By 1888 Sidgwick was convinced that in at least one field of its investigations—telepathy—the Society for Psychical Research was making progress. In July of that year when he was again president of the organization, he made an address to the group in which he appealed strongly for a more extensive research effort on these problems.[59] His own interest took him limitedly into psychology. In the summer of 1889 he and Mrs. Sidgwick attended the International Congress of Experimental Psychologists in Paris. Under the influence of Professor Richet, the Congress evidenced quite an interest in psychical research, particularly in the field of sensory hallucinations. As a result Sidgwick was designated president of the next Congress, which met in London in the autumn of 1892. He brought his excellent powers of organization into play by turning the psychological end of the meeting over to James Sully, a psychologist of European reputation, while he and Myers concentrated solely on mental telepathy. The response was sufficiently gratifying to cause him to attend the third Congress in Munich in 1896 where he read a paper regarding some experiments made at Brighton under hypnotic conditions while he had been working on the *Census of Hallucinations.*[60]

It is impossible, of course, to make a precise estimate of his contribution in obtaining a hearing from qualified psychologists for the theory of extrasensory perception, but it is safe to say that his election to the presidency of the Congress and his invitation to Munich are proof enough of an influential connection with the reception of this study, at least tentatively, into orthodox psychology.

The early nineties were especially busy times for Sidgwick. In 1891 he published *The Elements of Politics,* a deductive treatment of the functions and institutions of a modern liberal state. Although the work takes its starting point from utilitarian ethics, it is so much more thorough, balanced, and methodologically sound than either Bentham's *Fragment on Government* or James Mill's *Essay on Government* that his study must be considered a new departure in utilitarian political thought.

Sidgwick suffered one of his greatest disappointments as an educational reformer in 1891. Since the early 1870's he had been an active supporter of the attempts to allow the substitution of modern languages for compulsory Greek and Latin in secondary school preparation for the University. The matter having arisen again, a Syndicate was appointed by the Council of the Senate to consider a wider alternative for either Greek or Latin in the Previous Examination. Sidgwick served on the Syndicate and was a leader in the campaign to procure some changes. He published several fly sheets defending his views, but his efforts were in vain as the measure was lost by a big majority. The worst feature of the affair, to him, was the fact that even the support which he had had earlier seemed to have receded.[61]

The year following Sidgwick was asked to take part in the work of the Gresham University Commission to consider the draft of a charter for a Teaching University in London.[62] This body began its work on May 21, 1892, and for a time he gave two days a week to this task. The report of the Commission, whose recommendations were followed to a large extent in the Constitution of the University (1900), was issued in 1894. Sidgwick submitted with reserve, and with the addition of a cautionary note, to the plan for granting external degrees. His reluctance was due to his idea that university life was more than the mere passing of examinations and taking degrees. His long, happy association with Cambridge made him wary of anything that smacked of the degree mill; his belief in education by the symposium method presupposed an enveloping academic atmosphere.

24

Sidgwick joined one other organization that should be mentioned—the Synthetic Society. It was organized in 1896 as a discussion group somewhat along the lines of the Metaphysical Society, but with a stronger flavor of pure theology. Although pressed to join at the outset, Sidgwick did not become a member until 1898. In the two papers that he read to the group[63] he reveals more strongly than ever his desire to demonstrate a scientific basis for religion.

Sidgwick had never been especially strong physically, and the rather poor locale and climate of Cambridge dealt harshly with him. He had to leave each summer in order to get relief from hay fever. He had bouts of insomnia, too, which increased in later years, especially if he participated in an exciting discussion, a fact which caused the postponement of his entry into the Synthetic Society.

His general health had been none too good for some time when in May, 1900, he was advised that an operation was necessary. He was suffering from an internal cancer, but he did not give up his activities. One of his last public appearances was at the Ad Eundem dinner at Oxford on May 19, following which he stayed over until May 20 to address the Oxford Philosophical Society on T. H. Green's philosophy. His good humor was never lost right up to the operation on May 31, and into what looked like the beginnings of recuperation. There were hopes of a recovery until a relapse occurred on August 13. Sidgwick died on August 28 and was buried in the village churchyard at Terling.[64]

The tributes to Sidgwick by the close-knit society at Cambridge were very impressive. A sunken garden was placed in the lawn in front of Newnham with a stone fountain inscribed: "The daughters of this house to those that shall come after commend the filial remembrance of Henry Sidgwick." A Sidgwick Memorial Lecture was established; the first one was delivered by Bryce in 1902 on "Philosophic Life Among the Ancients." The University also founded a lectureship in Moral Science in his name. His friends paid tribute to him at a memorial meeting at Cambridge in November, 1900.

Several volumes of Sidgwick's work appeared after his death, the most noteworthy being *Philosophy, Its Scope and Relations* (1902) and *The Development of European Polity* (1903). The former makes explicit certain philosophical fundamentals which had

25

been presupposed in some of his other books, while the latter was, in the words of Bryce, "a masterly piece of work, and reveals a wider range of historical method than had been shown in his earlier books or indeed than some of his friends had known him to possess."[65]

Sidgwick had lived "the still and tranquil life of the thinker, teacher, and writer, varied by no events more exciting than those controversies over reforms in the studies and organization of the University in which his sense of public duty frequently led him to bear a part."[66] But it was nonetheless a full and useful life; and the breadth of Sidgwick's intellectual interests should number him among the last of the universal scholars.

Sidgwick's countenance reflected his gentle nature and engaging personality. Lady Frances Balfour, in *Ne Obliviscaris*, said that he had a child's eyes, the forehead of a dreamer, and the mouth of a talker.[67] Sidgwick wore a full beard, and when he meditated he usually stroked the underside of it. His only exercise was walking or running, and his academic personage must have presented a strange appearance trotting around the streets of Cambridge.

Sidgwick's greatest forte as a personality was his conversational ability. He spoke with a slight stammer which added charm to his discourse. He was the center of any discussion circle and the delight of Mrs. Sidgwick's breakfasts for the students of Newnham. The Sidgwicks entertained admirably and extensively, and Sidgwick's talk was regarded as the main treat of their hospitality. He had a subtle wit, which unfortunately seldom appears in his writing, and a useful facility for putting his fellow conversationalist at ease and meeting him on his own ground.

In national politics Sidgwick called himself an Academic Unionist Liberal. Because of his desire for a strong parliamentary majority and his preference for disestablishment, he hesitantly voted for the Liberals in November, 1885; after that, however, he went over to the Tories whose criticism of radical policy had previously impressed him. His change was due mainly to the Liberal party's handling of the Irish question; he felt that either coercion or home rule was necessary in place of what he regarded as vacillating policy.

In 1885 he was asked to stand as a Liberal candidate at the next election. His conscientiousness led him to make this comment: "I was tempted; but I communed with my political conscience and discovered that I could not come forward as a Liberal at this juncture without hypocrisy. I am a Utilitarian, and would be a hypocrite if I were convinced that the country required this sacrifice; but I cannot rate my political value so high. In fact the temptation was really this: I want to write a great book on Politics during the next ten years, and am afraid it will be too academic if I do not somehow go into the actual struggle. But how?"[68] His sense of political obligation is further borne out by an incident reported by Bryce. Sidgwick once came back from Davos, Switzerland, where he was vacationing, in order to vote in a parliamentary election which was in effect already decided.[69]

He was completely selfless in his service to his University, seeming to care only for getting the job itself done regardless of where the credit went. He reached into his own pockets frequently to support projects in which he was especially interested. In addition to his generosity to Newnham, he provided £200 a year for four years toward the expenses of the Indian Civil Service Studies; out of his own pay he contributed £300 a year for four years for a Readership in Law held by Maitland; for a time he helped underwrite the Professorship of Modern History; and he gave £1,500 for the building fund of the Physiology Department.[70]

He was equally generous with time and money in promoting better civic conditions. He joined the old Anti-Mendicity Society in 1871 when the beggars in Cambridge were a real source of trouble. Under his direction the Society was reorganized into the Cambridge Charity Organization Society in 1879, operating thenceforth along the lines of its London counterpart. Both he and his wife acted as president at various times, and Sidgwick gave up his place on the Executive Committee only in 1890 when he was appointed to the Council of the University Senate. Even then he came back often to preside over meetings; and as late as 1911 Mrs. Sidgwick made over a piece of her husband's property to the Society.[71]

His services in other ways achieved full fruition only after his death. For many years he had desired an organization on a national scale which would take care of those interested in scientific inquiry in fields other than mathematics and the natural sciences. He and Lord Acton were united in thinking that this type of society would be useful in promoting the study of history, philology, philosophy, and economics. The British Academy, embodying this ideal, was not granted its charter until 1902, two years after Sidgwick's death and a year following Acton's. Due acknowledgment, however, was given to their efforts. Bryce wrote a memorial to them for the

Proceedings which commended their long activity toward the founding of the Academy.[72]

A close scrutiny of the life of a figure from the past often brings with it a measure of disillusionment. Such is not the case with Sidgwick; familiarity with his life creates a new respect engendered by his ability to reflect most of the virtues of his age while he escapes many of its vices. It is small wonder that George Eliot remarked of him that he was expected by his intimates to conform to a higher standard of conduct than ordinary men.[73] Mrs. Sidgwick once commented that she and her husband were "grey people."[74] In the lack of surface ostentation in their lives this was certainly true. But the grey external coating only added luster to the bright whiteness of their influence. For the Sidgwicks not only lived a close approximation to the classical ideal of the good life, they taught a great many others to do the same.

CHAPTER TWO

Benthamic Utilitarianism

A S A PHILOSOPHER Sidgwick chose to place himself directly in line of succession to the utilitarians whose system "constitutes the largest contribution made by the English to moral and political theory."[1]* By his own designation as well as in the content of his work, Sidgwick was probably the last of the orthodox utilitarians.

In the period between the death in 1776 of David Hume, the recognized founder of the school,[2] and the beginning of Sidgwick's philosophical productiveness in the late sixties and early seventies of the following century, utilitarianism reached its greatest height of popular influence as a philosophy and as a philosophical basis for political, economic, and social reform. And this period of approximately a century was dominated by the three central figures of the school—Jeremy Bentham, James Mill, and John Stuart Mill. Their ideas, then, form the context into which Sidgwick's final modification of the utilitarian doctrines must be set. But the extent of their work is so enormous and subject to so many ramifications that any attempt to present the ideas of the Benthamites as a background into which later developments may be fitted must be highly selective.

The utilitarianism of Bentham and the Mills has two main aspects: a comprehensive philosophical system and a program of

*Notes to this chapter begin on page 175.

practical reform. The two are complementary, however, inasmuch as the reforms recommended by the group were direct practical applications of the philosophical fundamentals advocated by them. Although the moral and political theories of the Benthamites are the major concern of the present work, the practical application of their ideas often overshadowed the formation of principles in the lives and works of these utilitarians. Bentham himself was originally concerned with legal reform; and even when he vastly broadened the field of his writing, it was largely for the purpose of providing support for legal change by elaborating the principles on which a comprehensive theory of legal reform should be based.

As far as philosophical traditions go, it may be claimed for Bentham and his school that they fit into the broad movement of the English tradition of empiricism which was passed from Francis Bacon to Hobbes, Locke, Hume, Hartley, James Mill, and on to John Stuart Mill.[3] Despite connections with empiricism in parts of the work of the Benthamites, however, the commentators on Bentham and the Mills from Macaulay to the present have uniformly stressed the deductive nature of Benthamite principles. Utilitarianism, at the hands of this central group, takes the form of an elaborate interdependent system containing psychological, moral, economic, and political theories which are almost never supported by concrete examples. Sir Leslie Stephen characterizes this quality of the school exceptionally well when he says; "Their appeals to experience always end by absolute assertions. . . . They treat of what would be, if certain forces acted without limit, as a necessary step toward discovering what is when the limits exist. They appear to their opponents to forget the limits in their practical conclusions."[4]

The all-embracing nature of the system is reflected strongly in the sweeping practical reforms urged by the utilitarians. Bentham and the two Mills were the philosophers of the English reform movement in the early nineteenth century and, in consequence, may be regarded as the founders of modern English liberalism. They furnished the intellectual ammunition with which the Philosophical Radicals in Parliament attacked what they believed to be the strongholds of reaction.

In the development of utilitarian theory Bentham and his followers borrowed more than they originated. After all, they followed a long and distinguished line of thinkers to whom they owed great debts. But the Benthamites occupied a central position in the movement because of their indefatigable effort and ultimately their substantial success in reforming political institutions, the law, and economic policy along utilitarian lines.

Utilitarianism matured when the times were ripe for change. After 1780 technological innovations were intruding so rapidly into the life of England that there was no opportunity to assimilate them.[5] The Industrial Revolution piled up a backlog of social problems that could not be solved by the political ideas and machinery which had served a decentralized agrarian society. The rapid trend toward urbanization accentuated the lack of effective administrative machinery and the control of government by the rural gentry. The rapid rise to social importance of the middle class was unaccompanied by any change in its political status; the entrepreneur was largely unrepresented and almost universally disfranchised. A social theory was badly needed to provide a method by which these changes might be accommodated to the existing society. The utilitarianism of Bentham fitted this need precisely.

For a full generation and more following the French Revolution, however, the fear of extensive reconstruction of political institutions prevented the changes that would have accelerated the development of the liberal society, a society embracing representative government, a rationally codified legal system, and an economy as free as possible from governmental restraints. During this period of Tory reaction Bentham remained in relative obscurity in his own country while enjoying great prestige abroad. Even his elaborate prison reform scheme, the Panopticon, which he tried for twenty-odd years to put into effect, was repudiated by Parliament, after having been accepted once.

It was only after Bentham's meeting with James Mill in 1808 that utilitarianism as a system of thought began to furnish a basis for the reform program of the radicals. Dicey has conveniently catalogued the impressive list of legal, economic, and political changes which may be said to be based on utilitarian principles.[6] He notes that "from 1825 onwards the teaching of Bentham exercised so potent an influence that to him is fairly ascribed that thorough-going though gradual amendment of the Law of England which was one of the main results of the Reform Act."[7] The Reform Act of 1832 assisted above all in transferring political power to the hands of the middle class whose interests the utilitarians believed identifiable with that of the whole society. Despite the fact that the parliamentary movement based on philosophical radicalism "had . . . spent its strength in the history of English thought and English legislation"⁸ by the early 1850's, utilitarianism was so prevalent a force in English liberalism that changes attributed to Benthamite principles have been traced by Dicey throughout the latter half of the nineteenth century.

In his study of European liberalism Ruggiero found in this nineteenth-century remodeling of society on a utilitarian basis "a curious reciprocal influence between English and continental liberalism. Each tends to reproduce in itself the phase which the other was manifesting in the preceding century. English liberalism tends to model itself on the rationalistic and democratic attitude of continental liberalism, while the latter in its turn draws inspiration from the traditional forms and privileges of the former."⁹ But in spite of the fact that the historical empiricism of a conservative like Edmund Burke had no place in the deliberate philosophical calculations of the Benthamites, the English tradition of empirical social change modified the practical course of utilitarianism and forced the radicals to follow conventional gradualistic lines in their reform movement. And perhaps for this very reason we can note in the tendencies to collectivism in the last quarter of the nineteenth century important remnants of Benthamism. It might almost be said that we are all utilitarians now, not only because many of the doctrines of the school are still plausible even after coming under critical attack, but because ideas and institutions change only very slowly, and even when they do, the forms often change more slowly than the substance.

For the purpose of the work at hand it will be necessary to sketch in rather broad outlines the content of Benthamite utilitarian philosophy in several of its complementary aspects. These aspects may be reduced, without claim to exhaustiveness, to four fundamentals: the method and basic doctrines of the school, its hedonistic ethical theory, and the subsequent theoretical structures of representative government and economics.

Elie Halévy declares that "Utilitarianism, or Philosophical Radicalism, can be defined as nothing but an attempt to apply the principles of Newton to the affairs of politics and of morals."¹⁰ The utilitarians sought a universal law (or laws) of human nature comparable to the Newtonian law of gravity upon which they could erect a science of the mind and society as complete as Newton's explanation of the natural order. The constant laws of the human mind and of society were to be based on experience and arrived at experimentally. Following this process of "analysis," by which the "general laws" governing phenomena were discovered, a more inclusive theory could then be constructed by the process of "synthesis," or deduction of further principles from the fundamental laws discovered by the original analysis.

The subtitle of Hume's *Treatise of Human Nature* (1739)— "Being an attempt to introduce the experimental method of reasoning into Moral Subjects"—is a clear indication of this goal, although more modestly expressed than some later examples. Hume follows Newton in his objection to deductive hypothesis and in his insistence that speculation begin from fundamental experiences. "The first task of philosophy is therefore, by the method of analysis, to determine the fundamental experiences; the second task is, by the method of synthesis, to show how in terms of these fundamental experiences others of a more derivative character can be explained."[11]

Professor N. Kemp Smith has argued convincingly and has adduced much evidence to demonstrate that the use made by Hume of this Newtonian method has been widely misunderstood. It has been the usual practice among commentators to follow the interpretation of Reid and Beattie, which takes Hume's treatment of "the doctrine of ideas" to be the focal point of his work, and which results in the view that "Hume's teaching is sheerly negative, being in effect little more than a *reductio ad absurdum* of the principles which Hume's predecessors, and Hume himself have followed in their inquiries."[12] It is Professor Smith's contention that the central part of Hume's teaching is not the theory of ideas at all, but his theory of morals. That is to say that Hume began his philosophical analysis with ethics, and from that point he later proceeded to the epistemological problems which eventuated in the doctrine of ideas appearing in the opening book of the *Treatise of Human Nature*. Furthermore, not only did Hume first concentrate his energies on ethical questions, but the conclusions that he drew from his moral studies continued to form the core of his philosophy.

Hume's basic ethical doctrine may be stated in general terms as follows: to say that an action is good or bad means that upon contemplation of it a sentiment of approval or disapproval is felt towards it. The determining factor in moral judgments is feeling, not reason. Hume's conception of good is completely naturalistic; moral judgments have their source solely in the particular fabric and constitution of the human species. Reason plays no part in recognizing the distinction between good and evil, but is confined to matters of "truth and fact." Reason, in the study of triangles or circles, considers the known relations of the parts of the figure, and from them proceeds to infer some unknown relation which is dependent on them. In moral deliberation, on the other hand, *all* the facts have first to be before us; until they have been assembled and their relations known (a service which reason can perform), no sentiment of blame or approval should be made. But as every circumstance, every relation is then known, the moral approval or blame arises in the mind not as an act of knowledge but as a feeling to which we are immediately determined.[13]

According to Professor Smith's view, then, what is central in Hume's theory is not Locke's or Berkeley's "ideal" theory, "but the doctrine that the determining influence in human as in other forms of animal life is feeling, not reasoning or understanding, i.e., not evidence, whether *a priori* or empirical, and therefore also not ideas—at least not ideas as hitherto understood."[14] Further, it was from the facts of moral experience that Hume derived what he took to be convincing proof of the principle that reason acts, as it ought to act, in the service of feeling and instinct in practical life.[15]

If his ethical doctrine is central to Hume's philosophy in the manner just ascribed to it, then the sceptical conclusions concerning knowledge which Hume draws from his treatment of the doctrine of ideas are only preparatory to the naturalistic conclusions which Hume produces for morals and politics. "Not only . . . is Hume unshaken in his adhesion to Locke's doctrine of ideas by the sceptical consequences to which it leads; this is one main reason why he values the doctrine so highly, and opens the exposition of his philosophy, both in the *Treatise* and in the *Essay Concerning Human Understanding* with an exposition of its principles. His purpose from the start has been to give prominence to those negative consequences and to push them as far as they can be made to go. The more negative their character, the more evident must it become that 'ideas' cannot afford a sufficient basis for belief, and that belief must therefore be accounted for in some other, very different, manner."[16]

It is only in his treatment of the "artificial" virtues that Hume allows reflective reason a larger place in his ethical system. Such virtues as justice, fidelity, veracity, and integrity are numbered among the "artificial" virtues, and approval of them depends on the recognition of their utility in maintaining an ordered society. If the question is asked why justice is approved, "the only possible answer is by reference to its utility. Justice with all the machinery of law and government is necessary for the existence and advancement of society, and it is as being necessary that it is approved. And the *recognition* of this necessity, which the approval presupposes, is a function that only reason can perform."[17] But even in this instance, although the approval of justice presupposes the discovery of its utility, the approval itself cannot be ascribed to reason. Instead, the *approval* of the "public good" which justice subserves and which is discovered by reason rests upon feeling and instinct. In the case of the artificial virtues, the particular feeling which gives moral approbation is sympathy.

Hume's conservatism in ethics and politics follows logically from this central place which he gives to feeling in his theory. His basic position in both the *Treatise* and the *Enquiry Concerning the Principles of Morals* is "that it is the non-rational factual elements in experience, instinctive and traditional, which are ultimately decisive in the fields of ethics and politics.... It was not by any mere prejudice, whim, or inconsistency that Hume became a Tory in politics. In his use of the principle of utility, as in his own very distinctive type of sceptical empiricism, his kinship is more with Burke—with Burke in his early writings—than with Bentham. To the last Hume holds to, and makes central, the distinction between knowledge and belief. What, in his view, distinguishes thinking in politics from thinking in mathematics is that, in the absence of knowledge, we have to rely upon what at best is always only opinion. Our subjective convictions may be unqualified, but the objective assurances can never be other than precarious and incomplete."[18]

In moving from Hume's application of the Newtonian method and its results to the application of the method by the Benthamites, it is essential to recall of the latter that the "philosophers who belonged to the movement were primarily practical reformers."[19] In view of their concern with reform it is hardly surprising that many inconsistencies and gaps should appear in their theoretical system when it is examined in its entirety. Bentham, for instance, was influenced in his thinking by a wide variety of sources, and the breadth of his intellectual concerns did not always allow for the reconciliation of sources and theories applied to one subject with those affecting another.

Bentham, no less than Hume, wanted to place morals and politics on an empirical basis, to discover the irreducible elements of experience and to infer from these basic experiences others of a more derivative nature. Despite being influenced by this methodological conception, however, Bentham was so busy applying certain of his doctrines to the practical problems which confronted him that he often failed to see either the practical consequences of certain of his philosophical doctrines or the philosophical problems created by some of his maxims of reform. Benthamism is not, like Hume's philosophy, a system produced out of a steady concentration on an object of knowledge from the standpoint of a particular method. It is rather an amalgam of philosophical doctrines worked out at various times in the light of contemporary political, legal, and economic problems. In Benthamism "we are confronted . . . with something more challenging than a ready-made system—a series of possible approaches to central problems of society and politics, any one of which we may be able to utilize without committing ourselves to the others, and any or all of which may be capable of adaptation."[20]

In attempting to reduce experience to its basic elements, Bentham and his followers advanced the psychological doctrine that behavior is motivated solely by the expectations of the pleasures and pains which will accrue to the individual as the result of an action. Like Hume's moral theory, the pleasure-pain conception is naturalistic, although in comparison with Hume's it is greatly oversimplified. Furthermore, it is both egoistic and hedonistic, whereas Hume's doctrine is neither. Where the Benthamic utilitarians differed markedly from Hume was in advancing another quite different and nonnaturalistic doctrine on which most of their practical reforms were based. This other doctrine is the ethical principle that the sole end which morality, laws, and government ought to subserve is the greatest happiness of the greatest number. In carrying out the second step of their method—that of synthesis—the utilitarians were really deducing their derivative social laws from two different premises, a psychological premise and an ethical premise, and many of their fallacies may be traced to the fact that the relation between these two fundamental premises was never systematically analyzed.

Hume's scepticism with respect to the function of reason prevented him from formulating a theory of moral obligation in the strict sense of the term. "There is, that is to say, no intrinsically self-justifying good that with *authority* can claim approval."[21] But the Benthamites did not hesitate to establish the ethical proposition of the greatest happiness, even though their study of the facts of experience could not possibly yield such a principle of obligation, and in fact the psychological doctrine of egoistic hedonism to which their empiricism did lead them was incompatible with any such ethical premise. It is precisely because Hume claims to adopt a purely experimental method that he "does not think that it is the task of the moralist to issue commands. He seeks *that which is;* it is by a strange *petitio principii* that most moralists, having proceeded along the same lines, become all at once engaged in defining *that which ought to be.* Now if this involves a *petitio principii,* the objection applies to Bentham, since his dominating idea is just this—that he has discovered in the principle of utility a practical commandment as well as a scientific law, a proposition which teaches us at one and the same time what is and what ought to be."[22]

The conflict between their psychological and ethical doctrines hovers in the background of the theoretical structure of the ethics, politics, and economics of the Benthamites. Their psychology was too narrow and uncompromising a support for the grandiose vision of human progress before the eyes of the utilitarians. Even if one could conceivably overlook the philosophical problem of deriving an ethical end from a psychological "fact," there would still be a serious practical problem of finding a means of reconciling the interests of egoistic individuals in such a manner that the greatest happiness of the greatest number is achieved. In their ethical theory, as in their theory of economics and politics, it is sometimes the psychological and sometimes the ethical doctrine from which practical conclusions are deduced.

"Utilitarianism is above all a theory of morals,"[23] and the basis of its moral theory may be stated in very simple terms; the sole good is the greatest happiness of the greatest number.

However, the apparent simplicity of this doctrine covers an extraordinarily complex system of ethics, a system made more difficult by the failure of its central exponent, Bentham, to clarify his terms and make explicit his assumptions. Bentham's strength as a thinker may be found in his vigorous application of utilitarian principles, especially in the field of legal reform; his weakness lies in his inadequate philosophical formulation of the very principles on which his specific rules of action are based. Bentham always seemed

37

anxious to move away from fundamentals, which were clear and self-evident to him if not to his reader, in order to get down to the detailed classifications and refinements of pains and pleasures from which rules of individual action or legislation might be derived. The exactness demanded by Bentham in the moral sciences was much more nearly realized by him when he was cataloguing particular experiences as pleasurable or painful than when he was answering specifically ethical questions about the nature of good and the meaning of "rightness" in conduct. Bentham was confident that his principles were correct without extensive elaboration because workable rules of action could be deduced from them. A philosopher would have been more concerned with basic questions, but Bentham was less philosopher than reformer.

The main problems which were to lay out so rugged a path for later utilitarians are evident in the first page of the *Principles of Morals and Legislation*.[24] Bentham opens this treatise with the following frequently quoted sentences: "Nature has placed mankind under the governance of two sovereign masters, *pain* and *pleasure*. It is for them alone to point out what we ought to do, as well as to determine what we shall do. On the one hand the standard of right and wrong, on the other the chain of causes and effects, are fastened to their throne. They govern us in all we do, in all we say, in all we think: every effort we can make to throw off our subjection, will serve but to demonstrate and confirm it. In words a man may pretend to abjure their empire: but in reality he will remain subject to it all the while."[25] In an equally famous footnote[26] immediately following the quotation above, Bentham gives his definition of the "principle of utility" which is founded on the pleasure-pain dichotomy just indicated. The principle of utility or greatest-happiness principle is one which states "the greatest happiness of all those whose interest is in question, as being the right and proper, and the only right and proper and universally desirable end of human action. . . ."[27]

These two passages alone give rise to the basic problem confronting the utilitarians from Bentham to Sidgwick. In the first place the question may be raised whether Bentham is elaborating a psychological or an ethical theory. When he speaks of man being under the governance of the sovereign masters—pleasure and pain—is he implying that all of one's actions are determined completely by immediate or expected pleasures or pains? In other words, is the hedonistic end favored by Bentham psychologically dictated as a part of human nature or is it a product of a rational choice which it is desirable for all men to select? If hedonism is psychologically determined as the end of all behavior, what reason does Bentham have for referring to it as the "only universally desirable end of action"? Does he mean by "desirable" what is commonly meant when that term is used in ethical discussions—worthy of being desired—or does he simply equate desirable with what actually is desired by all people here and now?

A further confusion is introduced by Bentham through his failure to reconcile the idea that each person habitually pursues his own happiness as an end with the repeated avowal that the greatest happiness of the greatest number is the proper end of ethics. The principle that each man ought to pursue his own happiness as an end is identifiable by the term "egoistic hedonism," while "utilitarianism" or universal hedonism may be properly applied to the idea of the greatest happiness of the greatest number as an ethical end. It is obvious that a great difference exists between egoistic and universalistic ends of conduct, yet Bentham never makes clear the relation between the two. Very often Bentham asserts that no man can desire any pleasure except his own, and James Mill seems always to make that assumption, but this does not prevent both of them from insisting equally firmly that the only criterion of morality is the greatest happiness of the greatest number.[28]

Bentham himself does not seem to recognize any incompatibility in these ideas; at times he appears to be a psychological hedonist (as in the first quotation above) without any indication that the pleasure which is "sovereign" is either that of the individual concerned or that of all those sentient beings who are affected by the actions contemplated. At other times (as in the quotation from the footnote) it appears that he is making a straightforward ethical judgment without any psychological implications. And in perhaps even more places he gives the impression that he is judging it not only right and proper that each individual should pursue his own greatest happiness, but that every individual is constrained to do so by his psychological incapacity to desire anything other than his own pleasure. This means to say that many times Bentham appears to be a proponent of psychological egoistic hedonism. The problem is well summed up by Sidgwick when he says: "If, as Bentham affirms, on the occasion of every act he exercises, every human being is 'inevitably' led to pursue that line of conduct which, according to his view of the case, taken by him at the moment, will be in the highest degree contributory to his own greatest happiness, then, to any one who knows this, it must be inconceivable that Reason dictates to him to pursue any other line of conduct. But at the same time, as it seems to me, the proposition that he ought to pursue *that* line of conduct becomes no less clearly incapable of being affirmed with any significance. For a psychological law invariably realized in my conduct does not admit of being conceived as 'a precept' or 'dictate' of reason: this latter must be a rule from which I am conscious that it is possible to deviate."[29]

Bentham does not attempt systematically to reconcile egoistic hedonism (either in its psychological or rationalistic sense) with the greatest happiness principle. By implication there occasionally seems to be a naturalistic reconciliation of private ethics in which the general happiness is best promoted through each individual's pursuit of his own greatest pleasure on the whole.[30] Natural reconciliation of private interests may, however, be implemented by legislation designed to promote the greatest happiness, usually through attempting to realize the freedom necessary for rational pursuit of individual happiness. But this legislative implementation must be momentarily sidetracked since it takes us into the question of governmental activity before the full implications of the problem of private ethics have been exhausted.

In the posthumously published *Deontology* the principle of egoistic hedonism and utilitarianism are seemingly more explicitly reconciled by Bentham than in his other works "by the doctrine that it is always the individual's true interest, even from a purely mundane point of view, to act in the manner most conducive to the general happiness."[31] But if such a thesis is adopted, what happens to the idea of the greatest happiness as the sole desirable end of action? If one aims at the general happiness only to promote his own individual happiness, how can the general happiness be anything other than a means—a condition which logically precludes its being the sole criterion of ethics?

The more such deductions from diverse premises are made, the more apparent become the fallacies in Bentham's ethics. Plamenatz sums up this problem when he says that "Bentham, without quite knowing what he is doing, is trying to reconcile two couples of irreconcilable doctrines: egoistic hedonism with utilitarianism, on the one hand; and a psychological with an objective theory of morals on the other."[32]

In 1861 John Stuart Mill wrote his essay on *Utilitarianism,* setting out in brief but comprehensive form his defense of the ethical doctrines of his father and Bentham. This essay, then, is the final systematic statement of the hedonism of the small group of early nineteenth-century utilitarians who may properly be called Benthamites. The fundamental problem presented by this work is the extent to which it solves the difficulties presented by Bentham and thereby renders a consistent statement of utilitarian ethics.

To start with the basic factors: Mill advocates the Benthamic position that "happiness is desirable, and the only thing desirable, as an end; all other things being desirable only as means to that end."[33] And like Bentham, too, he equates happiness with pleasure. "By happiness," he notes, "is intended pleasure, and the absence of pain; by unhappiness, pain and the privation of pleasure."[34]

Mill recognizes the incompatibility of the psychological and ethical doctrines of Bentham, and gives careful attention to the philosophical problem of *proving* the greatest happiness to be the sole good. He admits at the outset of his arguments that "questions of ultimate ends are not amenable to *direct* proof. Whatever can be proved to be good, must be so by being shown to be a means to something admitted to be good without proof."[35] Nonetheless, the validity of the greatest happiness principle is open to rational proof, and it is not "solely in the way of intuition" that this appeal to the intellect is made.[36]

If Mill neither accepts the possibility of direct proof of utilitarianism as an end nor the intuitional proof of its clear and self-evident superiority to any other ethical end, what proof can he offer to support its claim? He says: "The only proof capable of being given that an object is visible, is that people actually see it. The only proof that a sound is audible, is that people hear it: and so of the other sources of our experience. In like manner, I apprehend, the sole evidence it is possible to produce that anything is desirable is that people do actually desire it."[37] Here again one meets with a difficulty already discerned as a possible source of difficulty in Bentham—the confusion of desired with desirable. Mill "has attempted to establish the identity of the good with the desired, by confusing the proper sense of 'desirable,' in which it denotes that which it is good to desire, with the sense which it would bear

41

if it were analogous to such words as 'visible.' If 'desirable' is to be identical with 'good,' then it must bear one sense; and if it is to be identical with 'desired,' then it must bear quite another sense."[38]

Mill, as much as Bentham, wants to produce an empirical science of ethics in contrast with the essentially rationalistic methods of the intuitionists. Even while admitting that his ethical end—the greatest happiness—cannot be proved, he still makes the attempt to prove it on the basis of a psychological analysis of what is actually desired. In other words, Mill attempts to do just what he refuses to admit can be done. Mill is not willing to pay the price that Hume did for pursuing an empirical science of morals. The question whether something is desired or not is open to experimental proof, but the question whether it *ought* to be desired for its own sake is not open to proof by the method Mill insists upon using.[39] Hume recognizes this condition, and in consequence his empirical method gives way in practical ethics to the enslavement of reason by the passions. Hume's careful analysis of the passions, however, leads him to a nonhedonistic position, far removed from the ethical end of the Benthamite utilitarians. In fact "no one could be more insistent than Hume that desire is not desire for pleasure: it is conditioned by the disinterested concentration of some passion upon its object."[40] Mill can not give up what is in fact a rationalistic ethical end, nor can he repudiate the claims of his ethical theory to be positive from a standpoint of both means and ends. His attempt to reconcile his ethical end with his psychological premises, therefore, leads to the same place that Bentham's does, even though Mill's position is perhaps even more exposed, because of its greater clarity, than Bentham's.

Mill is confronted also with the problem of reconciling the other two incompatibles inherited from Bentham. In direct continuation of the quotation given above, Mill attempts to deduce universal ethical hedonism from a presuppostion of psychological egoistic hedonism. Mill points out that "no reason can be given why the general happiness is desirable, except that each person, so far as he believes it to be attainable, desires his own happiness. This, however, being a fact, we have not only all the proof which the case admits of, but all which it is possible to require, that happiness is a good: that each person's happiness is a good to that person, and the general happiness, therefore, a good to the aggregate of all persons."[41] And Mill goes on in the next few pages to demonstrate not only that pleasure is desired, but that all desired objects really may be subsumed in the desire for pleasure and consequently that pleasure is actually the sole object of desire.[42]

Sidgwick exposed the fallacy in this reconciliation of utilitarianism and egoistic psychological hedonism,[43] and Broad expanded Sidgwick's presentation into a refutation of Mill's position:

Universalistic Ethical Hedonism is the doctrine that it is the duty of each to aim at the maximum happiness of all, and to subordinate everything else to this end. It is perfectly plain that this ethical theory is incompatible with *any* form of Psychological Egoism, and therefore with Psychological Hedonism. For Psychological Egoism denies that any one can desire as an end anything but some state of himself, e.g., his own happiness or the greatest development of all his faculties, and if, as would follow, no one can desire as an end the happiness of humanity in general, this cannot be the right or fitting object of anyone's desire, nor can it be anyone's duty to aim at this end.

Yet Mill [John], in his *Utilitarianism*, professed to deduce Universalistic Hedonism from Psychological Hedonism. Mill starts by assuming that "desirable" means "desired by someone." Though this rests on a confusion which we have already noted, there is no need to insist on that fact here. For Mill's argument involves another fallacy which would invalidate it even though the above premises were granted. The argument may be put as follows. If Psychological Hedonism be true, each man's happiness is desired by someone, viz., by himself. Therefore each man's happiness is desirable. But the happiness of humanity is simply the whole composed of the happiness of each man and of nothing else. Mill concludes that the happiness of humanity is desirable. But the only legitimate conclusion from these premises is that the happiness of humanity is a whole composed of a set of parts each one of which is desirable. It does not follow from this that the happiness of humanity is itself desirable. For on Mill's definition of "desirable," this would mean that the happiness of humanity is desired by someone. And it does not follow from the fact that every part of this whole is desired by someone that the whole itself is desired by anyone. On the contrary, it would follow from the premise that no one can desire anything but his own happiness, that no one can desire the happiness of humanity; and therefore, on Mill's definition, that the happiness of humanity is *not* desirable.[44]

If Mill had gone this far and no further, the strongest criticism that could be directed at him would be that he made the contra-

43

dictions of Bentham explicit by demonstrating through his own fallacies that both the psychological and ethical theories of the utilitarians and their egoism and utilitarianism were philosophically irreconcilable. But he actually adds to the problems of the school by his insistence that qualitative differences among pleasures must enter into utilitarian calculations. As with the other points on which he attempts a clarification of utilitarian doctrines, Mill is unwavering on this issue. "It is quite compatible with the principle of utility," he says, "to recognize the fact, that *some* kinds of pleasure are more desirable and more valuable than others. It would be absurd that while, in estimating all other things, quality is considered as well as quantity, the estimation of pleasures should be supposed to depend on quantity alone."[45]

Professor Moore has demonstrated quite clearly that "Mill's admissions as to quality of pleasure are either inconsistent with his Hedonism, or else afford no other ground for it than would be given by mere quantity of pleasure."[46] In the first place Mill's test for the superiority of one pleasure over another is the preference for the one on the part of people who have experienced both. A pleasure preferred under this test is more desirable, and since to think of an object as desirable is to think of it as pleasant, the consensus of experts merely proves that one pleasure is pleasanter than another. "But if this is so, how can he distinguish this standard from the standard of the quantity of pleasure? Can one pleasure be pleasanter than another, except in the sense that it gives more pleasure?"[47]

If we suppose the other alternative—that Mill does not really mean that the preference of experts merely proves one pleasure to be greater than another—then the basis of Mill's proof of hedonism is undermined. In this instance the meaning of "preferred" must be something other than "more desired," "since, as we know, the degree of desire is always, according to Mill, in exact proportion to the degree of pleasantness. But, in that case, the basis of Mill's Hedonism collapses, for he is admitting that one thing may be preferred over another and thus proved more desirable, although it is not more desired."[48]

The hedonistic ethical position of the Benthamites demonstrates again a major unresolved dilemma in Bentham and the two Mills. One horn of that dilemma is the result of the rationalism that actually pervaded the whole movement when its proclaimed method was empiricism. It is not possible to demonstrate empirically that the greatest happiness principle is the sole desirable end of action, the only end which is good in itself and the ultimate measure of behavior to which all other sound principles of action are related as means. The other horn is produced by the insistence that an empirical science of human nature—basically a science of the individual with social laws following as derivatives of individual laws—could be developed. The psychological egoism of Bentham and James Mill results from their efforts to give exactness to the laws of individual behavior. When these two opposing tenets, universal hedonism and psychological egoism, are brought together in the same system, the problems discussed in this section result.

The reformist inclinations of Bentham and the older Mill gave them an opportunity of escaping from their dilemma into the haven of practical programs of legislation, governmental organization, economics, and prison administration. Both these men were a little sun-struck by eighteenth-century enlightenment. They were quite confident not only that man could know what his own long-term interests are, but that he would through reason use the means necessary to achieve them if social conditions favorable to the individual pursuit of happiness were put into effect. And they were equally confident that under the impetus of rational utilitarian ethics the greatest happiness would be realized without extensive artificial reconciliation of individual interests. The incompatibility of an ethical end formulated as an ideal with the Benthamite conception of the nature of man as psychologically egoistic was not so much inadequately reconciled as ignored by Bentham and James Mill.

John Stuart Mill, on the other hand, in attempting a reconciliation of this dilemma deviated from what is central to the doctrines of his predecessors. As Plamenatz has so rightly said, Mill was, in the essay on *Utilitarianism,* "in the difficult position of a man whose loyalty is stronger than his faith, who cannot be blind and yet dare not see too much."[49] If this work is contrasted with the essay on "Bentham" in *Dissertations and Discussions,* it is not difficult to see that the younger Mill's inherited philosophy was not a satisfactory vehicle for his ideas. He accused Bentham of seeing man as governed only by self-interest in the pursuit of pleasure and the avoidance of pain, when he himself apparently felt compelled, in the essay on *Utilitarianism,* to follow Bentham in this same psychological egoism. "Man," he said, "is never recognized by him [Bentham] as being capable of pursuing spiritual perfection as an end; of desiring,

45

for its own sake, the conformity of his own character to his standard of excellence, without hope of good or fear of evil from any other source than his own inward consciousness. Even in the more limited form of Conscience, this great fact in human nature escapes him."[50] Again, he protested against Bentham's reduction of man, the complex being, to a very simple one and his refusal to accept qualitative differences in pleasures.

Even under the head of *sympathy*, his recognition does not extend to the more complex forms of the feelings—the love of *loving*, the need of a sympathizing support, or of objects of admiration and reverence. If he thought at all of any of the deeper feelings of human nature, it was but as idiosyncrasies of taste, with which the moralist no more than the legislator had any concern, further than to prohibit, such as were mischievous among the actions to which they might chance to lead. To say either that man should, or that he should not, take pleasure in one thing, displeasure in another, appeared to him as much an act of despotism in the moralist as in the political ruler.[51]

If his loyalty had not been so strong, Mill might have followed his faith in repudiating hedonism altogether in favor of some perfectionist ideal, which he implicitly does in the quotations above as well as in his introduction of the test of quality of pleasures into the hedonic calculus. Unfortunately, "There is not much left of Benthamite utilitarianism when John Stuart Mill has completed his defence of it. What is left is, strictly speaking, not utilitarianism at all, but a kind of naturalistic ethics that it would be misleading to call a variety of hedonism."[52]

James Mill's *An Essay on Government*, first published in the 1820 edition of the *Encyclopaedia Britannica,* is the authoritative pronouncement of the Benthamite utilitarians on political theory. The essay is a brief, simple statement of the principles of representative government, and it assumes greater importance from the fact that the utilitarians were later to rely upon parliamentary reforms as a medium through which their other reform measures might be promoted. This little work is uncomplicated by the exacting qualifications characterizing so many of Bentham's writings, and it provides a strikingly simplified example of the application of the philosophical basis of utilitarianism to the practical problems with which the group was concerned.

Typically Mill starts with the greatest-happiness principle. The end of government is the promotion of the greatest happiness of the greatest number and in order "to understand what is included in the happiness of the greatest number, we must understand what is included in the happiness of the individuals of whom it is composed."[53] Government as such deals with a particular class of happiness—the pleasures and pains that men derive from one another. The requirement of government stems from the motivation of self-interest which is the pivot point of all behavior. Since there is a shortage of the economic goods so important to happiness and since labor is required to secure these goods, men will try to avoid the pain of work by exploiting other men's labor and property if they are not prevented from doing so. "That one human being will desire to render the person and property of another subservient to his pleasure, notwithstanding the pain or loss of pleasure which it may occasion to that other individual, is the foundation of government."[54] In order that each individual may be as free to secure and to use the produce of his own labor as possible, it is necessary to unite them together under some power capable of protecting the individuals against mutual coercion.

The most important question for government, however, rises from this situation: how can this protective function be confided in those who exercise it so that they (the protectors) do not use the very powers of government for their own purpose? "All the difficult questions of Government relate to the means of restraining those, in whose hands are lodged the powers necessary for the protection of all, making a bad use of it."[55] This is the problem on which Mill concentrates his attention throughout the essay.

Mill reiterates as the possible forms of government the standard Aristotelian division into government by one, by the few, and by the whole of the community. He then proceeds *via negativa* to eliminate each of these types as unsuitable either from the standpoint of workability or from its inability to provide the requisite security against arbitrary power. Democratic government is rejected because of the impossibility of assembling all the members of the community and accomplishing the necessary tasks of government, while aristocracy and monarchy are successively moved toward the concentration of power into hands which will be opposed to the interests of the community in fostering their own ends. Mill also objects to any combination of these forms and to any attempt to balance them one against the other in a single government on the grounds that one form will tend to swallow up the others, first by combining with one of the other forms against the third, and then by elimination of the one with whom it conspired.

After making these sweeping objections, Mill moves into the positive part of the essay in which he attempts to isolate the necessary conditions of good government. He finds these conditions, as has been indicated, in the representative form, for "in the grand discovery of modern times, the system of representation, the solution of all the difficulties both speculative and practical will perhaps be found."[56]

Two factors must be present, however, to meet the requirements of an effective representative system: the governing agency must possess the power to check any usurpation of power threatening the general happiness; and the interest of the governing personnel who hold this power must be identical with the interest of the community. The fulfillment of the first condition is relatively simple: all the power necessary to check any other power or any combination of powers in the government must be given to the legislative body. On the second point, certain technical limitations are possible for preventing the abuse of political power. First, identify the legislator in his two capacities, that of legislator and that of private citizen or member of the community, and then see that his interests as a member of the community remain strongly fixed in his mind in opposition to the desire for political exploitation in the legislative capacity. This identification can be accomplished by having the power of the representative diminished, not by amount but by duration, through making him appeal for re-election at frequent intervals. This is the only and the essential security of the representative system.

Mill next moves to the consideration of the portion of the community which is to be allowed to choose the representatives. It is obvious that this electoral group must be identifiable with the whole of the community. Earlier on, Mill suggested a natural adjustment of the good of the community with the apparently incompatible atomism of individual self-interest by asserting that "the community cannot have an interest opposite to its interest."[57] Now he affirms that the community as a whole must participate in the selection of its representatives except for those special instances in which the interests of certain individuals are inseparable from that of others, such as the case of women and children whose interests are bound to those of husband and father. Mill does not advocate universal manhood suffrage, but he is concerned to see that only those persons whose interests can be adequately cared for by some other person will be disfranchised. He finds no special objection to a property qualification so long as it is sufficiently low to prevent aristocracy; but he does not concede any positive need for it since "the comparatively small number of those who have none . . . are naturally and almost necessarily governed by the minds of those who have."[58] In this case, as elsewhere in the treatise, Mill gives ample indication of the correlation between utilitarianism and that form of liberalism which sees in the middle class the exclusive possession of the virtues making for the progress of the state. The effort to place the middle class in what the utilitarians consider to be its justifiably important place is another recurrent theme of the system.

It is noteworthy that Mill takes only a single paragraph to consider the possibilities of the exploitation of the minority by the majority. The exploitation would, at the most, be minor since there would be less than one man for each of the majority to suppress, and anyway, the benefits of good government "accruing to all, might be expected to overbalance to the several members of such an elective body the benefits of misrule peculiar to themselves."[59] Here Mill returns to the familiar limitations of extreme individualism and of the attempt to reduce all social relations, however complicated, to definitely calculable quantities.

This essay by one of the central members of the school affords excellent insight into the application of the principles of the Benthamites. The method of analysis is characteristic; the arguments are deductive and almost completely lacking in any description of institutions that could be considered illustrative. As Sir Leslie Stephen puts it, Mill "speaks as from the chair of a professor laying down the elementary principles of a demonstrated science."[60] Indeed, Mill himself leaves little doubt as to his assurance that he is elaborating an established science. He points out that history, in a mere surface manner, shows us the most diverse examples of both good and bad government when the external arrangements seem the same, so we must probe to the springs of action if we are to find the requisites for a good government. And later he refers to the tendency of unrestrained individuals to acquire exploitive power over one another as a "law of nature" from which the utility of government is derived.[61] From a simple, egoistic law of human nature, then, Mill deduces not only the necessity for government, but the best means of operating that government in order to realize the greatest-happiness principle.

Another aspect of the essay which merits careful consideration is the nature of government power stressed by Mill. The utilitarians start with the dangers inherent in a social situation in which every individual is free to exploit to an illimitable extent the person and property of others in the pursuit of private interests. The solution to the problem lies in the imposition of a strong form of government over the whole of the community. But it is a government which is designed primarily to assure conditions which will afford the broadest opportunity for the free play of the natural forces of self-interest. Mill is confident that most men will behave rationally on the grounds of self-interest under proper conditions. Mill's government therefore is designed to achieve the security necessary for the intelligent pursuit of individual self-interest.

In the concluding section of the essay Mill is at pains to refute the charge that people are incapable of acting in their own interest. If the charge were true, the prospect of mankind would be deplorable. Fortunately, it is not true; most cases in which people do not follow their interests result from their mistaken views of those interests. And "the evils which arise from mistake are not incurable; for, if the parties who act contrary to their interest had a proper knowledge of that interest they would act well. What is necessary, then, is knowledge. Knowledge on the part of those whose interests are the same as those of the community, would be an adequate remedy. But knowledge is a thing which is capable of being increased: and the more it is increased the more the evils on this side of the case would be reduced."[62]

Mill, the staid and unemotional Scot, displayed an enthusiastic confidence in the likelihood that a sound parliamentary reform would provide a firm basis for rational pursuit of self-interest and that this same self-interest could, with the aid of an omnipresent, if somewhat inactive, sovereign, produce the utilitarian end.[63]

Bentham had begun his work with a different idea of government from Mill's. In his earlier Toryism he thought that his reform schemes could be imposed under the existing governmental arrangements and that the unreformed parliament might be willing to identify its own greatest happiness with that of the greatest number. But after his unfortunate experiences with his scheme for prison reform, and under the influence of James Mill, Bentham saw the necessity for securing constitutional changes along the lines of Mill's essay.

The end result of Mill's theorizing about government is a gratifyingly simple treatise in which all the complexities of political power and social cohesion are reduced to uncomplicated elements. History is of little consequence; that customary adhesion to existing society and institutions which played so important a role in Hume's politics is nowhere to be found in Mill. And even the tension between his egalitarianism and his stress on the security of previously established property rights does not spur Mill to elaborate on its problems. Man is rational and can see the utility of a common superior—which in this case is politically responsible—as a security against unenlightened egoists who might prey on him. Finally, the free pursuit of educationally enlightened self-interest will harmonize itself into the general happiness of the whole community with some help, when needed, from the government.

The role of legislation as an aid in harmonizing individual interests reopens the question of the irreconcilability of utilitarian principles, however. If the greatest happiness is the end of morality, why is this concept of legal reconciliation put forward as the only means by which egoistic desires can be achieved with security? Surely the acceptance of the sovereign as the producer of the greatest happiness becomes under these circumstances merely a means for obtaining the conditions by which self-interest may be pursued. And if the greatest happiness becomes the means to egoism, it cannot remain the ultimate end of morality. The problem raised by the ethics is still present in the politics: "Every man, says Bentham, is almost completely selfish, but painful experience teaches him that he has one great interest in common with all other men: the existence of a government that seeks to promote the greatest happiness of the greatest number and can be trusted to do so only if it is responsible to all the people and jealously watched by them. This argument of Bentham's is hardly consistent with his frequent assertions that the greatest happiness of the greatest number is an ultimate end, for what nobody desires except as a means can hardly be an ultimate end. But we are not to expect from Bentham the degree of consistency that we get from Hobbes."[64]

The utilitarians were bound by close ties to the classical school of economics. Although Adam Smith, the founder of that school and often called the father of political economy, was "no utilitarian . . . in the sense that Bentham, Ricardo, and Mill were, . . ." his system was "ultimately based on utility";[65] and some of his predecessors, including Locke, Berkeley, Mandeville, Hutcheson, and especially Hume, were also forerunners of the Benthamites. And David Ricardo, "without doubt the greatest representative of classical political economy,"[66] was in the first rank of the followers of Bentham and James Mill. Indeed, according to John Stuart Mill, it was only through the "entreaty and strong encouragement" of James Mill that Ricardo wrote and published in 1817 his epochal work, *The Principles of Political Economy and Taxation.*[67] James Mill's own *Elements of Political Economy* was to a considerable extent an additional exposition of Ricardo's main doctrines.

Bentham himself did not write a systematic classic on economic theory, although several of his tracts on economics, especially *Defence of Usury* (1787) and *A Manual of Political Economy* (1793), have attracted much attention and critical comment, so that in this branch of learning, as in the several others in which he engaged so prolixly, he must be accounted influential.

It is not within the scope of the present work to attempt a review of the economic theories of the classicists. It is more pertinent to examine the method, the underlying assumptions, and the theory of economic policy advocated by these thinkers. And it seems feasible, because of his unquestionable position as a major innovator, to begin with Adam Smith.

The philosophical implications of Smith's work are not present on the surface of *The Wealth of Nations*; "There is no special section set aside for a discussion of the scope of economic inquiry in relation to the study of human conduct in general; nor is there any explicit mention of the system of philosophy from which Smith's economic principles are derived. Yet this system is very much in evidence. It pervades the whole book even more than it does the work of the physiocratic writers."[68] The system thus underlying the whole of his work is naturalism. Smith used many particular economic arguments to emphasize the "supreme beneficence of the natural order and for pointing out the inevitable imperfections of human institutions."[69]

Smith put forward the idea that human conduct was actuated by six motives: self-love, sympathy, the desire to be free, a sense of propriety, a habit of labor, and the tendency to truck, barter, and exchange. Given these propensities, each man tended to follow his own interest, was likely to judge that interest better than anyone else, and should consequently be left free to pursue it in his own way. Added to this idea was a principle of natural harmony of interests. If left to himself, man not only would realize his own best interest, but would best promote the common economic good. "This result was achieved because Providence had made society into a system in which a natural order prevailed. The different motives of human conduct were so carefully balanced that the good of one could not conflict with the good of all.... Indeed Smith doubted whether the individual did not in this way promote the interest of society more effectively than if he had set out to do so."[70]

The consequence of this philosophy for a theory of economic policy is clear and well known. Smith was an advocate of the principle of laissez faire. Governmental noninterference in the economy was the general policy by which both private and societal interests were best promoted.

Nonetheless, there were important exceptions to this rule. Smith was willing to allow taxation of foreign commerce in order to achieve defensive self-sufficiency; he allowed some regulation of banking; he thought that interest rates might legally be fixed; and he was willing to see the government provide free schooling for those who could not afford an education. In addition, Smith was not entirely sure that class interests would always harmonize. However, neither the exceptions to the rule of noninterference nor the possibility of class conflict is sufficient to do more than slightly limit Smith's optimism; they by no means demand the relinquishment of the rule of noninterference in favor of a pragmatic, historically motivated approach to economic institutions. The general rule might allow for exceptions, but the exceptions did little more than prove the rule's applicability.[71]

Smith's method was a combination of induction and deduction, with the latter predominating. He, too, was building a science which would explain the interworkings of all the factors in man's economic relationships. As a result, Haney contends that one of his major faults is the absolutism of his theory. "In spite of bits of historical treatment, he lacked the concept of relativity, and was led to state his doctrines too narrowly and in too sweeping a fashion."[72]

The more empirical aspect of Smith's method is related directly to the social problems of his time. Smith's doctrines were founded on a thorough understanding of the rising capitalism of the late eighteenth century. And the attempt to apply his system of natural-ism to economic policy "involved a struggle against the still substantial structure of mercantilist foreign policy, against the mass of industrial regulation which had been left from preceding centuries, and against any attempts to add fresh monopolies and privileges to them."[73] But in translating the economic tendencies of his time into a complete systematic theory, it is doubtful that Smith showed sufficient awareness of the relativity of his own historical position, despite his acute consciousness that the mercantilist system was historically outmoded. It is at this point that his absolutism of theory conflicts with his empirical foundations.

It is not difficult to outline the common ground on which Smith and the Benthamites stood. The basic motivating factor of self-interest, the imposition of a completely deductive theory on a somewhat inadequate empirical framework, and the positive certainty about the conclusions reached by this method are almost identical in Smith and the utilitarians. Even Smith's naturalism was not entirely absent from the works of the utilitarians, although like his utilitarianism their naturalism is veiled and not articulated in any completeness. In *The Wealth of Nations,* then, the Benthamites found a well-formed economic theory which could be handily incorporated, with adjustment, into the body of utilitarian thought.

Although Ricardo was the representative economic thinker both within the utilitarian school proper and among the early nineteenth-century classical economists, we must turn ultimately to Bentham for the full implications of this economic system in its total setting of utilitarian ideas. But first a word about Ricardo. He carried the work of Smith to its furthest extent,[74] and in applying correctives and in elaborating the work of his predecessor, his own work seems to reflect some exaggeration of the assumptions and method of Smith. In his theory of rent he gives much more attention than Smith to the question of class conflicts and consequently displays a greater affiliation with the interests of the manufacturing middle class.[75] His exceptions to the laissez-faire rule are, if anything, narrower than Smith's; particularly is this true of his adherence to the principle of free trade. Again, in method and assumptions he illustrates even more vividly than Smith certain characteristics of his school. "Perhaps no other economist has been so abstract and hypothetical as he.... From a few premises he builds up his system like a mathematical proposition. But his premises are often taken for granted.... Enlightened self-interest, competition, the naturalness of existing institutions, are assumed. Then all 'disturbing' factors are practically disregarded. Single causes are taken, and an acute and generally accurate deduction follows. The trouble generally lies in the premises; for there is almost no verification with facts."[76]

Dr. Stark's essays on Bentham as an economist[77] attribute to Bentham far-reaching effects on the development of the classical, the historical, and the marginal-utility schools of economics. If this be true—and Stark's case is impressive—Bentham stands unparalleled as an influence on the development of economic theory in the nineteenth century. However, even allowing for some extravagance in the claims that he anticipated the fundamental doctrines of all these branches of economic ideas, his general social theory undergirded much of the thought of those in the various economic schools.

Stark contends that Bentham's sensationalist psychology is empiricist in nature while his moral theory is rationalistic and that Bentham has achieved a synthesis of the two. Man is, psychologically speaking, a pleasure-seeking animal born without innate ideas and formed by his experiences. Yet reason is able to direct the actions of men by calculating the means of maximizing pleasure and minimizing pain.[78] To this theoretical synthesis there corresponds a practical synthesis, that of the two ideals of liberty and equality. "Empiricism is thoroughly egalitarian; if men come into the world without innate ideas, filled only by an animal tendency toward pleasure, they are equal by nature; then it is only the influences received in society which cause their diversity. . . . Rationalism is thoroughly libertarian: it is in the power of man and his free will so to direct his actions by rational considerations that they serve the highest end of existence, the maximum of pleasure, in a perfect way."[79] In Stark's opinion these ideals of liberty and equality are the foundations of Bentham's economic theory, as they are the foundation of the whole of his practical philosophy.

Nonetheless, the emphasis in the economics is on freedom; by its maximization both liberty and equality will be achieved. In the matter of Bentham's theory of economic policy the primacy of liberty becomes clear, for "while the freedom of economic intercourse is to Smith only a postulate of opportunity, it becomes in Bentham a matter of principle."[80]

Bentham contested Smith's exceptions to the policy of governmental noninterference, particularly where Smith suggests the fixing of interest rates and the taxing of foreign trade. Not only are the exceptions illogical, but they do positive harm in limiting compe-

tition and subsequently in failing to apply the supply of capital to
the most productive places. Bentham starts, then, with a policy of
noninterference even more narrowly restricted than Smith's and
builds his science of economics on it. "With the view of causing
an increase to take place in the mass of national wealth, or with a
view to increase of the means either of subsistence or enjoyment,
without some special reason, the general rule is, that nothing ought
to be done or attempted by government. The motto, or watchword
of government, on these occasions, ought to be: 'Be Quiet!' "[81]

The question of equality, however, hovers in the background
of this scientific means of improving the national economic welfare
by government abstention. It must not be forgotten that it is the
greatest happiness of the greatest number which is the end in view
and that the harmonization of interests is necessary to this end. Stark
agrees with Halévy that of the three means of reconciling individual
interests employed by the utilitarians—fusion through sympathy,
natural identification, and artificial identification—the main method
employed in Bentham's economics is natural identification. But
Halévy has not seen behind this natural identification to the
principle of equality which is the common source of all identification
of interests. Bentham's principle was the *greatest happiness of the
greatest number*, not merely the increase of the happiness of any
minority to its highest degree. The social theory of the free play
of forces was thus not only productive of a greater amount of goods
than any other system, but with the presupposition in mind that
"individuals pushing against each other prove themselves equally
strong,"[82] it was the system which would be productive of the best
distribution of the goods which were so important a means to
happiness. "Hence it was an egalitarian society which appeared
to the philosophy and economy of utilitarianism as an ideal."[83]

Bentham's idea of the increasing and diminishing increments of
happiness in relation to wealth emphasizes this factor of equality.
An equal sum of money is productive of varying amounts of happiness to different persons, depending on the amount of money already
possessed. Bentham has formed a series of deductions based on this
axiom, the fifth and final one being: *"The nearer the actual proportion* [of wealth] *approaches to equality, the greater will be the total
mass of happiness."*[84]

In spite of this ideal of equality, however, liberty and equality
came into conflict with one another, "and here lies the great decision

between liberalism and socialism."[85] Liberty permits the rising of one man above the other, equality denies this right. "In view of this fact, Bentham rejects a system of strict equality in which the law removes all chance of ascent."[86] Neither on the basis of equal division of property nor on its common ownership is equality economically sound. In the conflict between liberty (called security in its juridical context) and equality, "The most important object is security. . . . When security and equality are in conflict it will not do to hesitate a moment. Equality must yield . . .";[87] otherwise this economic order based on free competition would break down. And on Bentham's calculations, if the system broke down, the most productive means—the one based on a scientific construction of the psychological nature of man—would collapse, and with it the potential of increased happiness.

Bentham was not entirely negative in his adherence to the idea of equality, however, in spite of the fact that much of his "agenda" of governmental activity was directed toward freeing the economy from arbitrary restraints imposed by law. Many of his recommendations for the advancement of equality rely on a somewhat puritanical advocacy of frugality by the individual. But in certain instances, for example in his stress on the use of the inheritance tax as an equalization measure, Bentham acknowledges a positive role for government in upholding equality. Never, though, does his support of equality outrun his emphasis on security; instead he seeks only to minimize inequality where it can be done without a threat to freedom of the acquisitive spirit and protection of the things acquired.

As Professor Robbins has recently shown,[88] the classical economists were far more concerned about the general welfare than many of their critics would lead us to believe. As a corrective to the idea that the classicists were more or less in the service of a deliberately self-seeking middle class, it is well to call to mind all their exceptions to the rule of laissez faire and to remember that they were concerned with implementing the total national economic welfare by the advancement of what they regarded as an authenticated economic science. At the same time it should not be forgotten that the exceptions, and even the doubts, which they voiced were faint compared to the confidence they reposed in their reasonings. Deductive rules were laid down which were only slightly qualified by empirical data, and even the qualifications were made from the standpoint of a rather constricted basis of experience and a rather narrow historical perspective. But the rules are formulated in so positive a manner that they sometimes appear to be given for all times and all circumstances, and perhaps the most unfortunate aspect of their work "was the opportunity which it gave to socialists to quote and misapply economic dogmas."[89]

John Stuart Mill illustrates the conflict of ends and means that became apparent in these economic doctrines. He made such extensive exceptions to the doctrine of laissez faire that he has been attacked by advocates of his school and embraced by the socialists. Haney holds that in spite of his presupposition in favor of laissez faire as the general rule, "Mill was not committed to individualism as an absolute generalization." Instead he was freer to apply the test of utility to any question of governmental activity, whereas Smith's confidence in naturalism forbade the immediate application of this test.[90]

When Mill, therefore, witnessed actual conditions resulting from a capitalistic development about which the early classical economists had only surmised, he measured these conditions by his ethical ideal of the greatest happiness and offered empirical correctives. Too often, though, Mill's framework of theory is drawn from his forebears. He sees man dominated psychologically by self-interest, yet in his idealism he asks this primitive man to accept and act in such a way that he realizes lofty social ends, and in these instances he shows a "lack of harmony or fusion in the elements of his philosophy"[91] which is again traceable to the old confusion of psychological and ethical theories. The utilitarians postulate a science of man based on psychological egoism, but at the same time they adopt as the ethical end which this science is supposed to serve the broadly humanitarian goal of the greatest happiness of the greatest number. In addition, the framework and foundation of the *Principles of Political Economy* "remain a priori. He set out with the same suppositions as Adam Smith and Ricardo, namely, that man is governed by self-interest in economic affairs, that the individual pursuit of selfish ends promotes the general welfare, that profits and wages are equalized, and that taxation is shifted about in such a manner as to make them so. Only in distinguishing the laws of Distribution from those of Production he breaks [*sic*] from the earlier idea, removing as the distinction does, a part of economics from the dominance of physical causes."[92]

CHAPTER THREE

Refutation of Positivism

I N THE BOOKS published while he was living, Sidgwick consciously avoided the entangling philosophical questions involved in the theory of knowledge and in metaphysics. His reluctance to commit himself on these problems is a reflection of Sidgwick's doubts about the possibility of reaching any satisfactory conclusions with respect to them. Coupled with this latent scepticism, however, was the very strong belief that some important problems could be handled by the philosopher without commitment to a precise ontology or a definite epistemology. In the Preface to the first edition of *The Methods of Ethics*, for example, he notes that he has avoided any inquiry into the origin of the moral faculty "by the simple assumption (which seems to be made implicitly in all ethical reasoning) that there is something under any circumstances which it is right or reasonable to do, and that this may be known." He points out that beyond this he makes no further assumption as to "the nature of the object of ethical knowledge...."[1]*
Again, after discussing the points at issue between determinist and libertarian moral theorists, Sidgwick concludes that the freewill question is one which does not have, for his purpose, the importance which some writers ascribe to it. Here, too, he substitutes an assumption for a final decision so that he may move on to the prac-

*Notes to this chapter begin on page 176.

tical ethical problems which confront him. In this case he assumes a subjective libertarianism on the basis of the introspective conclusion that in a situation in which he has a distinct consciousness of choosing between alternatives of conduct, it is impossible not to think that he may choose to do what he conceives to be right or reasonable.[2]

In spite of his failure to find a system of philosophy whose metaphysics and theory of knowledge satisfied him, Sidgwick never lost sight of the fundamental importance of the questions raised by these studies; he never lost hope that such a system might be created; and he was ever dissatisfied with his own scepticism regarding the establishment of verifiable conclusions about them.

As a matter of fact, both the internal evidence of the works of his later years and the more specific pronouncements in his letters demonstrate something of a change in his focus of interest in philosophy. Whereas in his early period he had been content to skirt the more abstract philosophical questions in order to move onto the firmer ground of practical ethics, economics, and politics, toward the close of his life he was occupied almost exclusively with the former matters. It would be absurd to deny that in earlier treatises (especially *Methods of Ethics*) Sidgwick was making, among other things, important critical analyses of the broader philosophical implications of the theorists on whom he concentrated. In articles and reviews dating from as early as the 1870's he also made specialized criticisms of some of the methodological, epistemological, and metaphysical conceptions of various schools of philosophy. But this criticism was secondary to the constructive work that he was attempting to do on more practical matters. For a good part of the last ten or twelve years of his life, however, he concentrated his energies both in teaching and in writing to a considerable extent on metaphysics.

There appears to have been two reasons for this shift of emphasis. In the first place, he became more and more dissatisfied with the lack of a metaphysical basis for some of his own conclusions. He recognized and accepted the fact that "somehow or other, morality will get on" in the practical sense, with or without the basis that he seeks for it. "But," he said in 1887, "my special business is not to maintain morality *somehow*, but to establish it logically as a reasoned system, and I have declared and published that this cannot be done, if we are limited to merely mundane sanctions, owing to the inevitable divergence, in this imperfect world, between the individual's

Duty and his Happiness. I said in 1874 that without some datum beyond experience 'the cosmos of duty is reduced to a chaos.' Am I to recant this conviction and answer my own argument—which no one of my numerous antogonists has yet even tried to answer?"[3] Is there, then, any point to professing ethics without some extramundane sanction? And from what source shall we derive the proof that such a sanction exists? Sidgwick reported that he tried all types of proof—revelational, rational, empirical—and all of them failed. But he continued to cling to the hope of success, because "it [was] premature to despair, and ... [he was] quite content to go on seeking while life [lasted]. ..."[4]

The second reason for Sidgwick's concern with metaphysics during this phase of his life lies in the great intellectual struggles over the underlying questions of philosophy, particularly ontology and knowledge, which ran through the second half of the nineteenth century. In the eighteenth and early nineteenth centuries the apparent success of the physical and biological sciences in solving their specialized problems had resulted in a form of positivism which had been reflected in the tendency of the Benthamites to reduce the problem of knowledge to reliance on methodological rules derived from the sciences and to deny the validity of any attempt to deal with metaphysics. Hardly had this trend run its course when the theory of evolution converted biological science from its traditional concern with the classification and functioning of supposedly static forms (morphology) to the study of the derivation and relationship (phylogeny) of changing forms.[5] To the emphasis on empiricism of earlier positivist conceptions there was now added the important new ingredient of historical relativism in the theories of those who attempted to find in evolution the source of their philosophical generalizations. After Darwin's work was published, issue was joined more vigorously than ever between the positivists and those who opposed them with traditional Christian, rationalistic, or idealistic philosophical systems. It seems safe to say that the evolutionary school with its numerous and often odd variations aroused far more philosophical controversy than any other doctrine of the nineteenth century. It is hardly strange that Sidgwick with his insatiable intellect and growing awareness of the lack of answers to basic questions implicit in his work should have thoroughly investigated the philosophical implications of the assertions of this new school.

A provisional answer to his own scepticism and a point of departure for his examination of positivism was furnished Sidgwick by the common-sense philosophy of Thomas Reid. In a paper on "The Philosophy of Common Sense" which he read to the Glasgow Philosophical Society in 1895 Sidgwick stated Reid's conception of the duty of a philosopher, a conception which, in view of Sidgwick's concern with practical problems of ethics and the extent to which common-sense moral beliefs had to be taken into account in dealing with these problems, was very close to his own view. Sidgwick pointed out that according to Reid, "it is the duty of a philosopher— his duty *as* a philosopher—to aim steadily and persistently at bringing the common human element of his intellectual life into clear consistency with the special philosophic element. And Reid is on the whole perfectly aware—though his language occasionally ignores it—that for every part of this task the special training and intellectual habits of the philosopher are required. For the fundamental beliefs which the philosopher shares with the plain man can only be defined with clearness and precision by one who has reflected systematically, as an ordinary man does not reflect, on the operations of his own mind."[6]

Sidgwick specifically acknowledged his debt to Reid in *Philosophy, Its Scope and Relations* by explaining that his own metaphysical position is "speaking broadly that of what has been called since Reid the Philosophy of Common Sense or Natural Dualism." He then went on from that point to explain that he believed that there was an "advantage in putting questions from the point of view of Common Sense" because its view is to some degree in the minds of all of us even when we are most opposed to it, and it is the view with which we all start when we begin to philosophize, "whatever metaphysical conclusions we may ultimately adopt (Materialist, Sensationalist, or Idealist): and therefore it will be a philosophical gain to bring it as clearly as we can before the full gaze of reflective attention, even though further consideration should lead us to abandon or modify it."[7] When Sidgwick comes to examine the philosophy of positivism, therefore, he concentrates on the claim that positive philosophy, in the service of science, has overthrown the beliefs of common sense and erected a naturalistic explanation of human and social phenomena in their place. As will become clear in the context of his criticism, the failure on the part of positivists to produce sufficient evidence to force an abandonment of the common-

sense beliefs about existence furnishes strong grounds for refusal
to accept the positivist premises. Just as Reid more than a century
before had reasserted the doctrines of common sense in the face of
the idealism of Berkeley and the scepticism of Hume, so now was
Sidgwick engaged in their reassertion against sociological and biological determination. It is important, therefore, to recall the place
that Reid occupies in the history of philosophy, together with some
of his doctrines, before enlarging on the problems presented by
positivism and Sidgwick's criticism of that school.

Dr. Thomas Reid, the founder of the Scottish school of philosophy, was born on April 26, 1710, at Strachan, Kincardineshire, near
Aberdeen. The son of a clergyman, he was entered in Marischal
College, Aberdeen, when he was about twelve or thirteen years
of age. In 1726 he received an appointment as librarian at his University, a post which he held until 1737. In the latter year he took
a living at Newmachar which he held until 1752, when he was
elected Professor of Philosophy, Kings College, Aberdeen. In 1764
he published his *Inquiry into the Human Mind on the Principles of
Common Sense*, the first of the three main parts of his philosophical
system. In the same year he succeeded Adam Smith as Professor of
Moral Philosophy at Glasgow, where he remained for seventeen
years. He retired from his chair at Glasgow in 1781 in order to
devote his full time to the completion of his philosophical studies.
The second treatise, *Essays on the Intellectual Powers of Man*,
appeared in 1785, and the final complementary volume, *Essays on
the Active Powers of the Human Mind*, in 1788. Reid died in 1796.[8]

The initial impetus for Reid's *Inquiry* came from his opposition
to the scepticism of Hume. As early as 1739, following the publication of Hume's *Treatise of Human Nature*, Reid began to speculate
critically on some of the supposedly established opinions on which
Hume's scepticism was founded. Earlier Reid had uncritically
accepted Berkeley's whole system, but when he questioned the
authority on which he accepted the "doctrine of ideas," he found it
to consist solely of the "authority of the philosophers."[9] Disliking the
sceptical consequences implicit in the doctrine, Reid proceeded to
trace its origin back through Berkeley, Locke, and Malebranche to
Descartes, the founder of modern philosophy.[10]

Descartes, by refusing credence to anything except that which
was "absolutely certain and evident," had countered the ancient
conception that knowledge proceeded from material effervescences

or "ghosts" which entered the mind to produce thought, after having been given off by external objects. But the difficulty of Descartes' dualism was his inability to solve the problem of how an idea accurately representing an external object *did* get into the mind. Reid held that the error of Descartes, and subsequently of Locke and Malebranche, resulted from the way in which they posed the problem; they were confused, he felt, in supposing that the development of an idea involved some sort of psychical translation of immediate sense perception into the cognition (or idea), which in turn implied the existence of the external object. The confusion probably resulted from the fallacy of philosophizing by analogy; in this case the philosophers concerned had apparently presumed that the relation between the mind and the external world was analogous to the action of one physical body upon another. But upon careful introspection one sees that the experience of normal perception does not consist of some unexplained impact of the external object on the subject's senses, followed by a mental image or idea which represents that sensation to the knowing mind. Instead the immediate act of perception in itself involves a judgment (cognition) of the object perceived. The certainty of the existence of the object perceived is not attained by an act of inference from some intermediary presentation to the mind; the conviction itself is a primary datum of knowledge.

By assuming the necessity of relating the external world to the mind in a step by step causal fashion, Descartes had already planted the seeds of doubt that were to bloom into full scepticism in Hume. Berkeley's failure to explain the connection of mind and matter, an explanation made necessary by the Cartesian method of presenting the problem, resulted in his rejection of the reality of an external world; and Hume "upon the same grounds, undoes the world of spirits, and leaves nothing in nature but ideas and impressions, without any subject on which they may be impressed."[11]

Reid's reliance on a form of naïve realism based on perceptional data as a basis for knowledge makes it necessary for him to explain how we can avoid the deception of the senses, not only in the case of illusions, but also in the more consistent fallacies of the senses, such as variations in the appearance of objects because of changes in the subject's physical relation to them. Thus, for example, an object appears to grow visibly smaller in size as the distance of the observer from it increases, in spite of the fact that the object (presumed real) remains unchanged. Reid's reply is that the very manner in which the objection is presented testifies to the belief in the object perceived. And further, it is by tacitly accepting the idea of the real existence of the objects perceived that we improve our knowledge of them and correct the distorted views yielded by the initial perceptions. This process is referred to as the alteration of original perception by the "acquired" perception of experience.[12]

Science carries acquired perception a step further: by relying on the vast collection of sense data which science assembles, our predictions become clear and unerring. Through acquired perception, for example, the ordinary man will soon learn to accept the fact that objects appear to diminish relative to his distance from them; but science will go beyond this point and find a method of determining the ratio of diminution to the distance of the observer.

In Reid's view, then, it is not the duty of philosophy to reject everything which cannot be made perfectly apparent to reason. Instead its function should be to accept tentatively the beliefs which present themselves to the common sense of mankind and to attempt to clarify these beliefs by critical examination and, finally, to create for them an ordered system.

It is fairly obvious from the foregoing that Reid's common-sense conceptions are better adapted to critical than to constructive philosophy. If, for instance, he fails to account satisfactorily for all the beliefs of common sense (a persisting, self-conscious mind, the reality of an external world, etc.), he does demonstrate that those who have opposed these beliefs with systems based on other doctrines have failed to produce satisfactory evidence to prove their falseness. And, additionally, he calls into serious question the positive systems of thought which have been put forward as replacements for common-sense beliefs. As Hume himself clearly recognizes, it is necessary in practical existence to act on principles quite different from those arrived at in the philosopher's chair. And Reid elevates this practical necessity into a philosophical first principle. "It is," he says, "a bold philosophy that rejects without ceremony, principles, which irresistibly govern the belief and conduct of all mankind in the common concerns of life, and to which the philosopher himself must yield, after he imagines he hath confuted them."[13]

In denying the validity of their conclusions concerning knowledge, Reid also makes an attack on the methodology of Hume and his predecessors. Although presumably basing their conclusions on inductive reasoning, they actually make hypotheses whose foundations do not meet the test of careful introspection. Introspection, which is the only satisfactory method of applying induction to the study of consciousness, does not tell us, for example, that notions of time and space, memory, and other forms of experience may be broken down into elemental sensations. On the contrary, introspection will actually yield Reid's conception of the irreducibility of these cognitions. Therefore, if the charge be made that Reid assumes "gratuitously, in all his reasoning, that theory of the human soul which the scheme of materialism calls in question,"[14] it may be replied that not only have opposing philosophies not proved this assumption false, but that their counterassumptions are not really based on the inductive ground which is claimed for them. Reid would be the first to agree that his common-sense beliefs leave much to be justified on rational grounds, but he would insist that in both method and conclusion they are less open to objection than are the alternatives in the way of idealism, materialism, or scepticism. In his view the only reason we have for holding a proposition concerning consciousness to be a fact is that careful introspection shows it to be such; all other conclusions are inferential. And critical common-sense conclusions, however much they may fall short of complete knowledge, are more practical, more readily drawn from introspective data, and internally no more inconsistent than those of the other schools.

The foundations of positivism were laid in the eighteenth century, and utilitarianism was certainly one of the participating schools. But the philosophers of the enlightenment were essentially striving after knowledge of objects whose forms and relationships were fixed and abiding; their conception of the potential knowledge of man and society was based on an analogy to the persisting laws of force discovered by Newton. Empiricism of the utilitarian type assumed the mental data which were the object of its knowledge to be unvarying and subject to analysis into irreducible sensations whose interrelations formed the content of experience. The analogy to the knowable relationship of objects in the material world is clear, and the discovery of the laws by which the relationships among the elementary data of knowledge are fixed permits the same objective control over the content of human experience as that obtained by the physical sciences over matter. The result was a "vague optimistic doctrine"[15] of human progress associated with an almost complete rejection of the past as a long succession of errors to be repudiated out of confidence in contemporary method. Of the relation of this thought to the later historical emphasis of the evolutionary school it may be said that:

During the eighteenth century men did believe in human perfectibility but they did not view this as a genuinely developmental process. Instead education and reform were thought sufficient to improve mankind. This view of human change lacked the notion of transformation through time; it was static rather than historical, as though each man was solely the product of his experiences and owed nothing to the past, and as though each institution could be torn up by its roots and a new one planted in the old soil to grow entirely according to present plans. There was little sense of the role of history and of the force of the past in moulding human institutions.[16]

But the nineteenth century saw history come of age.[17] Sidgwick notes that the nineteenth century was called, in contrast with the eighteenth, a pre-eminently historical century—the eighteenth being the "Seculum Rationalisticum."[18] Yet it was in the nineteenth century that historical thought, through its double alliance with the optimism of science of the eighteenth century and the scientific evolutionism of the nineteenth, came near to losing its claim to independence as a mode of experience. Under the influence of beliefs in the naturalistic objectivity of all social data and the inexorable change implied by evolution, the older static conceptions give way to the discovery of social laws indicating development in time toward perfection. There is, indeed, truth in "the epigram which affirms that, though the eighteenth and the nineteenth centuries were both self-satisfied, the eighteenth century was satisfied with what it was, and the nineteenth with what it was becoming."[19]

It was not, however, until the work of the "critical" historians was bulwarked by the sociologists that history was completely identified with natural causal processes.[20] Ranke's emphasis on "facts" did not destroy the dualism of material and spiritual factors in the historical process; all it did was to insist that the "idea" was knowable only in its "apparent" form. Though the idea appears only in the natural connections and can be understood only so, still it could not be subject to natural causality. Certain phenomena, and indeed the most significant, could not be grasped in their full meaning unless we resolved to look beyond the world of phenomena.[21]

The decisive break with this tradition of dualism in the study of social phenomena came with Auguste Comte who insisted on making the factual products of history into a science called "sociology," which would rid itself of nonnatural causes and discover in the relationship of historical facts the *laws* governing society. As Helen Lynd points out, "It was no great step from such a faith in science [as had permeated the intellectual climate of the nineteenth century] to the Positivism of August Comte."[22]

The first volume of Comte's work *Le Cours de Philosophie Positive* appeared in 1830, the final volume in 1842. His "law of the three stages" is the central thesis of the study. According to this thesis, man's opinions concerning any subject pass invariably through three historical phases: a theological phase, a metaphysical phase, and finally into a positive stage. In the first of these all events are referred by the thinker to the will of a supernatural diety, in the second to abstract essences, and in the third to the actual laws of nature. The only fields in which man's knowledge has reached the positive stage are the natural sciences. His opinions in other fields lag behind in the theological or metaphysical stages, social phenomena being now mainly in the metaphysical phase.[23] In order to produce the progressive results which should be forthcoming in society, the social sciences will have to emulate the natural sciences and pass into the positive stage.[24]

In history we find that our knowledge of the objective world is steadily growing on the basis of received scientific method. The earliest accurate knowledge is of the inorganic world, and from there we move to more and more complex sciences, each one of which is dependent for its development upon a fairly complete science of its predecessor. What is more important, the phenomena studied by the sciences are themselves structured in a relationship to one another which corresponds to the hierarchical order through which our knowledge of them moves. Thus when we proceed from the inorganic to the organic sciences, we encounter an increasing complexity, and when we move into the study of society, we arrive at the most complex phenomena of all. And since each study proceeds from the series immediately prior to its own (just as each successive object is of a higher order than the former), it is natural that man and society should have barely arrived at the point where real knowledge of them is possible. However, having discovered the governing historical laws, there remains only the task of applying the proper scientific methods to the study of society (the most complex and highest order of things) to make our total knowledge as complete as it need be, following which we can utilize this knowledge for making society over into Comte's perfectionist ideal of what it should be. Comte thus completed the first movement of nineteenth-century philosophy toward providing a complete explanation of the whole nature and development of man on the basis of laws derived from a temporal process, which explanation makes super-fluous all forms of metaphysics or systems of knowledge which have objects beyond those to be discovered in the facts of history.

Although with Comte we are already involved in a philosophy which derives its generalizations from a development concept going far beyond the older empirical tradition, it was the appearance of Darwin's *Origin of Species* in 1859 which brought the theory of biological evolution into the purview of the general public and stimulated the development of a school of evolutionary social theorists. But even before the appearance of Darwin's immeasurably influential treatise, Herbert Spencer, pre-eminently the English philosopher who developed a "social science" on the basis of biological evolution, had already sketched an outline of what is perhaps the most ambitious attempt to erect a complete philosophical system in the history of British philosophy. However little he may be read at the present time and whatever curious assortment of contradictory influences may be discovered in him today,[25] there can be no doubt that Spencer was to his contemporaries—philosophers and laymen alike—the representative of the evolutionary philosophical school and one of the eminent Victorians.

Spencer's earliest work of note was *Social Statics* (1851) which, although giving indication of his later developmental conceptions, was an enunciation of a perfectionist ideal of individualism which contained strong overtones of natural rights.[26] Spencer was never one to abandon an idea, no matter how incompatible it might be with his later postulates, and this early concept of individuation was later to become the teleological standard toward which evolution was carrying man and the standard by which human progress was to be measured.

The plan of the *Synthetic Philosophy* was sketched in 1858. The work began to appear in 1860 with the publication of the *First Principles*, and the other parts—biology, psychology, sociology, and ethics—came out intermittently for the next thirty years. Although biological evolution plays an increasingly important role in Spencer's work as he moves into the study of man and society, the evolutionary conception on which he builds is cosmological. In all of nature—inorganic, organic, and social—there is a constant redistribution of force, and this change is continuously in the direction of a state of equilibrium. The process of movement toward equilibration involves passing from a state of "relatively indefinite incoherent homogeneity to a relatively definite coherent heterogeneity."[27] This process of differentiation goes on in the physical universe in its advancement from nebula to the solar system, in the biological sphere in its advancement from the lowest organism to human individuation (the process is found very clearly in individual embryonic development in its stages corresponding to the hierarchy of the species), and on the social level from a warring primitivism to the peaceful industrial state based on liberal individualism.

Biologically Spencer was a Lamarckian rather than a Darwinian, accepting the idea of purposive adaptation in preference to natural selection.[28] However, this purposive adaptation has more effect than natural selection only in advanced stages of development when the end of individuation may be recognized and man and his environment consciously adapted to it. Spencer was unlikely to give up either his anarchistic utopia or the rigidly scientific laws by which man was directed there, but he was willing for the laws to be more scrupulously obeyed once they had been discovered. And above all, it must be emphasized that Spencer insisted that the laws of evolution were the laws of progress.

Positivistic historiography enjoyed a great vogue in the latter half of the nineteenth century, and it usually eventuated in a theory of progress. Following the earlier epochal development of Hegelian historiography, the most prominent figures in the movement were Comte, Spencer, and Marx, although claims were laid by many others to the possibility of finding in history not only important lessons from the past, but a complete knowledge of the laws of social development. And even the end of society was revealed historically by reason of our ability to project the discoverable laws of the past into the future. To be sure, both Comte and Spencer continued to talk of an area of the "unknowable," but the certainty with which their conclusions were expressed left little doubt that they felt they could know all they needed to know.

But to what extent does history so conceived really yield this culminating knowledge sought so long and through so many methods by philosophy? Perhaps the answer is in the variety of ends produced in the vineyard of history by the various tillers.

For the historical, or if the term is preferred, the genetic sciences do not in themselves, any more than do the mathematical or physical sciences, provide a scale of values by which men can guide their conduct. The historian, if he but search far enough, can find almost anything in the past. Unless he is willing to adopt a consistent monism, and apply the idealists' formula to the past, in the form of "whatever has been, has been right," he will be obliged to judge the past as Acton judged it, in accordance with standards which are his own, which do not derive automatically from the historical process itself. The historical method taught Marx the inevitability of socialism, and it taught Maine the impossibility of socialism. Each man must have held that the other was misusing history.[29]

When we come, then, to examine the philosophical content—the teleology, values, and ontology—which the positivist historians preferred to call the laws of historical evolution (or progress), we discover not the certainty of agreement of experts, but the same grounds for contention exposed by all philosophical systems. The ends, and even the means to these ends, envisaged by Comte, Spencer, Marx, Buckle, Bagehot, Maine, Nietzsche, and many other sociologists and historians of the period, cover as broad a variation of opinions as can be conceived. What was brought to history in this era was surely as important as what was found there. Extreme individualism, collectivism, the place of custom in society, institutional evolution, environment, and biological evolution were in the air; they were part of the intellectual setting around which philosophical controversy turned. The uniqueness of the situation was in the fact that history, scientifically studied, was supposed to verify these means and ends, thereby solving the problem of epistemology; and through the idea of progress, history also was thought to be solving the problem of ontology.

Sidgwick's critical examination of historical positivism occupies nearly half of *Philosophy, Its Scope and Relations,* published posthumously in 1902. This volume, which summarizes his conclusions on the subject, is the culmination of an investigation which dates from the 1870's and became intensified with Sidgwick's concentration on metaphysics in the nineties.[30] The fact that he places such emphasis on the question in a book of philosophical fundamentals points up the acuteness of the problem, not only in terms of Sidgwick's systematic position, but also from the standpoint of the tremendous impact of positivism on the Victorian world.

Sidgwick is concerned with the claim of history, in a positivistic sense, to have invaded and transformed all subjects of knowledge, leaving no philosophical method distinct from it. If such a method meant only induction, its invasion would not be so thorough, but it is actually much more: "For the historical method which is supposed to have invaded, and transformed, all departments of thought is mainly the method of studying the more or less remote past, so far as it is different from the *recent* past:—it is a method of studying in each department the whole series of changes either in things thought about or our thoughts about them in order to understand the general laws of these changes and so comprehend and explain the present as resulting from the past in accordance with these laws."[31] It is history so regarded that he is examining in a critical spirit.

Sidgwick's first approach to this criticism is to assess the supposed effect of the historical method so conceived upon each science. He begins with the physical sciences and presents significant and interesting arguments with respect to them, but it is the organic sciences and their penetration into the realm of mental activity by the Darwinian theory that have particular effect upon Victorian opinion. He refers to evolution as "historical biology" and examines its challenge to philosophy.

The first question to be settled is the extent to which the evolutionary school has resolved the problem of the relation of mind and matter. In spite of its important influence on science, evolution has not, in Sidgwick's view, affected the basic philosophical controversy respecting the reality of mind as a substance differing from matter. The great controversy over Darwinism results from a failure to distinguish between scientific and philosophical reasons for accepting the new biological thesis. There is nothing in evolution that should force a rejection of the old conception of the dual nature of man as a combination of spirit and body in favor of materialism. If the materialistic conclusion has been validated by Darwin, the invasion really would be complete, but the supposed achievement appears to Sidgwick "quite illusory."[32]

The old arguments respecting the distinction between mind and matter are untouched by the new encroachment. On the materialist side there is still the support offered by the invariable connection between organic and mental change and the absence of proof of disembodied mental activity, while on the dualist side there is the "unique disparity of physical and psychical phenomena, and the apparent arbitrariness of the connection between the two."[33]

One new argument is added, however, by historical evolution. This is the "argument from Continuity." The proposition may be stated in this manner: if the highest phenomena of mind are connected by an unbroken series of infinitesimal differences with the lowest organisms to whose operations we could ever attribute the term physical, and even to inorganic matter, there is no point at which the existence of mind as an entity may be said to begin. Mind could hardly be independent of matter "if man was gradually developed out of a monkey and the monkey out of a polyp and so on."[34]

Sidgwick believes that the argument from continuity presents no difficulty to the dualist that had not been present before the advent of evolutionary theories. He bases his belief on the similarity of the evolutionist's view of the whole development of the psychical element in men to the development of the human mind in an individual. Every individual man is developed gradually out of a portion of organized matter whose existence is no more psychical than the polyp's. What does it matter whether the race has gone through the same process or not? The difficulty is already present, and the relative rapidity of change of the individual soul-less organism to a human being compared to the longer process of evolution of the human race can hardly be taken as giving rise to a relevant philosophical difference.

Secondly, the philosophical evolutionist's argument against the independent existence of mind rests on the difficulty of believing that a new thing has come into existence quite gradually. But this difficulty has to be overcome by most modern schools of thought in the case of the individual mind: "For on the one hand they can hardly deny that any particular mind—even if we mean no more by this term than the stream of transient phenomena, thoughts, feelings, and volitions of which we have direct experience—is a new fact. That is, they cannot deny that it is totally unlike whatever physical facts antecede or accompany it; and they are not commonly prepared to contend that it is composed of pre-existent thoughts, emotions, etc., re-arranged in new relations. . . . On the other hand, we have equally to admit that this new fact, so far as known, actually begins

73

to be between certain limits of time. If this be granted, I do not see that a perfectly gradual beginning is harder to accept than an abrupt one; on the contrary I should say it was certainly easier."[35]

Sidgwick refused to accept the distinction made by contemporary thinkers between different types of mental phenomena. Some philosophers are willing to admit that the sensations and other relatively undifferentiated mental facts may have been completely caused by movement of organic matter, while holding that the higher types of mental phenomena are not attributable to a change in organic matter at all. Sidgwick, on the other hand, is unwilling to compromise his common-sense dualism by this concession to materialism. The hypothesis is invalid for him because the differences between mind and matter as such are so much greater than any demonstrable differences in mental activities. Once it is admitted that the movement of matter is the adequate cause of the most elementary feeling, there is no firm ground for not supposing all mental activity to have a similar cause; and Sidgwick was not willing, on the most careful introspection, to admit that sense data were separated from cognition and grounded entirely in changes in the body.

The conclusion is that "the historical method, as applied to Anthropology on the basis of Darwin's theory, leaves the metaphysical problem of the relation of mind and matter exactly where it was."[36]

These considerations, however, lead to a related question. That is, how far has psychology as an empirical science been dominated by investigations of the past history of the mind? This question, of course, touches the very roots of utilitarianism and the whole school of English associationist psychology.

Sidgwick finds that "psychogony," or historical psychology, has gradually taken over from other methods of empirical psychology. "A study of the history of the mind as it has gradually *become* what it is, has illegitimately presented itself as a Sensationalist theory of mind as it is now, all thought being reduced to supposed elements of feeling. And it is noteworthy that by a second illogicality the Sensationalism has led to Materialism. For when the more characteristic states and processes of the fully developed mind have been thus pseudo-chemically decomposed into their supposed elements, then— as all intellectual content has vanished in an imaginary chaos of atomic feelings, the material concomitant of the elementary feeling naturally becomes prominent to the reflective mind that is performing this analysis and presents itself as the real process."[37] In Sidg-wick's view Reid had long ago "exposed the unwarrantable assump-tions" generated by the "vague materialism" which had resulted from a similar attempt to analyze mind in terms of simple sensation.[38] The subsequent success of the natural sciences had provided assurance that the ultimate answer to epistemological questions lay in mate-rialism. As a result it was incumbent upon Sidgwick once more to explain the analogical fallacy upon which materialism was based and to demonstrate anew the misuse to which introspection had been subjected by the "psychogonists."

The difficulties of observation and analysis of mental activity by introspection have been factors in allowing this fallacious method-ology to take hold. Nevertheless, introspection, not associationism, is the only method by which the phenomena of mental activity can be assessed. No atomization or "analysis" of a belief can show it to be anything other than that which careful introspection shows it to be. Whatever its parts, conditions, or antecedents may be, an idea is, upon cognition, an entity distinct in itself. "For example, space does not mean to me successive feelings of movement, con-ceived as simultaneous from association with simultaneous feelings of touch, though this may describe the process by which I have come to have the notion of space."[39]

But it may be said that even if the nature of our thoughts, emotions, or volitions cannot be affected by an inquiry into the process by which they become what they are, this investigation of process may still give us insight into the question of whether these beliefs are what they ought to be. Introspection professes to give a criterion for determining the validity of beliefs. Can historical inquiry into the origin and development of belief affect this validity?

At this point in the discussion we are a step removed from an investigation of natural history under the impact of the doctrine of evolution. Hitherto, the questions raised could be considered as individual or set apart from social factors. Beliefs, however, are a different type of fact. "The current beliefs, the prevailing sentiments, in a given society at a given time, are no doubt beliefs and senti-ments of a certain aggregate of individuals; but we have generally speaking no means of tracing and explaining their development and diffusion in the consciousness of the great mass of individuals who entertain them: for the purpose of our cognition, they must be treated as social facts."[40] For this reason Sidgwick substitutes the

75

term "sociological method" for the term "historical method" throughout the remainder of the inquiry.

There is no doubt that the study of beliefs is an important sociological study, nor is there any doubt that the study should be conducted by historical method. However, the case is open to the same objection confronting historical naturalism. The claim of sociology overextends itself. The proponents of historical or sociological method want to do more than establish the sequence of social beliefs and the cause for this sequence; they also claim to demonstrate through this method the truth or falsity of these beliefs. Thus, they subsume under sociological method the whole epistemological question.

Two results follow from trying to construct a theory of knowledge solely by tracing the supposed development of ideas. One is a destructive or sceptical attitude on the part of the observer, the other is a positive or optimistic view of knowledge. In the negative sense scepticism often results from the historical study of beliefs. The student gains insight into a vast, bewildering succession of conflicting beliefs, held in each case, with almost fanatical tenacity; yet each belief passes away to be succeeded by another idea defended just as strongly as its predecessor. This demonstrable fluctuation in basic human concepts works an ill effect upon the witness. "Every portion of this series seems to have lost power to hold his own reason in the grip of true conviction; for peace's sake, he accepts the beliefs that are pressed on him by public opinion in his own age and country; but in his heart he believes in nothing but history."[41]

Sidgwick holds this sceptical position to be unwarranted. He argues here, as he had in the *Methods of Ethics*, that the ascertainment of the origin and development of beliefs cannot logically destroy confidence in accepted beliefs. Some thinkers have contended, for example, that an explanation of the *derivation* of the faculty of moral intuition (as opposed to the acceptance of that faculty as *innate*) would make a reasonable man regard the concept of moral intuition as invalid. This is not true. In order to disprove the intuitive factor's influence in ethics, there must also be proof that the causes producing it were such as to make it untrue. Mere demonstration of causes of beliefs is not sufficient to prove them false. We are aware in sociology, as in all other sciences, that every belief must have been caused in some particular way, the only ground for inferring untruth in a belief is to know some other belief to be true. Error is proved only by inconsistency with truth. General disbelief cannot logically be justified from a historical knowledge of successions of beliefs and their causes and development. Such scepticism tends to attack weakly organized systems of belief, but has no power against those systems in which there is an established consensus among experts. Mathematics, for instance, is unaffected by historical demonstration of the old beliefs held about its methods and conclusions through the ages. And to yield to general scepticism in the more controversial belief or opinion areas—ethics, politics, theology, philosophy—is a weakness that the historian should not indulge. The mind should not abandon its views on these, "the highest interests of reason and humanity,"[42] in order to become an investigator only of what happened, without trying to obtain knowledge.

Another aspect of the same question concerns particular scepticism. That is, how far does examination of the process by which particular moral or political beliefs have grown up prove these opinions false or misleading because of tendencies toward error involved in their development? It is true, of course, that any belief, if investigated from the standpoint of its origin, will demonstrate false opinions among its antecedents. Sidgwick suggests, however, that so long as these false opinions are not put forward as reasons for holding the belief, there is no cause to reject a particular belief on the basis of false antecedents alone. Truth grows out of error; because some accepted moral rule was at one time connected with a primitive custom now regarded as absurd does not destroy the reason for holding to the current truth of the rule.

The positive role played by sociology in establishing a philosophy of knowledge is probably more important than its negative effects. For the question is now raised as to the extent to which historical examination can provide us with a means of distinguishing truth among the diversity of opinions held by man. Sidgwick is prepared to admit that a study of the development of opinion in some fields may give valuable confirmation for conclusions otherwise arrived at as to the right procedure in a given case, but he does not see how these conclusions can possibly be established in the first place by a purely historical method. Suppose we had realized our utmost hopes in the pursuit of historical science; suppose we had ascertained completely the law of development of ethical, political, theological, or philosophical opinion so that we could predict the future views of these things. We still could not take the foreseen views as any more true than the opinions now held. Mere prediction does not pass a judgment of goodness on the foreseen facts. Indeed, "unless we start with a thoroughly sceptical or eccentric view as to the attainment of truth in any subject—ethics, politics, theology, or philosophy—unless we bring this to the study of history or somehow, not logically, derive it from the study, there will be a fundamental difficulty in forecasting the development of opinions, whatever insight into the law of development we may appear to derive from a study of the past. For we shall have some view of our own—say some theory of political or ethical end or method widely accepted here and now—which we shall regard as true; at the same time, as historians, we shall contemplate a long line of divergent opinions in past ages.... Surely the unique quality of being *true* which we attribute to the opinions of our own time must make inevitably a very profound difference between the past that leads up to our own truth and the future that takes it as a point of departure: so that the line of development in the past can hardly give us much insight into the line of progress in the future."[43] The present is taken as a culmination of the error of the past, and unless we see history as a pendulum movement from truth to error and back to truth, the truth of the future will be grounded for us in our own opinions.

The sociologists take two lines of approach to this difficulty: one may be described as the more philosophical view of the relativity of knowledge, the other as the more popular view of the progressive nature of knowledge.

Relativism is partially sceptical in holding that history shows us that absolute truth is unattainable, while offering in its place the consolation of relative truth. There are at least two types of relativism: philosophical relativism, or the relation of the objects of knowledge to the knowing mind, and sociological relativism, or the relation of a belief to the end of social preservation. Philosophically the attempt to conceive all truth as relative seems to Sidgwick to contain more error and confusion than accuracy. If philosophical relativism means that we can know only what is related to our faculty of knowledge, the idea is obvious and irrelevant. No one doubts that we know only what is knowable. But if the proposition means we cannot know things in themselves, then we may say that philosophical relativism is only expressing the limits of our knowledge, not its essential nature. In this sense knowledge is relative only insofar as it is not complete. What we know is really as we know it; but we have not reached, in the long process of error, the general ideal of complete knowledge. What we know is known rightly, but is limited as to extent. "If therefore we are to use the term 'relative knowledge or truth' with a meaning at once precise and useful (from a philosophical as distinct from a sociological point of view) I think it can only mean 'the best approximation to knowledge or truth' attainable by the mind to which the knowledge is affirmed to be relative."[44]

Sociological relativism, on the other hand, seems to discern the relation between beliefs (even though philosophically false) and the end of social preservation. This means that, while untrue, a belief may be contributory to the maintenance of the society and therefore called "relatively true." Some relativists go further, too, and insinuate an end greater than mere preservation to which these opinions contribute. To simple social preservation under the conditions of existence are added the ideas of development and welfare of the society. Thus, the divine right of kings or the conception of social contract may have been expedient to the preservation, welfare, and development of the society while being, in fact, untrue.

Where the proponents of this view are wrong, asserts Sidgwick, is in their application of the term *relative truths*. They are not truths at all, but expedient falsehoods serving to inculcate some necessary principle of action into people not prepared to accept the true end itself. Thus the idea of natural rights of man in a state of nature and the correlative social-contract theory may have been the only form in which prerevolutionary Europe could accept the proposition that a man ought to have freedom in a well-ordered society. But it is always necessary to suppose ourselves in possession of absolute ethical truth by which we judge the "expedient falsehood" to represent somehow a means to this absolute end. It is true that we may discover the expedient falsehood or means by sociology, "but what the end is at which we ought to aim we cannot learn from sociology. Any judgment we make as to the rightness of a practical end—that it is an end we ought to aim at—must be a fundamental ethical judgment; which we cannot regard as in its turn a merely relative truth."[45]

This brings us logically to the consideration of an extension of this method—the idea of progress. Progressivism is the special doctrine of the sociologist who cannot accept the impartial theory of relativity because of his particular application of the methodology of the natural sciences to social science. "He regards sociology as the latest born of the sciences, and so regarding it he necessarily accepts as valid, speaking broadly, the methods and conclusions of the other sciences and the general view of human thought and its objects which the modern sciences in the aggregate, when systematized by philosophy, are found to involve or suggest. And therefore, it may be said, he does not and cannot come to the scientific study of the history of belief as a social fact, without any other criterion than sociology itself affords: he necessarily has in his mind, whether implicitly or explicitly, the view of truth and its criteria which follows from assuming the general truth of the conclusions of the established and recognized sciences, and the validity of their methods—as to which there is no longer any general dispute or doubt among educated persons."[46] The progressivist foresees a long process of continuous progress, and his inferences for the future are derived from this view of the past.

Comte, of course, is the representative thinker of this group. Comte's law of the three stages, with his insistence on the investigation of the laws of phenomena as the legitimate method of all studies, relegates politics and ethics to the metaphysical and theological eras because their reasonings are based on conceptions of abstract rights and in some cases on the volitions of quasi-human wills. By refusing to admit theology or metaphysics as spheres of legitimate study, and by insisting on the absoluteness of the method dictated by the natural sciences, Comte combines philosophical relativity with a belief in the progress of knowledge. That is, he limits the knowable by making knowledge depend upon interrelated historical antecedents, while seeing almost limitless possibilities in the development of that which we can eventually know.

Sidgwick cannot deny the rapid advance of the natural sciences or the tremendous impact they have made on the opinion of his age. He questions, however, the limits of this type of knowledge and its effects upon the improvement of other fields of knowledge. Before investigating the epistemological problem of the rejection of any method not based upon or not used by the natural sciences, Sidgwick examines the notion of progress from a sociological point of view.

In what does "social progress," to which the narrower idea of progress in knowledge might be related, consist? What does progress carry us toward? Naturally we must reject the old periodic or cyclic course of change if we accept progressivism, even though history gives much support to the rise and fall of "forms of polity."

Progress may be described as movement toward an ideal always recognized as unattainable in the absolute sense, though we may draw ever nearer to it. The end or ideal toward which the social organism moves is regarded by the progressivist as self-adaptation or adjustment of the different parts of the organism to its preservation under its conditions of existence.

In Sidgwick's view the histories of societies exhibit no such tendency toward self-preservation in the self-adaptive alterations through which they have moved. Some of the very things we regard as higher developments of civilization have led in some political units to a decline in ability to defend the society and finally to subordination by conquest to a less civilized nation. Social adaptation to environment through survival of the fittest has not brought into existence beliefs tending to the preservation of the society. On the contrary, many of the beliefs called into being are actually hostile to the preservation of the society under its special conditions of existence. We may interject to allow the twentieth-century reader to apply for himself this fundamental truth to the facts relating to his society under its own special conditions. So far as I know, none of the societies which Professor Toynbee investigated managed to respond with sufficient intensity of belief or action to its challenges from within or without. And the application of the biological principle of the tendency toward organic balance cannot assure us that the social challenge presented this century by the creation of the scientific means to its own destruction will be met.

To return, however, to Sidgwick: we may go further than the mere end of preservation and introduce the idea of improvement as a part of progress. But if we introduce this additional concept, we require some definite criterion of the good which is the end of development. This criterion, Sidgwick contends, is not the prerogative of sociology pure and simple, but belong properly to philosophy. So long as we confine ourselves to concepts derived from biology—organism, adaptation, differentiation and correlation of parts, mutual dependence of coordinated functions—the end seems to be preservation alone. But how are we to attain a conception of social welfare and the means to it from sociology when history shows so much diversity in all such fundamental conceptions?

81

Sociology makes a claim to establish this fundamental criterion of truth and falsehood, and with the aid of this criterion to show changes in beliefs down through history as steps in progress toward fuller and purer truth. The natural sciences furnish the method of arriving at truth by meeting the tests of agreement of experts (acceptance) and of continuity of development (the way new truths fit in and confirm the old generalities). Using these bodies of real knowledge as our guides, we may correct and improve those departments which still are badly organized. This is the way in which Comte generalized his law of the three stages—only the natural sciences have reached the positive stage, the other departments lag behind. Sociology, however, allies itself to the natural sciences, accepts their conclusions as real knowledge, and claims through their method to have established "an exclusive right of deciding as to truth and falsehood on all matters of interest to man . . . theology and metaphysics being relegated to the position of different stages of error, through which the human mind progresses in its advance towards truth."[47]

Sidgwick cannot accept the validity of such an approach. The fundamental controversies of politics and ethics turn mainly on the definition of a single basic principle: the ultimate end by which all particular rules and institutions are to be tested. In the Victorian period that controversy revolved around the question of which of two ends to choose—happiness, an aggregate of pleasures realized successively through time in the lives of individuals, or some universal good, which is the good of each because it is the good of all rather than the summation of individual goods. It is only natural that one's thinking will be greatly affected by the choice of one or the other of these two ends, but that does not mean that this controversy can be treated by some positive rather than metaphysical method. "Ultimate ends are not phenomena or laws or conditions of phenomena: to investigate them as if they were seems futile as if one inquired whether they were square or round."[48] Philosophy can find no substitute in sociology as a means for coordinating beliefs.

The inference drawn by both Spencer and Comte as to the matters with which theology and metaphysics deal is entirely negative. Both feel that what these disciplines seek to know is unknowable and that philosophy's only work is to comprehend the natural sciences (the only area of knowledge in which progress has been made) and to make a higher generalization from them. In Comte's view theology is opposed to science. The universe, from the theological standpoint, is governed volitionally by unseen beings. On the other hand, science has exhibited the invariable laws of co-existence and sequence which actually control the facts. As a result, theological explanation in every department recedes as science establishes itself. Sidgwick feels that this opposition between science and theology holds true only in so far as the Divine Will is conceived as capricious, irregular, and inscrutable. The opposition vanishes when the Divine Will is conceived, as it now is in most educated minds, as invariable, regular, and open to human investigation.

It may be argued further, however, that another point of opposition between religion and science is created by the scientific discoveries which deny the order of the universe to be a perfectly good order—ethically the world discovered by science is an imperfect world. Finally, there is the additional opposition which results from science's presentation to us of a rational, intelligible universe from which the conceptions of practical reason (end, design, adaptation of means to end) are excluded. In this case science must conflict with any form of metaphysics that retains the notion of end or good as a fundamental conception in the universe, even where unconnected with the conception of personality.

Sidgwick holds that there is no opposition between science and theology or metaphysics on either of these latter counts. Science deals only with phenomena. It does not profess "to tell us anything of the First Cause of the whole process, its final end or significance, its underlying reality, and the relation to this of the human spirit, not as a mere series of phenomena or consciousnesses, but as the conscious, thinking, aspiring, self-determining subject of such a series."[49] These are precisely the questions on which metaphysics and theology reflect, however. Instead of regarding such problems as conflicting with science, one may view them as complementary. The only conflict would come from the negative assertions of positivism—that nothing can be known about the universe except the laws of existence and sequences of phenomena. "And this negative assertion is just *not* a scientific conclusion: it is, in fact, a metaphysical dogma."[50]

Comte's claim for sociology in itself involves a form of teleology because he assumes that the real comprehension of early social developments depends on viewing them in the light of later stages. Neither the final development nor the contribution of earlier social organisms to later stages could have been foreseen by earlier societies. The contribution can only be seen now that the end approaches realization. Then, too, when we think of scientific knowledge, on which Comte places so much emphasis, we are led to look forward to understand its significance. We assume as real a complete knowledge, going beyond the imperfect, fragmentary knowledge of the human mind. Any claim of science to have defeated the argument from "design" should stop short of the world of mind, for mind is itself a designing subject.

It may readily be seen that all the notions refuted by Sidgwick stem from a common source—the transvaluation of all values by science. At the basis of the concept lies the discovery of absolute laws governing mankind and the restriction of legitimate philosophical inquiry to the search for these laws and an understanding of their application. This conception carries with it a theory of materialistic determinism, as Sidgwick has shown. The form of this determinism may vary with each positivist, but not the content; and the results are rather startling. The values implied in the older Christian and humanistic complexes are completely undermined. The possibility of voluntarily creating in society the conditions of freedom necessary to secure the greatest potential development of individual personality is no part of positivism. Invariable laws, not free human choice, are the significant factors in history. Even Spencer's insistence on a particular form of individualism is authoritarian inasmuch as it is not advanced as a condition of free human choice, but in order to place rigid limits on the area of man's activities so that the objective laws of biological evolution can operate. This abstinence from social activity on Spencer's part and Comte's authoritarianism play a similar role in the general positivist conception. The two ideas are similar outgrowths of a desire on the part of the person who purports to understand the laws of society to make certain that the laws are not circumvented by religiously opiated man who may regard himself as a free spiritual agent.

Science, through its knowledge of phenomena, can control the operation of the world of nature because of nature's objective structure. This condition has led to a fallacious idea that the same objectivity and possibility for control exists with regard to humanity. For while "the knowledge of phenomena (natural) is certainly the key to their utilitarian mastery ... the understanding of human substance is not the key to the mastery of science and society."[51]

Politically these ideas have had far too broad an adaptability. Modern man, caught between totalitarian collectivism of positivist social engineers and the anarchistic individualism of biological positivists like Spencer, tries to work out his destiny as a free spirit in a world of material determinism. The limitations imposed by this determinism have taken a number of forms, nearly all of them being founded on the domination of a single aspect of human personality or condition of existence.

The attempt to retain for philosophy the function of synthesizing the particular sciences into a more comprehensive system of generalities seems to have broken down as a result of the growing trend toward specialization. The positivist philosophers consequently fell back upon the methods and conclusions of specialized areas of knowledge as sources of their philosophical generalizations.

Sidgwick is basically opposed to these attempts to erect a monolithic philosophical structure in which the use of a single science or a single methodology drawn from a particular science is taken as the basis of ethics and politics. Thus he rejects the psychologism of the Benthamites, the biological basis of Spencer's assumptions, and all other forms of historical positivism which became so prevalent in the late nineteenth century. In all of these schools the attempts to answer the fundamental questions of moral and political ends and of moral and political obligation not only lack philosophical completeness, but in Sidgwick's view they offer the practical difficulty of submitting individuals and societies to a state of external causality which he finds incompatible with the free moral and political development of man. Sidgwick was, in effect, trying very hard to do much the same thing that T. H. Green and the other idealist opponents of positivism were attempting; that is, he was trying to demonstrate the independent philosophical basis on which ethics stands. And, of course, it followed that political theory as an extension of ethics is possessed of a similar independence. It seems beyond question that he would have agreed with Sir Ernest Barker's argument that:

Biology, political economy, jurisprudence, psychology, history, are all studies which, though they lie in different fields from social philosophy proper, nevertheless deal with a subject-matter that is connected with and acts upon the peculiar subject-matter of social philosophy. The moral nature of man is isolated in no vacuum; it stands in intimate and organic relation with physical structure and economic motive, with legal enactment, with social instinct, with historic or pre-historic, institutions. Such relations social philosophy must necessarily consider. What it cannot admit is that any of the studies which deal with these other matters can solely or even primarily explain the reason and the value of society. They can throw additional light on the ultimate moral factor; in themselves they are necessarily one-sided and therefore misleading guides. They cannot absolve us from the primary duty of studying the State as the product and organ of the moral will of men.[52]

Since the whole of the dominant trend of philosophy, including that of Sidgwick's own utilitarian school, was opposed to this conception, it seems no more than natural that criticism should loom larger than systematization in his work. However, the fact that Sidgwick remained essentially a critic rather than a constructive philosopher was due more perhaps to another factor than to the dominance of the intellectual scene of his time by positivism. That factor was the common-sense philosophy on which his criticism was based; the doctrines of common-sense philosophy lend themselves far more readily to criticism than to the construction of a metaphysical system or a theory of knowledge. Common sense has essentially the negative qualities of naïve realism on which it is built; it suggests the absurdities of the logical projections of doctrines of other schools, but it produces practically no explanation of the internal consistency of its individual beliefs. Introspection thus told Sidgwick that mind and matter are diverse, that consciousness is not a matter only of sensation produced by the movement of matter; but it did not produce for him, for example, the transcendent "eternal consciousness" through which Green found not only self-realization, but a common substance of mankind as well.[53] That is not to say that Sidgwick was wrong and Green was right, but it does mean that Green's opposition to the system of positivism was based first and foremost on a system of his own, while Sidgwick's criticism was unattended by any metaphysics or theory of knowledge capable of displacing the one under attack. Sidgwick remained a doubter; he was too sensitive an introspectionist to accept either the atomism resulting from the analytical method of the eighteenth century (which formed the background for early utilitarianism) or the relativistic or progressive conclusions of the evolutionary school. Like Goethe he wanted to find that satisfactory position which would enable the "eternal to be seen in the transitory" insofar as the study of man as a moral and political being was concerned. But on the other hand, the world of nineteenth-century positivism was too much with him to allow him to accept some form of transcendentalism; he demanded proof which would satisfy the requirements of the most rigid positivist. It could with truth be said of him that his philosophy lacked a satisfactory metaphysical basis or "world view."[54] But his criticism raises serious doubts that the systems of philosophy contemporary with him had a "world view" which could stand up. And he was certainly not unprepared to assert certain of the beliefs derived from common sense which are at variance with the more dogmatic positions taken by other systems.

Sidgwick's remarks with regard to the "metaphysical dogma" and "teleology" of Comte are a clear challenge to the claim of the positivists to have rejected all metaphysics in their reliance on the objective methodology of the natural sciences. It is ironic that the exponent of progressivism, after depriving man of all specifically human characteristics, should be placed in the position of divinizing him. Nevertheless, the conditions of progress seem to demand this elevation of human clay to some form of earthly immortality. Comte's religion of humanity, Spencer's ultimate harmony, Nietzsche's superman, and Marx's dream of the final era of human contentment, all point toward the heavenly city. This element of intramundane perfection, together with the closure against human choice discussed above, must be accounted the two great perversions of history in nineteenth-century positivism. For the closure against human choice denies the influence of humanity itself in historical development,[55] and the progressivist theology denies any reality to historical experience apart from its connection with material advancement, which is the key to progress.

The question of the connection between Sidgwick's refutation of positivism and Benthamite utilitarianism cannot be overlooked at this point. Bentham's position is basically antihistorical in the eighteenth-century sense. That means that Bentham does not seek to find through history the working of the laws of progress. In fact he regards history as demonstrating little more than the past misdeeds and false opinions of mankind. There is a clear barrier between the past with its false basis of human action and the present with its correct utilitarian position.

Nevertheless, there are close connections between the earlier, general conception of progress and the later historical demonstration

87

of its actuality. Benthamism insisted as strongly as any later positivist on the absoluteness of objective laws of human nature discoverable by scientific investigation, including the possibility of establishing by the empirical method the validity of the utilitarian ethical end. For John Stuart Mill, Comte supplied a philosophy of history which had been missing in the Benthamites. In reconciling Comte with early utilitarianism Mill made obeisance to the "static" nature of his father's conception of knowledge by denying that a "law of nature" could be drawn entirely from historical speculation. He thought that only "empirical" laws could be ascertained by historical study of society and that these laws must be connected with, and ultimately derivative from, fixed psychological laws of human nature. But at the same time Mill felt that Comte alone of the new historical school had seen the necessity of making a connection between the generalizations from history and the laws of human nature.[56]

Mill is, in fact, effusive in his praise of Comte's earlier positivism. The only strenuous objection that he makes is to the antiliberal position.[57] He does satirize mildly the later phase of Comtian positivism, especially the religion of humanity; but his obvious sympathy with Comte can hardly be called into question.[58] Most of what the younger Mill finds important in Comte, in fact, establishes the relationship between positivism and Benthamic thought: the discovery by the empirical method of invariable laws of human nature and their scientific application for the purpose of constructing a utilitarian society.

Sidgwick, on the other hand, is denying precisely those postulates of positivism which have the most affinity to early utilitarianism. Instead of following Mill, who expends much of his philosophical energy in an attempt to reconcile the empiricism of the utilitarians with Comte's work, Sidgwick abandons the positivism of the early utilitarians. Ultimate values are not derivative from laws of phenomena, whether those laws are based on associationist pyschology or some other materialistic analogy. Knowledge is not limited to the succession and coexistence of naturalistic facts. There is a real world of self-conscious individual personality and even of society as an independent reality. Values are entities in themselves, introspectively derived from a recognition of objective moral obligation. They are products of mind as it is opposed to matter; they are ideals which ought to be willed by man. In his critique of positivism Sidgwick makes a decisive break with early utilitarianism. He rejects its narrow egoistic limitations and its materialist psychology. As a result he rejects the subordination of human will to deterministic laws, whether mechanistic or evolutionary.

When Sidgwick rejected the analytical empiricism of the utilitarians, he cut himself off from the epistemological and methodological doctrines which had been developed in their philosophical system.[59] But in doing so he placed ethics in a position of primacy which it had not clearly held in earlier utilitarianism because of the attempts of the Benthamites to tie ethics to an empirically ascertainable end. In Sidgwick for the first time the greatest-happiness principle became an end consciously desirable as a matter of free moral choice, unencumbered by the epistemological negativism concerning values which had been present in the works of all the previous utilitarians.

CHAPTER FOUR

Reconstruction of the Utilitarian Ethic

I N A BRIEF intellectual history of the maturation of his ethical theory, Sidgwick remarked that his "first adhesion to a definite ethical system was to the Utilitarianism of [John Stuart] Mill,"[1]* and the doctrine of universal ethical hedonism which he found there continued to be the foundation of his philosophy. However, when he recognized the contradiction between psychological and ethical hedonism in Mill's ethics, he began a thorough study of the methodological approaches to ethics which culminated in his earliest and best-known work of general social theory, *The Methods of Ethics*. In this book he examined critically the two systems of ethics—intuitionism and utilitarianism—which he regarded as the most prominent competing ethical theories of that time (1874), theories widely held to be completely opposed to one another.

In the course of the examination of the respective methods of intuitionism and utilitarianism, Sidgwick elaborates his own conception of the good, how it may be known and the basis of the obligation to realize it in action. Out of a criticism of both schools he extracts what he regards as the valid contribution of each and welds them into a completely reformulated utilitarian ethic. It is this restatement of utilitarian ethics which forms the point of departure for his theory of politics.

*Notes to this chapter begin on page 177.

Reconstruction of the Utilitarian Ethic

It should be reiterated at the outset that Sidgwick has no such ties to associationist psychology as John Stuart Mill and other utilitarians had. In his view complex cognition may be judged as irreducible without reference to the atomistic material sensations out of which they were formed. In part the distinctness of mental phenomena from material objects lies in this irreducibility. As a result Sidgwick needs no general psychological "law" by which complex cognitions may be related to their simple antecedents.[2]

When Sidgwick comes therefore to examine the basis on which we make ethical judgments, he discovers a rational principle opposed to the principle of egoistic psychological hedonism which denies the possibility of anyone's desiring anything other than his own happiness. The notion "ought" as it appears in ethical judgments is a rational categorical imperative. This means that judgments involving the notion "ought" cannot be reduced to any mere sorting out of various self-regarding impulses and choosing rationally among them. Instead, the judgment carries with it an elementary rational dictate of its own, a dictate which would apply to the same act regardless of the particular person involved. Thus, if the judgment is made, "x ought to be done," the implication is that the particular act x has characteristics which make it universally obligatory any time the special condtions now producing it appear. If in any circumstances an individual makes such a judgment, he must have some end or ultimate principle by which the particular act could be judged to be intrinsically correct or universally applicable. And if so, we make our common moral judgments with reference to an end which may be said to be reasonable for all rational creatures to will. In this conception of the independent nature of a moral judgment and the corresponding rational obligation to act on it, Sidgwick is at one with the intuitionists from the Cambridge Platonists of the seventeenth century to G. E. Moore.

Egoistic psychological hedonism, on the other hand, holds that the sole motive for human action lies in the anticipation of pleasure or avoidance of pain by the individual performing the action. If this be so, then the individual cannot accept the rational dictates of *any obligation*, either as an individual end or as a universally valid principle. The only thing that may be done in this case is rationally to select, on the basis of the expectation of pleasure or pain, that action among several alternatives which promises the greatest excess of personal pleasure over pain. The end of all action is already

91

set; one cannot be said to be obligated to do something which, by reason of his invariable nature, he *must* do.

The conflict, then, is quite clear. The exponent of psychological hedonism denies any such a priori "moral consciousness"[3] as Sidgwick affirms, holding instead that the end of conduct is given and is not subject to rational choice.

The issue being joined, refinements remain to be made in Sidgwick's position. The first is that the mere awareness of obligation is not finally decisive in moral conflicts. While this cognition of duty gives a motive to action, it is only one motive among several competing with it and has no certainty of being the predominant motive.[4] Sidgwick nowhere assumes that man always, or even in most cases, acts on a rational basis, however much one may desire that he do so. Secondly, the possibility of rational choice of ends of conduct and its conflict with the pre-existing end prescribed by psychological hedonism does not mean that egoism may not be accepted as the right or obligatory end of action. One may judge it right that any person should aim consciously at his own greatest happiness. If so, any time the criterion "ought" is applied to a particular act, it is thought that the person whose happiness is in question should take that course of action which will be most conducive to his own greatest happiness. This does not mean (as it would with the psychological hedonist) that it was necessary that the person act on an egoistic principle. It means only that it is a good end for any individual to will.[5] Finally, Sidgwick knows of no way to impart a sense of moral obligation "to any one who is entirely devoid of it."[6] When thorough self-examination does not render a consciousness of the type of "unconditional or categorical imperative" he is trying to ascribe to the notion of obligation, there is nothing further to be said.

Sidgwick finds two general ends which might be chosen rationally as self-evident goals of human conduct. These are happiness (either general or individual) and perfection or excellence.[7] Naturally, any person who has a clear undoubtable end of behavior in mind will wish to employ the most adequate means of achieving that end, hence Sidgwick's concern with methods. It would be inconsistent to adopt an end while rejecting the means by which it may be most effectively realized.

There are three methods which are distinguished as means of realizing the chosen ends. These three are intuitionism, egoistic hedonism (as distinct from psychological hedonism), and universal ethical hedonism (or utilitarianism).[8] Intuitionism as a method of ethics involves the acceptance of unconditionally prescribed moral rules seen to be self-evident and complete in themselves as forms of moral perfection. Intuitionism is the method commonly used by those accepting perfection as the end of ethics. The egoistic hedonist[9] measures good by the contribution of any action to the total quantitative happiness of the individual concerned. The utilitarian judges conduct by its effects on the happiness of the totality of sentient beings.

Having explained the general aim of ethics, the rational content of moral judgments, the general ends on which such judgments are based, and having indicated the systematic approach to these ends, Sidgwick then proceeds to examine each method in detail and to correlate and evaluate them.

The intuitionist method seeks to formulate general principles of behavior which are intrinsically good without reference to consequences.[10] It should be noted here that even the methods of egoistic hedonism and utilitarianism cannot do without self-evident propositions altogether. "If Hedonism claims to give authoritative guidance, this can only be in virtue of the principle that pleasure is the only reasonable ultimate end of human action: and this principle cannot be known by induction from experience."[11] Thus both perfection and happiness as ends owe their origin to intuition. Behavior judged right on the perfectionist principle is dependent on its conformity to some one of several moral rules, each designated as good; on the hedonistic principle actions are right according to their productivity of happiness.

Intuition as a specific method, however, tries to extend deduction beyond cognition of a first principle by framing rules to be applied categorically to all specific instances in which an ethical decision has to be made. On its premises good manifests itself in behavior in a number of ways and each rule is self-evident and complete in itself as a form of good. In order to pronounce this or any method valid, we must discover on application of the method a clear basis for individual decisions as well as consistency among the various actions taken in accordance with the system. To meet this test, all the propositions advanced by intuitionism must be self-evident, however closely examined; they must be mutually consistent; and they should receive a clear consensus about their validity.[12]

In order to test conformity to these requirements, Sidgwick

examines the most common rules postulated as self-evident moral principles. The main moral axioms considered are wisdom, benevolence, justice, obligation to law and promise, and truth. Since the present work is not an examination in detail of Sidgwick's ethical theory, there is no need to summarize each section, interesting and varied though all of them be. There will be occasion later to revert to such a concept as justice, but for the time being his conclusions are sufficient. In each case he finds a lack of clearness and consistency in the individual's moral judgments, and discrepancies among different individuals over the rules and their application. Most people would certainly agree in general to the desirability of benevolence, justice, and other virtues of their type. When these terms are examined for precise meaning, however, they elude definition. Further, when we try to determine their application in particular cases, conflicting claims of duty are apparent. For example, benevolence calls on us in some way to cultivate affections and kindliness, but when we try to formulate self-evident rules covering all cases, we are up against the problem of evaluating the relative merits of competing claims of affections from widely varying individuals and groups. In what proportion are we to assess our obligations of being kind to neighbors as opposed to kinsmen, or of duties owed out of gratitude as compared to those arising from pity? Each intuitionist axiom of specific moral good breaks down similarly when examined in this manner.

Apart from these problems of finding clear, self-evident rules by which the general moral categories may be applied, there are other objections to intuitionism. These may be stated briefly as the difficulty of (a) eliminating the concept of consequences altogether from our judgments of good; (b) the tendency for variations in common-sense judgments of rightness of action to arise because of the entry of subjective factors into our decisions; and (c) the tautological fallacy involved in assessing an action as right because it is good and, in turn, good because it is right. Whatever importance intuitionism may have in its wider sense (that is, of defining an ultimate end at which it is right to aim), it is deficient as a complete method because its systematization of ethics through the establishment of a number of categorical rules leaves the application of those rules so much in doubt. "There are certain absolute practical principles, the truth of which, when they are explicitly stated, is manifest; but they are of too abstract a nature, and too universal in their scope, to enable us to ascertain by immediate application of them what we ought to do in any particular case; particular duties have still to be determined by some other method."[13]

Sidgwick's concern with ends accepted by rational choice has already been demonstrated by his rejection of psychological hedonism and by his arguments in favor of the rational basis of the notion of obligation. The ethical end that he accepts as valid is happiness. That is, happiness is the characteristic by virtue of which any experience is judged good. And happiness to him is "a feeling which, when experienced by intelligent beings, is at least implicitly apprehended as desirable, or—in cases of comparison—preferable."[14] In Sidgwick's view there are two forms of hedonism, either of which might be adopted as an ethical end—egoistic hedonism and universal ethical hedonism.[15]

Egoistic hedonism is the principle that the sole end of action should be the happiness of the individual concerned. Sidgwick can find no logical inconsistency in accepting this principle as an end at which it might be proper to aim. He attempts to discover, therefore, what method may be used to realize this end once it has been adopted. As always, he considers carefully all the possibilities put forward and comes to the conclusion that empirical hedonism (or assessment of relative quantities of pleasure, followed by choice of the action most likely to produce the greatest excess of pleasure over pain for the individual) is the only method acceptable to this type of theory. In moving to that conclusion, he rejects a number of alternatives and makes several important refinements in the general problem of hedonism.

The first nonempirical method considered is the use of common-sense morality as the guide to the greatest good on the whole for the person involved. This method would insist that by following the ordinary currents of opinion about the different objects sought as sources of pleasure, one can achieve his greatest happiness. However, Sidgwick finds the variations so great in the judgments of different persons about the same or similar pleasures that one can find very little exactness of result through this approach. This does not mean that common-sense judgments may not be used as supplements to introspection in cases of indecision, but this use is only supplementary and not a complete means in itself. Similarly, the attempt to demonstrate that happiness may be achieved by the performance of duty fails to satisfy the exacting conditions of completeness and definiteness as a test of method. There is no rational assurance to the egoist that virtue will be rewarded with an equivalent amount of happiness for the agent. Nor do duties prescribed by legal or social sanctions coincide with the moral dictates of rational self-love. Finally, all attempts to ascertain the causes of pleasure or pain by psychological or biological investigation have failed. Therefore, the attempt to deduce the correctness of actions from such theories is altogether deficient.

This leaves us with the empirical method as the only satisfactory means to the realization of the end of egoistic hedonism, and this method is by no means free from problems. Sidgwick is under no illusions about these difficulties. Aside from direct objections by other writers, he points out that it is not easy to make a quantitative evaluation of relative pleasures and pains, especially when we have to consider the whole future of the agent. Then, too, direct reflection on pleasures while those pleasures are in process may dull the pleasant feeling through the intrusion of nonhedonistic cognition. Also, the agent may under different times and conditions find wide variation in the relative pleasures produced by various actions. Sidgwick warns that much of our pleasure will be derived incidentally and will best be served by losing oneself in objects for their own sake, without directly forcing cognition of pleasure at the time. In spite of manifest disadvantages, one *does* introspectively measure quantities of pleasure and pain and relies on the result for choosing among alternative actions. Thus, the empirical method seems the one by which individual happiness can be realized most fully.

Universal ethical hedonism, or utilitarianism, is the nonegoistic form of the greatest-happiness principle. In its view that conduct is right "which will produce the greatest amount of happiness on the whole; that is, taking into account all whose happiness is affected by the conduct."[16] Unlike the egoist, who is concerned only with his personal good, the utilitarian recognizes a universal good. This universal good is realized in the pleasant experiences of individuals. The duty of the utilitarian, then, is to maximize the total amount of happiness, disregarding his own or any other particular person's pleasure when the net happiness requires such personal sacrifice. In order to act consistently on the principle of utilitarianism, one must be willing to relinquish one's own happiness if by so doing one can improve the total happiness.

The universalistic ethical end is the one which is most acceptable to Sidgwick. Although this form of hedonism is obviously incompatible with psychological hedonism, when its relation to egoistic ethical hedonism is considered, we come face to face with the main dilemma in Sidgwick's intellectual position. He has already admitted the appeal exerted by the prospect of aiming at one's own greatest happiness as the ultimate end of conduct; now he seeks to make valid the principle of general happiness as the ultimate end of ethics and to insist that an individual ought to give up his greatest good on the whole if it comes into conflict with the realization of a quantitatively greater good among the totality of conscious human beings. Egoistic psychological hedonism can be disproved for practical purposes if the exponent of the theory can be made aware of non-rational motivations other than personal pleasure upon which actions might be based. But if a man deliberately chooses the rational dictate of self-love to the complete exclusion of the rational dictate of universal obligation, it is hard to see on what grounds Sidgwick proposes to persuade him to adopt the latter principle instead. And yet it is equally clear that egoistic hedonism and universal hedonism cannot both be held to be the ultimate end of ethics, even though separately each seems self-evident. The self-evidence of both egoistic hedonism and utilitarianism or universal hedonism when considered separately, and the equal self-evidence of their mutual incompatibility when taken together, are referred to by Sidgwick as the "dualism of the practical reason."[17] The egoist cannot admit any total good because for him there are only personal goods. He admits the importance of *my* happiness to *me* and of *his* happiness to *him*, and his expectancy will be based on each individual's pursuit of his particular happiness. The only duty one has is to improve one's own greatest happiness on the whole; no one is under rational compulsion to aim at maximizing the happiness of all sentient creatures. Professor Broad is correct in his finding that Sidgwick does not profess to give any solution to this logical difficulty.[18]

Sidgwick does indicate time and time again his own acceptance of the utilitarian or universalistic form of hedonism. And he attempts also to demonstrate the importance of self-love in the utilitarian method. Even if one has recognized the moral obligation to act on a universal utilitarian principle, he is still under obligation to act in his own interest much of the time. After all, a person is concerned with his individual happiness in a manner quite different from the concern he may have for anyone else's good. The acceptance of universal good by no means demands that one act always on the intuited principle of rational benevolence. Most of one's actions will still be concerned primarily with oneself. If individuals are not personally responsible for enhancing their own happiness, the general happiness, which is the sum of individual pleasures, will fall far short of maximization. It is nonetheless true on utilitarian grounds that an individual must consider the social consequences of the pursuit of individual happiness and weigh actions which will produce a surplus of pleasure over pain in himself against the corresponding pleasures and pains likely to be produced in all persons directly or indirectly affected by the proposed action, and is obligated to alter his action if the result is likely to produce on the whole more pain than pleasure.

Sidgwick has produced only a limited reconciliation of individual interest with the utilitarian end, and for this reconciliation he offers little in the way of explanation except that it is a personal choice with him. Both egoistic and universal hedonism are reasonable principles of conduct. They are also regulative principles; that is, they carry with their acceptance rational motivation which is one element impelling the individual to action on the basis of duty. In this sense both help to control nonrational impulses to action which, as undirected motivations, are indiscriminate in the production of any sort of desirable end.[19]

This reconciliation is still made at the price of subjecting the general principle of egoism to utilitarianism as a higher end, a subjection for which Sidgwick gives no persuasive reason. In this context, however, individualistic hedonism has become an important subsidiary to the ultimate end of universalism. It is obvious that one can select a universal good, yet at the same time hold that some particular aspect of that good is important to its full realization. But if the particular good comes into conflict with the universal end, the former must still give way. On the other hand, if the particular individual end is conceived as the final one, it cannot be placed in a position of subordination to any other end. A whole may conceivably be only the sum of its parts, but a thing complete in itself can hardly be considered merely a part. Thus it is possible to convince the utilitarian that self-interest is important in achieving general happiness, but to the confirmed egoist it would be inconsistent to sacrifice personal happiness to a general happiness whose very existence he doubts.

There are more complete means of bringing these contradictory ends into conformance, but they would entail the sacrifice of Sidgwick's independent philosophical position. A hedonistic religious conception might be held in which the individual could achieve his ultimate happiness only by sacrificing it for the present and adopting a universalistic end of conduct. On the other hand, the earlier theory was often argued that there are universal laws by which the good of the whole is advanced exclusively through the pursuit of individual interest. There is the third possibility of claiming for the impulse of sympathy a sufficient role in ethics for it to serve as a reconciler of egoism with utilitarianism. On such a premise the feeling of sympathy (regarded solely as a generator of pleasure or pain in the individual) could be construed as a motive so strong that action undertaken to produce the individual pleasures or remove the pains of sympathetic feeling would promote the general happiness.[20] Since reliance on any of these solutions would rob Sidgwick's ethics of far more consistency than he gains by leaving the matter without a satisfactory conclusion, the question is left open. But Sidgwick still would insist, it seems, that the careful introspectionist would conclude that universal hedonism exercises a superior rational claim over egoism.

Little need be said at this point about the method of utilitarianism. The approach is predominantly empirical and closely in keeping with the method advocated for realizing the end of egoistic hedonism. The important variants lie in the connection between utilitarianism and intuitionism, discussed in the next section of this chapter. However, the problems confronting an empirical approach to the realization of egoism are still present in the case of utilitarianism, and in a more complex form. In addition to assessing one's own greatest happiness, there is now the added difficulty of taking into consideration all other persons affected by the action. And this gives rise to a related question—the variation of intensity of pleasure produced in different individuals by different objects. This variable is responsible for the peculiar complexity involved in attempting to compare quantities of feeling when one has no direct experience of their relative strength. In view of these entanglements our calculations at best will be rough rather than scientifically exact; empiricism as a method implies restraint in guarding against overgeneralization from inadequate data, and the data of social phenomena are never complete. Sidgwick cannot be accused of demonstrating excessive moral "enthusiasm." The correlation that he makes between utilitarianism and intuitionism is indicative of a strong feeling for historical continuity operating as a conservative check on reformist zeal.

The largest part of the section on utilitarianism in *Methods of Ethics* is devoted to the reconciliation of utilitarianism and intuitionism. The concluding chapter of the book seeks to sum up the relationships among the three distinct means of realizing good in human conduct. The most characteristic facet of Sidgwick's writing is subtle refinement, and it is quite in keeping with his usual pattern to give careful consideration to connections existing among different approaches to the same problem. In actual practice the ordinary person adopts no precise method, but applies to his conduct a diversity of moral rules and judgments, some of which are certainly inconsistent. The problem, then, is to discover whether there is some logical relation by virtue of which the individual methods may be connected or whether they are mutually exclusive.

Early nineteenth-century utilitarians had rejected outright any form of a priori rationalism. Sidgwick points out that "since Bentham we have been chiefly familiar with the negative or aggressive aspect of the Utilitarian doctrine."[21] By that he means that utilitarianism has been concerned primarily with demonstrating the falseness of received moral rules and their inadequacy as a logical ground for social action. To the earlier utilitarian any rule claiming rational rather than empirical evidence as its basis was invalid. Consequently, the antipathy between utilitarianism and common-sense intuitionism had apparently been made absolute and irreconcilable. Sidgwick, in his struggle to assimilate the conflicting claims of interest and duty, finds that the opposition between utilitarianism and intuitionism rests on a misunderstanding. "There was indeed a fundamental opposition between the individual's interest and either morality, . . ." i.e., utilitarianism and intuitionism. The very opposite of the supposed conflict between these latter two is true, however; utilitarianism has to have a basis and that basis "could only be supplied by a fundamental intuition."[22]

The fact that the important conflict is not between utilitarianism and intuitionism, but between egoism and the universal forms of morality, is borne out by a historical example. When Hobbes called forth the first opposition to his egoism, it came from the intuitionists. And Sidgwick finds the axiom of his own utilitarianism—that a rational agent is bound to aim at universal happiness—present in some form in the intuitionist moral theories of Cumberland, More, Clark, and Shaftesbury.[23] Cumberland's intuitionist reply to Hobbes, in which the common good is the single standard by which moral rules are determined, is voiced in such terms that he may be referred to as "the precursor of the later utilitarianism."[24] And, in fact, although the intuitionists did hold to the self-evidence of a number of moral principles, and although their ethical end was generally the vague idea of perfection, they did not eliminate the idea of happiness from this conception, but rather for the most part regarded happiness as an invariable accompaniment of perfection. Thus, the early search for a philosophical, nonegoistic morality found intuitionism "in friendly alliance with Utilitarianism."[25]

In addition to the fact that the basis of utilitarianism is intuitional, the methods of intuitionism and utilitarianism complement rather than mutually exclude one another. This occurs in two ways: first, the intuitive moral rules perceived as productive of good are frequently justifiable on utilitarian grounds and indeed may have originated by experience of their productivity of happiness; secondly, (and reciprocally) utilitarianism furnishes a means of clarifying common-sense moral rules and settling current conflicts between them. As Sidgwick puts it, one may show how "utilitarianism sustains the general validity of the current moral judgments, and thus supplements the defects which reflection finds in the intuitive recognition of their stringency; and at the same time affords a principle of synthesis, and a method for binding the unconnected and occasionally conflicting principles of common moral reasoning into a complete and harmonious system."[26]

The first part of the reconciliation (the demonstration of the presence of a utilitarian basis in common moral judgments) shows no exact coincidence between the two, but does indicate that intuitionism is "inchoately and imperfectly Utilitarian."[27] Self-evident (common-sense) rules, such as distributive justice, kindliness, truth-speaking, etc., come to be accepted as moral dictates over a long period of time. During this gradual formation experience teaches that conformance to certain standards of conduct leads most frequently to pleasant results for the affected persons. As a consequence the rule comes to be applied more and more stringently until it becomes accepted for itself without recourse to an ultimate end with which it accords. Thus experience brings about this form of

101

common-sense moral generalization. Sidgwick then elaborates to some extent the important intuitionist rules in order to illustrate the "latent Utilitarianism of Common Sense."[28]

Inasmuch as this development of intuited rules from utilitarian considerations has taken place, utilitarianism has at hand, already prepared, a set of ethical rules which have proved themselves by long experience to be productive of the greatest happiness. These immediately apparent first principles, then, may be said to be "middle Axioms"[29] of utilitarianism, furnishing a previously calculated utilitarian solution to many of the problems faced by the moralist. If the common-sense rules may be taken as valid, some of the difficulties of the universal hedonic assessment will be overcome. A word of caution is required, however. Adoption of current moral rules will not furnish a fully formulated utilitarian morality; the resemblance is general, not complete. It still remains for the utilitarian to prescribe an empirical hedonic calculation as the final test of ethics, and also as a method for solving moral problems where no received rule exists or where two or more variant common-sense rules conflict. Sidgwick may have been a utilitarian "on an Intuitional basis,"[30] but he was nonetheless utilitarian. The answer always lies ultimately in the estimate of the total pleasures and pains resulting from a given course of conduct, and this principle will overrule any other opposed to it.

With the relationship between utilitarianism and common-sense rules of morality established in his own mind, what should the utilitarian do about bringing these rules more into conformity with universalistic hedonism where obvious differences occur? The utilitarian is faced with the problem of his obligation from a standpoint of moral conservatism as opposed to reform. The answer that Sidgwick gives is important because it states the necessity for change, but with important qualifications. Since common sense does not yield a consensus on the kind of conduct likely to produce the greatest happiness on the whole, the utilitarian has a manifest obligation to reform these rules so that they conform more closely to the end of universal hedonism. In this respect the utilitarian is a reformer. But if his projected reform is to be consistent with the utilitarian end and if his decision is to be rendered by the empirical method, he must take account of important consequences for the general happiness likely to result from change. A delicate operation is required of one interfering with accepted traditions. The careful

102

utilitarian must take cognizance, from the personal standpoint, of the penalties of social disapprobation which he will incur and the effect on his own mind which may be brought about by a breach of customary morality. And he must also consider the effect of disrupting social habits which are conducive to good morals. It is always easier to pull down than it is to build up, especially where a whole system of expectancy is based on established standards. The conclusion is that much of utilitarian morality will consist of applying more carefully the old rules rather than in making innovations.

The utilitarian basis of customary common-sense morality is indicated also in Sidgwick's *History of Ethics* in which he demonstrates some of the constants among moral rules as well as the occasional disruption and creation of whole new systems of morality. Sidgwick says fairly directly that received moral rules, and the historical inheritance of moral standards which are residual in new generations, form important restraints on seductive impulses and appetites. And he suggests further that these historical residues exhibit characteristics which strongly imply their rational generation from the utilitarian principle. Sidgwick recognizes the tendency among earlier utilitarians to make society over, and "he pours buckets of cold water on the reforming fires of such Utilitarians."[31] In this respect Sidgwick is closer to the traditionalism of Hume than to the Benthamites, although the basis of his ethics is as much opposed to the naturalism of Hume as it is to the confusion of ethics and psychology in Bentham.

The ethical theories of Henry Sidgwick provide the foundation for a complete revision of the utilitarian philosophical position, ranging from metaphysics to political institutionalism. In one sense Sidgwick might be said to represent the beginning of the third period of utilitarianism.[32] From Hobbes to Hume there is a struggle to advance the philosophical system in the face of criticisms drawn from older schools of thought. In this era the main concepts are developed—psychological atomism as a theory of knowledge (based on a materialistic metaphysics), a psychological theory of morals, and empiricism as the method of utilitarianism. At the same time the political framework is conservative, except with Locke, because of the necessity for a close check on the dangers of the unleashed passions of man. The second stage is the reformist period extending from Bentham through John Stuart Mill. While retaining the philosophical bases of older utilitarianism, the system now seeks its

103

culmination in the new social system of economic and political liberalism. This process had hardly run its course, however, when its last exponent, John Stuart Mill, vainly tried to adjust new social conditions and new systems of thought to the framework of the old fundamentals. It was necessary, instead, that a figure more dissociated from the earlier period reformulate the whole system in order to avoid some of the inconsistencies of the younger Mill's position.

In the first place Sidgwick, like John Stuart Mill, was greatly influenced by the schools of thought that stood in direct opposition to Benthamism, but he had the advantage over Mill of not feeling compelled to try to preserve the philosophical doctrines of the Benthamites when there were better ones available. In a letter written in 1866, at a time when his reflections on ethics were leading him to break his somewhat dogmatic adherence to the philosophy of the younger Mill, he said: "I am at present an eclectic. I believe in the possibility of pursuing conflicting methods of mental philosophy side by side."[33] Later, in his revealing commentary on his intellectual development, he explained the ways in which the reading of Kant and Butler contributed to his merger of utilitarianism and intuitionism.[34]

Certainly Kant influenced Sidgwick's conception of the independence and universality of moral obligation. And like Kant, although in a manner far more provisional, Sidgwick returned to a conception of religion through ethics. Whereas Kant inferred a moral need for immortality in order that the moral experience of finite wills might attain to the full realization of perfected ideals, Sidgwick, in a simpler frame of reference, felt the moral need for immortality both as a sanction for the performance of duty and as a state in which redress could be made for the failure to equate happiness with desert in the finite world.[35] In Butler, on the other hand, Sidgwick was able to discover the influence of rational self-love (and its relation to other forms of duty) on the realization of universal good. Even more important, perhaps, is the fact that Butler's influences led him "to abandon the doctrine of Psychological Hedonism, and to recognize the existence of 'disinterested' or 'extra-regarding' impulses to action. . . ." On this point, so far as a psychological basis of ethics was concerned, Sidgwick found himself "much more in agreement with Butler than Mill."[36] The internal evidence of his work further supports the idea that the impact made on Sidgwick's thought by these and other nonutilitarian thinkers, together with his own critical powers, was sufficient to distinguish his whole ethical system from its Benthamite antecedents.

Perhaps an even more basic influence than Kant and Butler, however, was Sidgwick's working hypothesis of common-sense beliefs. Common-sense philosophy led him to realize the validity of certain of the inferences of the intuitionists and idealists, because common-sense beliefs, however hypothetical, were the only basis that he had for unifying his practical ethical conclusions into a body of knowledge. And these common-sense beliefs ("rectified" by philosophy)—including the rational nature of the concept of obligation and the notion that perception involves immediate cognition and is not analyzable into simple sensation—were far removed from the metaphysics and conception of knowledge of Benthamic utilitarianism. In Sidgwick's case philosophy is not reduced to associationist psychology because mind performs, in a manner which cannot be explained in terms of elementary "feelings" or sensations, the functions of thinking, judging, and believing. These functions have a philosophical concern which is not present in the psychological studies dealing with "feelings" and attempting to ascertain the laws of sequence and coexistence of mental facts. Thus, the choice of ethical ends is a philosophical generalization regarded as true of certain relationships apart from the source of the ideas. For those who resolve all thought into feelings, philosophy cannot be distinguished from psychology; but "the assertion 'All is Feeling' is a philosophical, not a psychological proposition, as the assertion 'All is Matter' is a philosophical and not a physical proposition."[37] As a consequence Sidgwick maintains that the type of generalization drawn by the earlier utilitarians from their empirical psychology was not a scientific result of the type sought by psychology in its role as a positive science. Instead, it was an affirmation about the very nature of mind, a subject on which science yields no objective results.

This metaphysical difference from the positivistic utilitarians stems from the active role Sidgwick assigns to mind in generalizing humanistic questions, and it leads to an important methodological shift. The early utilitarians insisted on regarding the structure of mental substance as objective in the same sense as the physical universe. James Mill's remark to the effect that what he was attempting in the *Analysis of the Phenomena of the Human Mind* was to make the human mind as plain as the road from Charing

Cross to St. Paul's typifies this attitude. Consequently they held the empirical method to be the key to knowledge. At the same time they drew rationalistic conclusions about their objects of study which could certainly not be verified by induction. This inconsistency between the claims of the early utilitarians and their method was exposed much earlier by Macaulay in his famous essay on James Mill's government. Macaulay makes the criticism, so often made later, that Mill relies too much on a priori deduction from an inadequate conception of the nature of man, and recommends the use of a more extensive historical, inductive method.[38] Bentham, too, used an "unduly deductive method"[39] in arriving at his results. The proposition that man is motivated solely by apprehension of his own pleasures and pains is a hypothetical generalization from which the moral and political theory of Benthamic utilitarianism is largely deduced, yet it is quite clear that observation does not warrant such an egoistic conclusion. In addition, many of the other social and economic "laws" promulgated by the utilitarians are deductive; but they are often left uncorrected when empirical data appear to demonstrate the need for qualifying them.

It is interesting that Sidgwick, who makes no claims to exactness of result in the social sciences and who frankly admits the necessity for use of methods other than empiricism, should be the utilitarian who makes the most extensive use of empirical observation in his social and political theory. Sidgwick's social theory originates with the clear recognition of a problem. With the problem in mind, a hypothesis is produced and is then stringently tested by experience to discover whether it is complete as a generalization. Thus Sidgwick begins with the problem of ethics—what should the basis of individual behavior be and how may it be realized? He also differentiates between the normative and factual aspects of the problem. The normative in this case is, of course, the question of the end of behavior, while the methodological problem involves the means for realizing the end. Both norm and method, however, must be fitted into a consistent whole and should yield results which are in accord with the natural conditions and experience of man. The ultimate end of behavior, however, is a matter of rational choice which, while it may be verified in a limited way by the consensus of experts, by its clarity, and by the consistency with which it accords with other beliefs and experience, remains undemonstrable in terms of purely empirical methodology.[40]

The contrast with the Benthamic utilitarians is striking. Their theory originates with generalizations about the nature of man for which an empirical basis is claimed. Therefore, the problem which follows must fit into preconceived categories whose sources are obscured by methodological inconsistency. Since man is by nature an egoist, the problem is to relate his egoism to the necessary social conditions under which he lives.

Psychological hedonism, or naturalistic egoism, is discernible as the motivating factor of human conduct in all the utilitarians down to Sidgwick, with the exception of Hume. The Hobbesian man, a creature of passions, is a precursor of all the subsequent types.[41] The sovereign governance over the individual of pleasure and pain is the Benthamic statement of this basic fact of earlier utilitarianism. In adjusting these atomized, self-interested wills to social obligation, the early utilitarians have produced a variety of regulative forces for obtaining order. In Hobbes' view the fear of death induces man to accept the protective order of the Leviathan. Among the other utilitarians the regulative order is also externalized in the form of the natural harmony of interests and the artificial identity of interests through a mechanistic political formula. The utilitarians desired that people behave as though they were promoting the general interest, even though psychologically they were incapable of doing so.

Sidgwick fortunately does not have the self-complacent assurance of Bentham, who can shrug off all theory in conflict with his position; neither is he traumatically tied, like John Stuart Mill, to a psychological dogma contradictory to the end of action that he wills. He has, therefore, not lost the technique of philosophy in his zeal for reform or in an attempt to justify incompatible postulates. Sidgwick's regulative order for man in his social condition is internal. By universalizing ethical obligation Sidgwick has reintroduced into secularized ethics a concept of *amor dei* which is both opposed and superior to the principle of *amor sui*. Man is capable of adjusting his own behavior to social conditions and is indeed under obligation to do so. The fact that it is not easy to adopt and follow a nonegoistic end does not preclude the possibility or even the necessity of making this adjustment. In fact, such an ethics is one of the prerequisites of political freedom in a democratic society, for "unless a little more sociality is allowed to an average human being, the problem of combining these egoists into an organization for promoting their happiness is like the old task of making ropes of sand. The difficulty that Hobbes vainly tried to settle summarily by absolute despotism is hardly to be overcome by the democratic artifices of his more inventive successor."[42]

Sidgwick takes Bentham to task for his insufficient theory of the moral nature of man, indicating that "while he is as confident in his power of constructing a happy society as the most ardent believer in the perfectibility of mankind, he is as convinced of the unqualified selfishness of the vast majority of human beings as the bitterest cynic."[43] He notes further that for Bentham "psychologically analyzed, morality appears as a simple result of common selfishness. . . . How, on this theory, men's moral judgments come to agree as much as they actually do is not sufficiently explained; and in any case there is no rational transition possible from this psychological theory to the ethical principle that 'the standard of rectitude for all actions' is 'public utility.' Nor does Bentham really maintain that there is: when pressed, he explains frankly that his first principle is really his individual sentiment; that, in fact, he aims at the general happiness because he happens to prefer it."[44]

Sidgwick is fundamentally opposed to the social physics of the utilitarians and the related positivists. And this opposition stems from his view of the basic ethical potential of man. The fact is that where Bentham wanted to make man over in his own image, Sidgwick was on the whole more content with God's product.

CHAPTER FIVE

Sidgwick & English Liberalism

THE CRITICISM and corrections of the philosophical doctrines of the early utilitarians which Sidgwick made greatly influenced his development of a later utilitarian political theory. In no case is this influence manifested more clearly than in his discussion of the relation between economics and politics.

Dicey has no hesitation in placing Benthamic utilitarianism at the very center of the development of classical liberalism; in fact he uses the terms "utilitarianism" and "liberalism" practically interchangeably. He points out that "Utilitarian individualism, which for many years under the name of liberalism determined the trend of English legislation, was nothing but Benthamism modified by the experience, the prudence, and the timidity of practical politicians."[1]* He further holds that one of the three guiding principles of legislative utilitarianism as expounded by the Benthamites was the "dogma of *laissez-faire*," whose major proposition may be stated as follows: "*Every person is in the main and as a general rule the best judge of his own happiness. Hence legislation should aim at the removal of all those restrictions on the free action of an individual which are not necessary for securing the like freedom on the part of his neighbours.*"[2]

*Notes to this chapter begin on page 178.

109

It seems clear that this major principle was one which could have furnished a guide to legislation in cases other than those where economic policy was involved; but it is also fairly clear, on the basis of the treatment by Dicey and others,[3] that it was in the particular area of economic policy that this rule held sway most fully. The fact that "in 1830 the economists and the Benthamites formed one school"[4] was undoubtedly an important factor in the extent to which this principle gained practical influence.

This influence was sufficiently strong not only to dominate the formation of public economic policy down to about 1870, but it was so widely held that its more authoritative proponents could practically overlook criticism directed against the assumption of laissez-faire principles. "From 1832 onwards the supremacy of individualism among the classes then capable of influencing legislation was for many years incontestable and patent."[5] The attitude expressed in the doctrine quoted above worked its way into the thinking of leaders of opinion drawn from the most widely varying sources. The leaders of the Manchester School, although neither "philosophic Radicals nor philosophers of any kind," followed out the ideas of Bentham in politics "more nearly than did any other body of English liberals"; and while the Conservatives who followed Peel would have derided the idea of their being utilitarians, they nonetheless "had accepted to a great extent the doctrines of Bentham," in common with the others of their generation.[6] This is not to deny that specific acts of legislation based on principles contrary to the laissez-faire doctrine came into being during that doctrine's ascendancy, but only to say that its sweeping success as a basis of economic policy has seldom been paralleled by that of any similar doctrine.

Despite this connection of Benthamic utilitarianism with the practical success of individualistic liberalism, however, there were other aspects of early utilitarianism which gave support to collectivistic doctrines.

Dicey, who was a firm laissez-faire liberal himself, called attention to the fact that the extension of democracy after 1832 meant a renewal of state activity partly, at least, because the right to vote meant the right to combine for securing economic benefits. Utilitarianism, in spite of its suspicious attitude toward the interference of government in the economy, achieved its dominance through governmental activity. Dicey holds, therefore, that collectivism

110

owes a debt to Bentham, since from him the socialists inherited a legislative dogma, a legislative instrument, and a legislative tendency. Utility, in itself fraught with a revolutionary egalitarianism, was the dogma; parliamentary sovereignty ("democratic despotism") the institution; and constant extension and improvement in the machinery of government was the tendency.[7] In part, then, the extension of some of the principles of early utilitarianism other than those on which its economic premises were based was a factor in breaking down the strong hold that its economic doctrines had on practical problems of public policy.

It is difficult to discover the precise time at which early liberalism began to recede in favor of the new liberalism in which the state's active interference in the economy is accepted as a valid function. As early as 1802, with the Pauper Apprentice Act,[8] social legislation in the industrial area made its appearance. Thus in the period of Tory reaction, the Tory philanthropist was already seeking to modify the conditions of the industrial order. Even in the heyday of Benthamic liberalism (1832-1867) the working-class-Tory compound, united largely by the catalyst of Evangelicalism, was active in moderating the harsher doctrines of laissez-faire economics, especially in extending regulation over the employment and conditions of work of women and children.

Dicey dates the advent of effective collectivism from about 1870.[9] He holds that its influence is due to the following factors: (1) Tory philanthropy and the factory movement; (2) the changed attitude of the working class after 1848, particularly its demand for collective bargaining; (3) a modification of economic beliefs resulting from an odd assortment of critics including Carlyle, Kingsley, Mrs. Gaskell, Comte, and John Stuart Mill; (4) the changing character of commerce, especially the rise of the joint-stock company and protectionism; and (5) household suffrage.[10] The free-trade idea was confronted with demands for protection; stringent regulation of contracts was replacing the free contract principle; action in combination began supplanting individual enterprise; and equalization of advantages was stressed more than the laissez-faire demand for complete liberty to rise economically without assistance.[11]

What the extreme individualistic liberal was faced with in these changing opinions was an attack both on the philosophical assumptions of the earlier form of liberalism and on the conditions resulting from the practical application of its doctrines. "In the judgment of

111

the so-called 'critical school,' the hedonistic-rationalistic bias of the orthodox economists led them to frame their science in a rigid deductive cast, thereby imparting to it that abstractness and arid scholastic quality that was once the bane of the natural sciences. Instead of attending to man as he behaves in the here and now of concrete circumstances, they described how man would behave *if*, propelled by pleasure and repelled by pain and careful to calculate the units of each so as to procure a favorable balance, he competed freely in an economy based upon private ownership."[12]

Added to this critical attack on the method of the classical economists was the practical problem arising because the older liberal had not been sufficiently aware of the extent to which the principle of equality was involved in making every man count for one and no man for more, and of the tendency of egalitarian democracy and liberty to conflict. "Whereas liberty involves differentiation and division, equality entails levelling and centralization. Liberty and equality, which find their embodiment respectively in liberalism and in democracy, are thus complementary and at the same time antithetical: complementary inasmuch as absence of equality, at least equality of opportunity, degrades liberty to the level of exclusive and therefore oppressive privilege; antithetical, inasmuch as equality is conducive to indiscriminate levelling and indirectly to excessive centralization—to the detriment of such bulwarks of liberty as local associations and institutions."[13] Looking back over the nineteenth century after the results of this transformation were becoming apparent, Dicey could write that "liberalism itself has at last learned to place no small confidence in the beneficent effects of State control; but this trust, whether well founded or not, is utterly foreign to the liberalism of 1832."[14]

If 1870 can be accepted as the approximate date of origin of a general trend toward collectivism, Sidgwick's active intellectual life falls in the early period of the shift away from laissez faire. The rationalization of the social structure by the classical liberals had largely been completed by that time. The reform movement had set commerce and industry free, enfranchised the middle class, created a professional bureaucracy, and developed a local administrative structure capable of performing the services demanded of it. But the Industrial Revolution had also created a new social class, which after 1848 was a self-conscious political force and after 1867 was qualified as an active participant in the political process. The voting strength of the laboring class was capable of turning the parties away from conformance to deductive principles of economics to economic pragmatism based on intermittently expressed political demands. Politics once again was to supersede economics, but it was to do so primarily in the interest of fulfilling economic desires.

Sidgwick's treatment of the problems involved in the theory of economic policy required two closely related analyses. In the first place he gives full recognition to the practical consequences of the political opposition between extreme individualism and doctrinaire collectivism, while at the same time he appears to feel confident that an examination of the common-sense moral (and political) judgments which form the basis of these respective attitudes will demonstrate a certain amount of utility in the opposing views and may even furnish a "common ground on which a profitable discussion may be conducted between them."[15] In the second place, he is concerned with the extent to which classical economics provided a basis of support for individualistic liberalism. Consequently he examines the development of economic thought, its methods, and its pronouncements on policy in order to see what corrections will have to be made if valid conclusions are to be drawn about the functions of the state relative to the national economy.

Sidgwick's earliest treatment of these problems in his examination of the ethical concepts of liberty (or "freedom") and equality in the chapter on "Justice" in *The Methods of Ethics*. This chapter is in Book III ("Intuitionism") and it, like the other chapters of that book, deals with the problem of determining whether common-sense intuitive concepts, such as "justice," can be clearly defined in relation to their ethical application. That is, is it possible to draw from these conceptions any generalized rules of conduct which are universally applicable and independent of an empirical estimate of their result?

There are, he finds, two distinct notions respecting the realization of ideal justice—the individualistic and the socialistic theories of a political community. In the individualistic idea, freedom from interference is thought to be the principle which systematizes all human rights, thereby producing justice. "It has been held that freedom from interference is really the whole of what human beings, originally and apart from contracts, can be said to *owe* to each other.... All natural Rights, on this view, may be summed up in the right of freedom; so that the complete and universal establishment of this Right would be the complete realization of Justice,—the Equality at

113

which Justice is thought to aim being interpreted as Equality of Freedom."[16] On the other hand the socialist ideal is founded on the principle of requiting desert. Those who hold to this conception feel "that Justice requires a mode of distributing payment for services, entirely different from that at present effected by free competition: and that all labourers ought to be paid according to the intrinsic value of their labour as estimated by enlightened and competent judges."[17] Neither of these ideals is self-evident and immediately practicable as a basis for social action which will realize our sense of justice.

Although "it commends itself much to ... [his] mind," Sidgwick cannot perceive the self-evidence of the idea of total freedom.[18] In the first place it needs limitation in its application. Certainly no one would deny that freedom's negative principle—that no one should be coerced for his own sake—cannot be applied to children or mental defectives. Once this exception is admitted, is there any intuitive way of knowing that the idea should be applied without exception to sane adults? Even those who favor the idea of freedom often admit that some adults in a low state of civilization should be subject to the decisions of others. If these exceptions, then, are valid, there is no criterion for applying the principle except that it should go into effect where individuals are intelligent enough to provide for themselves better than others would do it for them. And if this is the only possible means of determining its practicability, the principle of freedom is not an absolute, but a subordinate of the general-happiness principle.

The idea of freedom is open to other objections, also. In the first place it is ambiguous, since on an a priori basis we cannot know the extent to which freedom of action of an individual should be limited in order to avoid annoyance to others. Secondly, since freedom of contract is presupposed and in making a contract a man may voluntarily limit his freedom, upon what deduction from the idea of freedom are we to base a limitation of contractual freedom in order to prevent a contract of enslavement?

It is almost inevitable that the economic question should be raised in this connection; and if it is difficult "to define freedom as an ideal to be realized in the merely personal relations of human beings, the difficulty is increased when we consider the relation of men to the material means of life and happiness."[19] The question of appropriation of property is fundamental to the idea of freedom, and all sorts of problems arise from this right. For example, to what extent should a man's prior occupation and ownership of property permit him to exclude more intensive productivity of that property? Or, what right does a man who has acquired property have to dispose of it after death? Again, once nearly all available property is appropriated, equality of freedom in the acquisition of property is denied the propertyless man, and he may be even less free than if no appropriation at all is allowed. It seems that none of these problems can be settled by taking freedom as the sole end of distributive justice.

On the other hand, the socialist attempt to establish principles by which the comparative worth of different activities may be measured is open to serious objections. On common-sense standards, how can we rationally compare the values of skilled and unskilled labor or the relative worth of different types of labor in a common enterprise, or the reward due management as against that due the worker? In order to deal with these problems, we have to fall back on the market value of these services and ask, not what they are intrinsically worth, but what reward will procure them. Our sense of social justice may be more completely satisfied "by the Socialistic Ideal of Distribution, founded on the principle of requiting Desert: but when we try to make this principle precise, we find ourselves again involved in grave difficulties."[20]

On a purely philosophical basis it appears that Sidgwick recognizes the values implicit in the intuitive concepts on which both individualism and socialism are founded. However, in his analysis any generalized principle of social action must be subordinate to the ultimate end, which is the greatest happiness. In his view economic freedom seemed to supply the most practicable means to the attainment of this end. In a larger sense the intuitive concept of freedom, on which liberalism rests, satisfied some distinctly human demands intimately connected with happiness.[21] Nonetheless, he could not accept the conception of freedom adhered to by some individualists who "hold the realization of freedom or mutual noninterference to be not merely desirable as most conducive to human happiness, but absolutely desirable as the ultimate end of law and of all governmental interference: an ideal good which would be degraded if it were sought merely as a means of obtaining pleasure and avoiding pain."[22]

The basis of Sidgwick's position on questions of economic policy, then, is ethical—the question asked by him is: Does a particular theory of economic policy provide the mode of production and the distributive pattern that it *ought* to do in order to realize the hedonistic end? To choose absolute freedom without qualification would not solve the ethical problem any more effectively than the advocacy of the absolute principle of equality (on which socialism largely rests) will solve it, even though each principle, for reasons which differ, have some application as means to the utilitarian end.

Sidgwick opens his *Principles of Political Economy* with an explanation of the change in attitude that had taken place in England with respect to economics. He remarks (1883) that:

Some twenty years ago, both the Theory of Political Economy in its main outlines, and the most important practical applications of it, were considered as finally settled by the great majority of educated persons in England. Two causes appear to have chiefly cooperated in producing this result. The prosperity that had followed on the abolition of the corn-laws had given practical men a most impressive and satisfying proof of the soundness of the abstract reasoning by which the expediency of Free Trade had been inferred; and a masterly expositor of thought [J. S. Mill] had published in a convenient treatise [1847] a skilful statement of the chief results of the controversies of the preceding generation; in which the doctrines of Ricardo were presented with many of the requisite explanations and qualifications, and much of what was sound in the objections and supplementary suggestions of other writers was duly taken into account. It seemed that the science had at length emerged from the state of polemical discussion on fundamental notions and principles, and that whatever further remained to be done would be building on a foundation already laid. J. S. Mill's language had a considerable share in producing this belief.[23]

Sidgwick goes on to observe that many of the generation taught by John Stuart Mill were probably not aware that this confident tone was of such recent origin. He cites a number of instances in which classical economists in the earliest part of the century had expressed concern about the "rudimentary and unsettled" condition of their study.

He then goes still further and points out that by 1871 the "Halcyon days of Political Economy" which had prevailed in the middle years of the century had passed away. He dates this passing from 1869 and gives a general outline of the way in which it occurred. Just as the triumph of the theory of classical economics was sustained by the apparent success of its application, so, too, was the attack on economic theory which occurred in the 1860's and 1870's reinforced by a loss of confidence in the effectiveness of the theory's recommendations on economic policy. According to Sidgwick, John Stuart Mill himself contributed to the uncertainty about economic theory by the ease with which he abandoned the wages fund theory in a review of Thornton's book *On Labour* in 1869. In the early 1870's Cairnes and Jevons questioned various doctrines put forward by Mill, and Cliff Leslie attacked the "Ricardian" or a priori method of orthodox economics along lines similar to the criticism made by the German historical school. At the same time, according to Sidgwick, the opposition of influential artisans "did not diminish, it only changed somewhat from sullen distrust to confident contempt"; and even free trade, on which so much of the prestige of political economy had rested in the halcyon days of the subject had "been called in question by an apparently growing party of practical men...."[24]

If Sidgwick's description of the rise and decline of the confidence with which classical economics was viewed both by economists and by the country as a whole is true (and it is borne out in various ways by other observers), an understanding of the way in which the dogma of laissez faire became "the philosophy in office" in the middle years of the nineteenth century should throw some light on the sources of conflict over the meaning of economic liberalism. For there seems to be little doubt that whatever the economists themselves may have said or implied, the triumph of orthodox economics in the practical sense meant the application of the doctrine of laissez faire to questions of economic policy. The general acceptance of that doctrine has been described by Dicey in the following manner: "The Exhibition of 1851 had a significance which is hardly understood by the present generation [the generation of the turn of the century]. To wise and patriotic contemporaries it represented the universal faith that freedom of trade would remove the main cause of discord among nations, and open an era of industrial prosperity and unbroken peace. The ideas of the political economists, and above all the dogma of laissez-faire had, it was thought, achieved a final victory."[25]

The question that is debatable in this connection is the extent to which what the classical economists said, implied, or left unsaid contributed to the growth of this dogma and sustained it after it had become accepted.

On this particular question the work by Professor Lionel Robbins, *The Theory of Economic Policy*, is a *tour de force*. Robbins argues with great effect that the attribution to the classical economists of certain attitudes on questions of economic policy and of a bias in favor of the middle class is not founded on a study of the facts. In particular is this ignorance of the facts true of popular writing on the subject, which "is far below the zero of common knowledge or decency. On this plane, not only is any real knowledge of the classical writers non-existent but, further, their place has been taken by a set of mythological figures, passing by the same names, but not infrequently invested with attitudes almost the exact reverse of those which the originals adopted. These dummies are very malignant creatures indeed. They are the tools or lacqueys of capitalist exploiters—I think that has the authentic stylistic flavour. They are indefatigable opponents of social reform. They can conceive no function for the state other than that of the night watchman. They 'defend' subsistence wages and are supremely indifferent to the well-being of the working classes."[26] Nor is such an attitude towards the classicists confined altogether to popular writers, as an examination of some of Professor Robbins' citations will show.

In the course of removing the stigma attaching to the classical economists (including Hume, Smith, Ricardo, Matthews, Torrens, Senior, McCulloch, and James and John Stuart Mill), Professor Robbins produces much evidence in the form of excerpts from the classical texts themselves to show that the writers were far from advocating a complete absence of state regulation in the formation of economic policy and were even, criticism to the contrary notwithstanding, very much concerned about "the condition of the people." Supplementary to this presentation based on the exceptions to laissez faire and the proposals for amelioration of the lot of the people expounded by the classicists is an ingenious argument about the differences between the practical character of English utilitarianism and the sweeping assertions of the natural-rights school of French economists. This argument takes the position that from the historical standpoint, "The great individualist movement of the eighteenth and nineteenth centuries is seen to rest not on one but on two different points of view. On the one hand, you have those who, like Mercier de la Rivière and Bastiat, conceive the system of economic freedom arising spontaneously in a *milieu* in which the functions of the state are minimal and more or less cut and dried for all times and places. On the other hand you have the English Classical School who, while urging just as strongly the claim for the freeing of trade, and enterprise, conceive the functions of the state in a much more positive and experimental spirit and who are not prepared to lay down in advance prohibitions of state action resting on conceptions of a natural order of things at once simple and universally applicable."[27] Since these two schools were at one in their attack on mercantilism, it may be asked why their theories of society proceed on divergent lines. The real difference, according to Robbins, is in the philosophical origins of these two liberal theories. "On the one hand, you have the tradition of natural law and natural rights, according to which the criterion of policy consists essentially of conformity to a pre-established natural order capable of very easy definition and invariant in time and space. . . . On the other hand, you have the Utilitarian tradition, influential conspicuously through Hume and Bentham, according to which all laws and rights were to be regarded as essentially man-made and to be evaluated according to their effects on the general happiness, long term and short."[28]

Now there are some commentators, as detached and scholarly as Professor Robbins, who differ with his interpretation. While admitting that Robbins proves much of his case, Eric Roll contends that "he tries, perhaps, to prove too much"; and in the case of the argument about the difference between the English and French economists Roll says that it seems to him, "in spite of its ingenuity and brilliant exposition, somewhat exaggerated."[29] Roll does not believe that the classicists were free from the naturalism characterizing the French economists; indeed the assumption of a "natural harmony of interests" plays a very important part in their theory of economic policy. Despite specific exceptions to the guiding rule of laissez faire (some of which reflected the presence in classical economics of the egalitarian rather than the conservative political theory of their utilitarian background), Roll denies that the attitude of the classical economists toward problems of economic policy was pragmatic. "No doubt . . . some economists had transcended the narrow confines of doctrinaire *laissez-faire*. But attempts to portray the whole post-Ricardian school as social reformers whose interest in *laissez-faire* was only that of opponents of monopoly and privileges have not been generally successful."[30] Nor, in the opinion of Roll, is the classical school altogether free even from the charge that it

119

favored capitalist interests as against other groups in the society.[31] Roll sums up his statement on these questions of the responsibility of the economist for the rigid views imputed to him by saying that his (Roll's) position is the product of "a strong general impression left by a study of the literature of the period; and it was during that period [the era of the classicists] that economics, not altogether unjustly, got its bad name as a rationalization of and apologia for the evil conditions in which the vast majority of the population were obliged to live."[32]

The fact that a careful reading of the classical writers by two scholars of the ability of Roll and Robbins yields such different results seems to imply a measure of confusion in the sources which is not explained away by the acceptance of either view to the complete exclusion of the other. On the whole Sidgwick's explanation of the complex set of factors out of which this confusion emerges sheds more light and less heat on the problem than most of the subsequent ones.

Sidgwick's discussion turns on two main points, both of which constitute problems characterizing nearly all the various aspects of Benthamic utilitarianism. One point is the tendency to confuse empirical and ethical propositions (the "is" with the "ought"), and the other is the method used by the economists. Both contribute to the uncertainty about what the classicists were actually saying with regard to the scope of economic theory and its role in the determination of economic policy.

With respect to the first of these points Sidgwick suggests that the English economists had actually drawn a "sharp distinction" between economic theory and its application to practice, but the general tendency to merge the two makes it "important to examine carefully the causes and the justification, if there be any, of this widespread confusion—or at least fusion—of distinct inquiries."[33] He finds that the causes are complex, being "partly historical or linguistic; partly again, they lie deep in the nature of the subject and the normal conditions of the application of the human intellect to practice."[34]

He notes that the generic term "economy" had always denoted an art or method of attaining a practical end rather than a science. Historically "political economy" had been associated with "the art of government which had for its aim the replenishment of the public treasury, and—as a means to this—the enrichment of the community by a provident regulation of industry and trade."[35] Before the close of the eighteenth century, however, a different view of the statesman's duty in relation to industry and trade had begun to be taken, largely as a result of the work of the Physiocrats and Adam Smith. The studies by Adam Smith and the Physiocrats still asked the question: "How to make the nation as rich as possible?"; but the answer now was: "By letting each member of it make himself as rich as possible." In other words, the previous attempt by political economists to guide the ruler by suggesting methods of governmental intervention in order to create a "system" designed to realize the political aims of the ruler was being countered by arguments that what was done by government to encourage one part of the national economy, for example, was not only detrimental to other parts of the economy, but in fact was harmful even to the end on behalf of which intervention was made. This argument, of course, is basic to Adam Smith's attack on mercantilism.

The central point in this matter, however, is that in reaching this point of view on the way in which men "ought to be governed," Smith traversed the entire field of the way in which men actually do behave in their economic relations apart from other influencing factors. "In short, the substance of his [Adam Smith's] doctrine naturally leads him to expound it in the form of a science to which later writers have applied the name Political Economy; before entering (in Book V) on the discussion of the Art of Political Economy, of which the legitimate sphere is, in his view, reduced to the principles of governmental expenditure and taxation."[36] However, Smith has "really not seen the extent to which, in the hands of the Physiocrats as well as his own, the method of Political Economy has changed its fundamental character and become the method of a science rather than an art...."[37] As a result the transition from art to science was incomplete. "Political Economy became primarily a study of 'what is' rather than of 'what ought to be done': but this was because the two notions were, at least to a considerable extent, identified in the political economist's contemplation of the existing processes of the production and distribution of wealth. He described and analyzed these processes, not only to show what they were, but also to show that they were not likely to be improved by human restraints and regulations. This is true not only of Adam Smith, but of almost all his disciples and successors for more than half a century."[38]

Sidgwick feels that this problem of the failure completely to separate moral judgments from the economic studies of the classicists is made more difficult because of the ambiguity of their use of the term "natural." "For by the term 'natural' as commonly used, the notion of 'what generally is,' or 'what would be apart from human interference,' is suggested in vague combination with that of 'what ought to be' or 'what is intended by a benevolent Providence': and it is not always easy to say in what proportions the two meanings are mixed by any particular writer."[39]

Although he does not use such a term, it seems clear that Sidgwick recognizes that the assumption of noninterference is, when properly used, a regulative idea which enables certain aspects of economic behavior to be isolated and examined in their relative purity; and it seems equally clear that he holds that most, if not all, classical economists had failed to use the assumption of noninterference only in this scientific sense. Instead, either because of a naturalism like Adam Smith's or because of their lack of restraint in stating their case against interference, they had tended to merge their advocacy of laissez faire as a basis for governmental policy with the results of their scientific study. From this somewhat ambiguous treatment by the economists themselves it does not appear to be a great step to the kind of conclusions drawn by organs of opinion primarily concerned with practical decisions on matters of economic policy. In reviewing Marshall's *Economics of Industry* in 1879, the *Economist* made the following statement in which the merger of the ethical and factual is made by apparently giving sanction to a completely naturalistic economic order: "The labour of the economic thinker is only successful when he explains the real working of natural forces however overlaid they may be by social habits, however unwilling social prejudice may be to admit that they are ultimately irresistible."[40] Or as Sidgwick himself puts it: ". . . it is hardly surprising that practical persons have connected this conclusion [i.e., the general presumption by the economists that laissez faire ought to be the rule of practice] with the economic doctrines with which it was found in company, and have regarded it as an established 'law of political economy' that all contracts should be free and that every one should be paid exactly the market-price of his services."[41]

On the contribution of the method used by the economists to this obscuring of the line between science and art, somewhat less need be said. One of the major debates which had reawakened the dispute over the certainty of economic theory had turned on the question whether economics should be primarily inductive or deductive. The critics of orthodox economics concentrated their attention on the deductive nature of the classical approach and accused the classicists of not attending sufficiently to induction from historical experience. Although when Sidgwick discusses the methods of economic science, he is more concerned with expounding his own views on the uses of induction and deduction and their respective limitations than with imputing views to his classical predecessors, he strongly implies that there are certain weaknesses in their primarily deductive method. In fact, much of his discussion of this subject is in the form of corrections which need to be applied to that combination of induction and deduction which he regarded as characterizing the actual methodology of economics.

It is significant that in outlining the major propositions from which economic reasoning starts, Sidgwick is taken back to the controversy between factual and moral premises. He remarks: "Two distinct propositions, one being important as a premise in the deductive reasoning of the science, the other in the *rationale* of the leading rules of the art, have been more or less blended together— under some such name as individualism or economic egoism—or at any rate regarded as logically inseparable, and forming part of one doctrine."[42] These two propositions are, respectively, the factual proposition (expounded with varying degrees of qualification) that economic man always prefers a greater apparent gain to a lesser one and prefers to attain any desired result with the minimum expenditure, and the normative proposition that the best possible result will be attained by the system of economic freedom. Although there may be a certain affinity between these propositions, there is certainly no logical connection, and the limitations required to make either of them useful are quite different. They belong to different departments of inquiry; "the first is important in explaining scientifically the facts of economic experience, but has nothing to do with economic ideals or rules of governmental action in economic matters; while the second leads immediately to a fundamental maxim of policy."[43] It seems reasonable to presume that Sidgwick would not have bothered to restate this distinction unless he felt that the characteristic predominance of deduction in the method of orthodox economists had played a part in merging these two propositions.

123

However, even if these ethical and empirical propositions are separated, it is necessary in dealing with the science of economics to draw attention to certain problems. Although in handling questions of production the reasoning of the economist is influenced at practically every step by induction, in the theory of distribution and exchange, "Political Economy, as commonly treated, uses mainly an abstract, deductive, and hypothetical method."[44] In this connection it is necessary to recall that "the general applicability and utility of hypothetical reasonings of the kind described above will depend largely on two conditions: first, on the degree of success attained in forming our original suppositions, so that they may correspond as closely as possible to the facts, without becoming unmanageably complex; and, secondly, on the extent to which we recognize and attend to the divergence from facts which is—in most cases—inevitable in such abstract reasonings, and the insight and skill which we show in conjecturing roughly the effect of modifying causes whose operation we cannot precisely trace."[45] Thus induction is "certainly an indispensable supplement" to deduction in the formulation of economic theory.

Sidgwick next discusses the necessity for qualifying the basic propositions about economic behavior from which inferences are made, and he finds no ground for assuming such propositions to be a priori and capable of explaining or predicting economic phenomena of any given society without additional data of an inductive nature.[46] There is no doubt that Sidgwick thinks that the deductive economists have overstated their case. "I certainly think," he says, that "the languages sometimes used by economic writers, suggesting that the doctrines they expound are entitled in respect of scientific perfection to rank with those of physics, is liable to be seriously misleading."[47] On the other hand, his aim is not, in economic theory at least, to give up the study of economics as a science, but to "avoid mistaking a generalization from limited experience for a universal law; and so far as we are treating it hypothetically, we should take care not to use words in different meanings without being aware of the difference, nor suppose our notions to be quantitatively precise when they are really indefinite."[48]

Lord Keynes has stated the simplest (and probably the most frequently appearing) form in which the deductive method leads to the dogmatic assertion of laissez faire and ties the moral judgment to the supposedly factual account:

The beauty and simplicity of such a theory [of economic freedom] are so great that it is easy to forget that it follows not from the actual facts, but from an incomplete hypothesis introduced for the sake of simplicity. Apart from other objections to be mentioned later, the conclusions that individuals acting independently for their own advantage will produce the greatest aggregate of wealth, depends on a variety of unreal assumptions to the effect that the processes of production and consumption are in no way organic, that there exists a sufficient foreknowledge of conditions and requirements, and that there are adequate opportunities of obtaining this foreknowledge. For economists generally reserve for a later stage of their argument the complications which arise ... they reserve, that is to say, for a later stage their analysis of the actual facts. Moreover, many of those who recognize that the simplified hypothesis does not accurately correspond to fact conclude nevertheless that it does represent what is "natural" and therefore ideal. They regard the simplified hypothesis as health, and the further complications as disease.[49]

Sidgwick was anxious to avoid the fallacy of merging empirical and ethical propositions and sustaining the particular form of liberalism which advocated the doctrine of laissez faire in a naturalistic form. He recognized the practical implications which had resulted from the widespread and dogmatic manner in which this doctrine had come to be held, and he saw that the tenacity with which it was defended as a basis for the economic organization of society was producing an equally dogmatic opposition. His treatment of economics therefore aims at preserving in a corrected form the body of knowledge which had been built up by classical economics, while at the same time examining its assumptions as well as the conclusions drawn from them. In particular he makes a complete separation between the discussion of the theoretical science of production, consumption, and distribution, and the treatment of the art of formulating governmental economic policy. The result is an examination of economic liberalism within the framework of a utilitarian philosophy freed from its connections with the fallacy discussed above.

With the view discussed above in mind Sidgwick devotes the first two parts of his *Political Economy* to the theories of production, exchange, and distribution, which are treated by him in a classical manner, largely following J. S. Mill's treatment. The third division of this work is entitled "The Art of Political Economy" and consists of an extensive discussion of the problem of governmental interference in the economy as a means of improving the system of production and exchange. In addition to the treatment here, *The Elements of Politics* contains several chapters dealing with the assumption of an individualistic order and the role of government in such a society. These two sources are the most important for estimation of the manner in which Sidgwick's views of governmental interference modify the liberalism of the laissez-faire utilitarians.

The exponents of laissez-faire individualism make two important assumptions, according to Sidgwick. The first, psychological in nature, is that men are better able to discover and aim at their own interests privately than government can do it for them. The second is a sociological postulate to the effect that the common welfare is enhanced by each individual's pursuit of his (and his family's) welfare exclusively.[50] Neither of these assumptions has proved entirely true, and as a result two tendencies toward governmental regulation have sprung up. The first (which contradicts the psychological assumption of the advocate of political quietism) is paternalistic interference, or interference to prevent mischief to an individual caused by himself or with his consent. The second type of regulation is termed socialistic and aims at realizing through governmental activity a more equitable social system of production and distribution than is achieved by reliance solely on the free activity of individuals. The socialist, then, rejects the sociological proposition that the greatest common good is achieved by the pursuit of individual welfare alone.

Sidgwick accepts neither laissez-faire assumption as "even approximately universal truth"; but empirical evidence indicates that the individualistic motivation does work powerfully and that there seems to be no system which offers a satisfactory substitute for it in its entirety. Inasmuch as there are empirical weaknesses in the extreme individualistic society, however, he does criticize its shortcomings and attempts to determine the degree to which interference is warranted as a corrective, and on what basis it should be applied.

In regard to paternalistic interference the question of controlling an individual for his own good can hardly ever be separated from the problem of the effects that his uncontrolled actions might have on others who had not consented to them. Thus the man who is forced to participate in a common drainage or sanitary arrangement is being coerced partly for his own sake, but the main justification for interference is the protection of the whole community. The regulation of the sale of alcoholic beverages, too, is mainly to control the social effects of drunkenness, and not protect the alcoholic. In such cases the effect of the regulation is indirectly individualistic, since individualism presupposes protection of the individual from interference and from harmful actions by others.

The same axiom holds good when the interference is undertaken to protect the individual against deception, a protection deemed valid even from the extreme laissez-faire position. Where the government regulates entry into medical practice, certain conditions of hazardous employment, and some occupations, it is, if the regulation is kept within a certain framework, merely applying to specific cases the hazy principle of individualism which advocates nondeception of the parties engaged in an economic exchange. Sidgwick suggests that where the government prohibits absolutely the sale of foods considered unhealthy or the consultation of an unqualified physician, it is a paternal action and should be regarded warily. However, the effects of such harmful practices can be controlled by less direct means. The government might, for example, supply information as to dangerous commodities, unfit medical practitioners, and the hazardous conditions of certain types of employment. It might also decline to enforce contracts which facilitate practices deemed detrimental to the general welfare. The government may also depend to some extent upon the moral pressures of the community to react against these undesirable practices and even upon voluntary combination to apply sanctions against them.

For the most part, then, Sidgwick feels that the controls in the paternalistic area should be indirect and even negative. However, all direct paternal interference ought not "therefore to be rejected without further inquiry."[51] The principle of noninterference rests upon a rough induction from ordinary experience, but is in no wise an ultimate truth. "Hence, if strong empirical grounds are brought forward for admitting a particular exception to this principle ... it would ... be unreasonable to allow these practices to go on without interference, merely on account of the established general presumption in favour of *laissez-faire*."[52]

The more important aspect of governmental intervention—socialistic interference to improve production or to achieve a more equitable distribution—is of greater complexity. In this area regulation may not always mean simply an indirect extension of recog-

127

nizable principles of individualism. Here one is up against such diverse problems as natural monopoly, protectionism, and the moral question of the extension of happiness by controls tending in the direction of an equalization of wealth.

Typically Sidgwick makes no attempt to simplify his solutions by abstracting economic motivation from its personality and social setting. We cannot determine what government ought to do without considering what private persons may be expected to do, which, in turn, depends upon the recognition of their duty. And "in the performance even of the ordinary industrial function with which economic science is primarily concerned men are not merely influenced by the motive of self-interest, as economists have assumed, but also extensively by moral considerations."[53]

Nonetheless, Sidgwick does feel somewhat sceptical about the possibility of motivating individuals to economically useful actions by means other than economic incentives. However much the environment of thought may have been moving toward collectivism, the overt presumption was still overwhelmingly in favor of governmental quietism. The stimulus to initiative and self-help, the necessity of abstinence from immediate consumption in order to accumulate capital, and the rewards to diligence are all acceptable arguments in favor of a general thesis that free enterprise is an effective economic arrangement. Sidgwick does give a slant to these arguments, however, that is somewhat different from that of the classical economists. He does not assume that work is always disagreeable and therefore undertaken only under the pressure of economic necessity.[54] He suggests instead that there may be an overemphasis on leisure as a source of happiness which might lead many of the poorer classes into imprudent action if they were freed from the sanctions imposed by economic freedom. In addition he gives some credence to the socialist argument that abstinence could take place in a collective economy and that the workers would eventually share the extra reward resulting from this saving, a reward which now goes to the capitalist.[55] And he certainly does not assume that rewards are always equivalent to desert in a capitalistic society, even though he knows of no general means of improving the system.

Sidgwick also adopts the traditional attitude of the reform era in his suspicion of government. He regards governmental enterprise as less efficient than private production, and considers that even where laissez faire fails, it is not always best to have government supply the deficiency. This attitude is based on the danger of corruption accompanying a concentration of power, the tendency toward domination by special interests, and the wasteful expenditure of government acting under the influence of popular sentiment.[56]

In addition to these economically based reasons for adherence in general to the individualistic economic order, even while contemplating some empirical changes in it, Sidgwick adds an ethical point of view which is conservative in nature. He notes that many economists have tried to exclude all questions of fairness from their "scientific" economic reasonings. This omission is not satisfactory. Economics always relates to human beings ultimately, "and actual human beings will not permanently acquiesce in a social order that common moral opinion condemns; and if common moral opinion is tolerably satisfied with the competitive system, this is surely because it is not conscious of any wide and glaring divergence between the distribution of wealth which the moralist approves and that which the economist assumes."[57] This statement is typical of Sidgwick's ultimate reliance on the moral considerations involved in any social question. It is also characteristic of his attitude favoring the preservation of traditional social patterns which have developed in a given society. In it there is an implicit theory of gradualism which is thoroughly utilitarian, but which differs from the positive utilitarianism of Bentham who advocated sweeping changes followed by what he apparently regards as a static utopia of the felicific calculus.

Considered from a practical standpoint, the application of the unmodified principles of economic individualism demonstrates a number of shortcomings. Sidgwick carefully points out that there is no doctrinaire theory which would solve these problems, but that some of them might be corrected empirically. Some interference to promote production is fully justified on pragmatic grounds. In this respect he recognizes, first of all, the government's role in providing services which would not otherwise be provided or would be provided on an unsatisfactory basis. Thus highway systems, postal service, currency, and banking are examples of services which promote production without being remunerative to the private entrepreneur; or if made remunerative to him, these activities do not always fulfill the needs of the society.

Secondly, Sidgwick clearly recognizes the problem of monopoly, particularly that of natural monopolies. In these cases (e.g., the railroads) the government should regulate the effects of monopoly

129

after the period of development and if clearly necessary may eventually take them over upon payment of just compensation. He is also a staunch conservationist, accepting the idea of government reservations of forest lands and of fairly strict regulation of the extraction of minerals.[58]

There are grounds, too, on which governmental interference might be considered for the purpose of improving the distribution of goods in a society. From the standpoint of utility Bentham had held two propositions: (1) an increase of wealth is ordinarily productive of greater happiness to an individual; and (2) after a certain amount of wealth is amassed, there is a decreasing ratio of happiness to the individual from additional increments of wealth. From these two propositions taken together Sidgwick draws the conclusion that "the more any society approximates to equality in the distribution of wealth among its members, the greater on the whole is the aggregate of satisfactions which the society in question derives from the wealth that it possesses."[59]

This moral justification of interference is always conditioned, however, by the stipulations that the total amount of wealth remain the same and that there be no change insofar as other factors involved in happiness are concerned. However, within this framework a number of alterations might be considered in regard to the distributive arrangement. Sidgwick raises most of the issues so avidly debated by the nineteenth-century exponents of collectivism and individualism. The problems of the justice of private property, social security, labor organizations, free education, and methods of taxation are all touched upon.

A careful reading of Sidgwick's views on the validity of the principle of private ownership of land (in both the *Principles of Political Economy* and the *Elements of Politics*) will demonstrate the extent to which his opposition to land nationalization has been exaggerated.[60] From a theoretical standpoint he is prepared to argue that while there is certainly no absolute distribution on the basis of merit which results from the system of private property, there are economic advantages accruing to the whole society from the abstinence of the owners in the interest of improving the productivity of the land. As a result society as a whole is compensated to some extent for the appropriation which made this productivity possible. He also argues that we have to ask whether the nationalized land would yield a greater aggregate of utility than privately owned land.

In this connection he feels that the inefficiency of public management, the divergence of interests between the owner and lessee, and the loss of special satisfactions and stimulus of ownership would outweigh the advantages of large-scale activity in most places, at the time.[61]

Again, he holds that the historical fact that property was confiscated by force is not a satisfactory argument in favor of nationalization in view of the current utility and expectations that have resulted from the institution of private property. The deciding factor in the question of land nationalization can only be utility—will a greater aggregate of utilities be yielded to the society through public ownership than under private ownership? If such is the case sweeping measures, "including even the complete abolition of private property in land—are theoretically defensible *on the basis of individualism.*"[62]

Most of Sidgwick's views on interference to achieve a more equitable distribution are based on his general acceptance of individualism, subject to the possibility of collective intervention on an empirical basis. However, some of the contemporary collective demands were justified on somewhat different, if related, grounds. Free education was acceptable both from a productive and a distributive standpoint; it provided skills and intellect for greater output and a greater equality of opportunity for gifted persons. If anything, its distributive effect was the more important reason for its commendation.[63] Inheritance taxes, too, are valid on both the distributive and productive sides.[64] Finally, the protective tariff, while generally unsatisfactory from a productive and distributive standpoint, can be promoted on the political ground of the national interest in self-sufficiency.

Two rather lengthy quotations from the *Principles of Political Economy* will generalize Sidgwick's empirical, gradualistic, and undogmatic economic liberalism.

To sum up: the general presumption derived from abstract economic reasoning is not in favour of leaving industry altogether to private enterprise in any community that can usefully be taken even as an ideal for the guidance of practical statesmanship; but is on the contrary in favour of supplementing and controlling such enterprise in various ways by the collective action of the community. The general principles on which the nature and extent of such collective action should be determined have been given in the present chapter; but it would hardly be possible to work out a system of detailed practical

131

rules on the basis of these principles, by the abstract deductive method here adopted; owing to the extent to which the construction of such system ought reasonably to be influenced by the particular social and political conditions of the country and time for which it is framed.[65]

At the same time, as I have already explained, I see no reason to regard unqualified *laissez-faire* as tending to realize the most economical production any more than the best possible distribution of wealth: and it seems to me quite possible that a very considerable extension of the industrial functions of government might be on the whole advantageous, without any Utopian degree of moral or political improvement in human society. But at any rate to be successful such extensions must, I think, be gradual; and the first experiments in this direction ought to be made in departments in which the defects of private enterprise, and the advantages of unitary administration, have been shown to be greatest—e.g., in departments where there is a manifest tendency to the establishment of monopolies in the hands either of single individuals or of associations. And, moreover, it ought to be an object in any such extension to maintain as far as possible in the governmental organisation of industry an effective stimulus to individual exertion, and to allow scope for invention and improvement of methods.[66]

In summary, Sidgwick's liberal theory represents a reformulation of some fundamental tenets of laissez-faire liberalism. At the same time his attitudes are direct outgrowths of his transformation of the utilitarian ethics and are, therefore, internally consistent with his philosophical principles. In the first place, he rejects the laissez-faire idea that the greatest happiness is most effectively realized by the assurance of complete individual freedom in economic relations. Freedom, while filling an important psychological need, is not an ultimate end. Nor does it contribute to the realization of certain scientific laws which operate in the social environment apart from human volition. Insofar as the psychology of an individual is egoistic, the system of economic individualism is a sanction under which the individual is responsible for seeking his own welfare. It is possible that the general welfare may additionally be promoted by this attention to private interests. However, there is no psychological impediment to group action where conditions prescribe interference in the natural economic order. The independent obligation to seek the general happiness remains as an ultimate ethical proposition alongside the individual's egoistic obligation. Thus Sidgwick allows scope for free human activity of a collective type, and regards it as necessary for the realization of his philosophical end in some cases.

Sidgwick also reorients the methodology of classical liberalism. There is no naturalistic system by which scientific social laws are put into effect to promote the end of happiness. This conjunction of ethical ends with a positive, deductive theory of economics is not valid. Instead economic policy should be subordinate to the ethical ends which one tries to effect by means of social institutions. Applied economics, therefore, should be based on an empirical estimation of social needs and the end likely to be achieved by a given course of action. Since we are in a fundamentally individualistic society, and certain expectations accrue from this situation, any interference in the economic order should be pragmatic and not based on a deductive absolute. There is no completely scientific means of fixing the limits of governmental interference in the economy; this is a matter for political decision. The application of political economy is not a science, it is an art; just as most ethical and other social problems are arts. It is beyond our capacity to assemble and evaluate scientifically all the factors influencing an economic decision.

Sidgwick is neither a political quietist nor a collectivist. He is primarily an individualist, but an individualist on a nonclassical basis. What he has done is to reintroduce a humanistic element into classical individualism. He does not regard the individual as completely egoistic nor as entirely prone to inactivity when freed from the compulsion of the threat of starvation. On the contrary, he is a complex personality, dynamic rather than inert, and capable of respect and even concern for others. His actions are subject, therefore, to an indefinite degree of modification through his own volition. Nonetheless, he has certain egoistic obligations and requires some scope for free individual activity. As a result of this combination, man can act individually and collectively; he can (where the pressures are too severe) free himself from the state, but he can also (in collectivity) free himself through the state for the realization of a greater degree of happiness.

As a humanistic liberal, Sidgwick stands, in the late nineteenth century, on the threshold of the doorway through which L. T. Hobhouse passes early in the twentieth century. Sidgwick still belongs as much to the negative tradition of the early nineteenth century as he belongs to the positive tradition of the later period. Yet in some respects he is far closer to Hobhouse than to the Benthamites, for he has rejected dogmatic individualism in favor of empirical individualism, the liberty that he recognizes as valid is directed toward an ethical end and not toward the satisfaction of a psychological state of egoism, and he holds that a greater degree of equality (where it is merited) can be achieved by the positive action of the state.

Sidgwick took an early step toward a compromise between laissez-faire individualism and collectivism, each of which represented itself as a form of liberalism. His compromise was based on the primacy of his ethical end—the greatest happiness—and his recognition of a dual ethical obligation which embraced both the self and society.

His intellectual formulation of the problem of liberalism may be discovered in practice in the working arrangements of the English political parties, with their respect for both individual and social values, their spirit of tolerance and compromise, and their economic gradualism. All these matters belong historically to English political empiricism, a tradition which Sidgwick clearly recognizes and draws upon.

There is no satisfactory way to trace the direct influence of political ideas on action nor even to discover whether ideas preceded the political institution or vice versa. Nonetheless, Sidgwick has, in merging the tradition of rationalism and empiricism, produced a statement of liberalism that is logically more consistent and practically more acceptable than Benthamism. If it has been less overtly influential, it is because it lacks the appeal of dogma and because the times for which it was designed demanded compromise, not social reconstruction.

CHAPTER SIX

The Conservative Idea

I N THE FORM that it took in the hands of the Benthamites
utilitarianism was a philosophy of revolutionary import. The
radicals demanded a complete reorganization of the institutional structure of society in order to realize what now seems
at best a prosaic utopia. It is fortunate that the older empirical
political tradition in England had an implicit acceptance sufficiently
strong to produce change without violence. Certainly the confidence
in the reasonableness of the electorate and the flexibility of existing
institutions were factors in ensuring that 1832 would not repeat the
process of 1789. But comprehensive social theories such as those
characteristic of Benthamism have an inherently conservative side.
This conservative element results from the fact that the doctrines of
reform are so complete and so final that the society can, after the
ideology is translated into practical politics, rest in the satiety of
fulfillment.

The Philosophical Radicals exemplify this latent conservatism
which follows on sweeping change. The intellectual disciples of
John Stuart Mill did not recognize his shift in the direction of
collectivism as a logical extension of utilitarianism, but regarded it
as an abandonment of tried and true principles. The doctrinaire
liberalism which gained ascendancy after 1830 was held as a dogma

by its proponents; any further attempted change, whether rational or empirical, was to be regarded with suspicion.

Roberto Michels holds that there are two chief uses of conservatism: "The first is technically political, in which it means a tendency to maintain the *status quo* regardless of what that may be."[1]* The successors to completed revolutions belong to this class of conservatives. It is through verbal adherence to the fixed principles out of which the social upheaval grew that the privileged group justifies and protects its position. The dogmatic laissez-faire liberal exemplifies such revolutionary reactionism almost as well as the communist.

There is, however, a second conception of conservatism which may be referred to as philosophical conservatism.[2] In this sense of its usage, the very name of Burke signifies all that we mean by the term "conservative." In contrast to the technical political conservative's uncompromising adherence to the status quo, the philosophical conservative is primarily concerned with the difficult problem of social order. Characteristically he believes that change should be empirical and related closely to the accepted mores of the society for which the change is designed, and that a revolutionary alteration of institutions is likely to disrupt the delicate balance of social forces which has been worked out in the historical development of a political unit.

In a succinct statement Francis Wilson has recently given an excellent working definition of the philosophical conservative.

First, conservative thought has attempted to find a pattern in history that may give some clue as to the possible and impossible in politics. Second, conservatives have generally been somewhat distrustful of human nature, viewing it as a mixture of the rational and irrational. Third, the conservative has in general believed that there is a moral order in the universe in which man participates and from which he can derive canons or principles of political judgment. Fourth, conservative thought has accepted as sound politics the idea that government should be limited in its power and that such limitations should be based on principles which favor the free development of individuals and groups. And fifth, the conservative mind has defended the institution of property, I think, long before the rise of modern capitalism, and, it will, no doubt, continue to do so after capitalism may, perhaps, have ceased to exist.[3]

*Notes to this chapter begin on page 179.

This definition provides excellent tools for an analysis of Sidgwick's position as a conservative and for assessing the relation of his attitude on political change to that of the philosophical tradition of utilitarianism.

Radicals may reject the use of history in the formulation of their principles, but conservatism largely rests on a sense of the value of preserving continuity with the past. The conservative usually feels that the past forms a residuum of experience on which the present depends and from which it grows.

Sidgwick had an excellent grasp of the larger movements of history and a sense of its usefulness in empirical methodology in the social sciences. He always remained wary of generalizing too broadly from history, however, because of his sceptical attitude toward positivism. Nonetheless, the concern with history which permeated the Victorian intellectual scene was too pressing to ignore. The result of his historical reflections are contained in the posthumously published *Development of European Polity*. This book, which, like so much of his other work, was the cumulative result of lectures at Cambridge, furnishes an excellent insight into Sidgwick's view of the role of history in political studies. It should be emphasized that the book is primarily political history and could hardly merit the description "philosophy of history." At the same time a sufficient number of "clues as to the possible and impossible in politics" are given so that it might be called an *interpretation* of Western political history.

Sidgwick is careful, as he also is in *Elements of Politics* and in *Philosophy, Its Scope and Relations*, to delineate the limitations of the application of historical lessons to contemporary problems. First, the study of history cannot of itself provide knowledge of the ultimate end to which moral or political action should be directed; instead this end is brought to history when judgments are made regarding the past. Second, even where an end of action has been accepted, history can only give us limited clues as to the means of attaining that end.[4] In spite of this warning Sidgwick had gradually come to realize the necessity for including an historical analysis of the development of the national state in any extensive treatment of politics.[5] This attitude is indicated as early as 1886 when he writes: "I find History studied as inductive sociology more and more interesting, and quite wonder that I have neglected it so long. It seems to me that, without genius or originality, one might produce a really important work combining Hegelian view of evolution of the *Idea* of State with Spencerian view of quasi-biological evolution of the *fact* of the State, and testing both severely by history."[6]

The Development of European Polity is by no means an interpretation of history in the tradition of positivism, which generally produces a secularized theory of progress. Even though he seems to regard the modern liberal state as a culmination of western political development, Sidgwick does not suggest that it is the final or complete form of political union. Instead, he cautiously excerpts from political history certain limited generalities regarding constant elements in politics. Some of these factors serve to preserve political societies, others to make changes in them.

The most frequently recurring, and consequently the most important, of these concepts for a philosophy of historically based conservatism are the theory of unity among the members of a body politic, the ideas of continuity and imitation as principles of political development, and, above all, the tension between a priori theories of politics and the historically existing community.

In explaining the social cohesion of political societies, Sidgwick hardly goes as far as formulating a theory of the myth of the state. But he does advance certain ideas concerning membership in a political unit which suggest a serious concern with the problem of community among the individuals in society. He begins by pointing out that political society (which in advanced stages takes the form of the state) means a group of people united among themselves and separated from others by virtue of the fact that they habitually obey the same government. But he goes on to point out that in order to comprise a state, a political unit must have a clear consciousness of the fundamental distinction between the rights and obligations of the community in its *corporate* capacity and those of the individuals who make it up. Even though no bond other than the habitual obedience of the common government is implied in the definition of the state, "it should be recognised that a political society, whose members have no consciousness of any ties uniting them independently of their obedience to government, can hardly have the cohesive force necessary to resist the disorganising shocks and jars which external wars and internal discontents are likely to cause from time to time. If a political society is to be in a stable and satisfactory condition, its members must have—what members of the same state sometimes lack—a consciousness of belonging to one another, of being members of one body, over and above what they derive from the mere fact of being under one government, and it is only when I conceive them as having this consciousness that I regard the state as being also a 'nation.' "[7]

Here, then, is a statement of the necessity for the individual members of a society to be conscious of an evocative idea of the polity. This awareness of a corporate idea in politics is in striking contrast with the egoistic utilitarian conception of the state as an artifact in which the individual members obtain assurance of mutual noninterference so that there may be an unimpeded pursuit of self-interest. Sidgwick's idea of a universal ethical obligation enables the unity of political society to become a reality, an historical experience conveyed to every new member of the state through all the traditions and institutions of the community. In this theory, too, there is an expression of the strength of the community idea, an idea which is neither fully rational nor irrational, but a combination of both. The experience of belonging to the society is so pervading that it goes unquestioned; it is an experience deeply embedded in the subconscious. To rationalize it is to destroy it. All the institutions in the polity are dependent upon it; consequently, serious disruption of the idea is likely to create disorder.

Closely connected with the idea of unity are the symbols which publicly represent the consciousness of membership in the state. In the formative stages of the society these symbols are especially important, and the ability of the polity to maintain itself, to expand, and to achieve an advanced governmental form depends upon the suitability of the symbols. Thus the Greek use of the idea of kinship through blood as a unifying symbol presents an almost insuperable barrier to the broader unification of the *poleis* for defensive purposes. On the other hand, kingship in the modern national state furnished an early symbol that was useful in unifying widely dispersed groups into a common citizenship. And the adherence to the symbol meant that its institutional function as a producer of order would receive the support of the populace. "It is from this point of view that the transition to absolute monarchy is, when we now look back upon it, seen to be a stage in the direction in which the constitutional monarchy of the nineteenth century is a further stage. The triumph of monarchy represents the first introduction of approximately complete unity and order, by the effective subordination of all other authority in the state to the authority of the monarch.... As the slow process of civilization goes on, the need of more perfect order is keenly felt, and the completer repression of the anarchical resistance of powerful individuals or groups has consequently more and more the support of public opinion."[8]

Sidgwick recognized the unifying symbol of the Church in the Middle Ages, holding that "the unity of Western Christendom was the source of such unity as was maintained in West European society in this chaotic period."[9] However, he never perceived its universalistic content which created an open basis for unity in opposition to the closed national state.[10] The sense of security afforded the historian of the nineteenth century by the vision of peacefully coexisting rational liberal states was rudely shaken only with World War I. Sidgwick did feel that the institutional device of federalism might open the way to a more broadly based political society, especially since history demonstrated a tendency toward the formation of ever larger political areas.[11] His political history is, therefore, an open one in which the contemporary form of the state is regarded favorably, but not as an ultimate.

The element of philosophical conservatism in these ideas lies in the recognition of a gradual historical process by which a consciousness of unity as an ordering factor in politics is created. There is also present a sense of danger from the possible disruption of this ordering cohesion. Since order is the first requisite for the preservation of a political society, the idea of conservation is an important aspect of Sidgwick's political history.

The concepts of continuity and imitation represent other conservative elements in his historical attitude. The process of development of the modern national state is a continuous one with roots in antiquity. The influence of the Roman Empire is always present, if not always direct. "Though only some of the modern Western European states are formed out of the fragments of the ancient Roman Empire, still it is an important factor, though more indirectly, in the causes which have made the others what they are."[12] It is not, however, the generally accepted fact of the influence of antiquity on the modern world that gives the idea of continuity a conservative flavor. It is rather the tenacity with which old forms cling to new institutions and set limits to the rate of change that can be produced without disorder for the polity. For "even in revolutionary times, when there are widespread aspirations after something very different from what actually exists, any political ideal that aims at being practical is likely to be modelled on something that is known to exist—or at any rate is believed to have existed elsewhere."[13]

Imitation is, of course, so closely related to continuity as to form with it, in effect, one concept. Sidgwick regards imitation as especially important to political history. In fact, modern parliamentary government is largely due to direct or indirect imitation of the English system. And through all political history in the West "we must allow a large place for such imitation, even when we have no direct proof of it."[14] Even though imitation is an important means of extending institutional arrangements, it has a tendency to be a disruptive factor if not handled warily by the reformer. The adoption of the ideas and institutions of a political society with a different set of traditions will not produce an identical development, but will be modified by the customary pattern of the copying polity.

There is a striking resemblance between Sidgwick's use of continuity and imitation and that of Sir Henry Maine in his *Ancient Law*. In fact, there is a general similarity which is difficult to analyze between the *Development of European Polity* and *Ancient Law*. To say that the former does for politics what the latter does for jurisprudence would be overstating the case. Nonetheless, they are mutually concerned with generalizing tendencies among two important social institutions, and with tracing the main lines of continuity from antiquity to the present in their respective fields. The difference is a matter of degree. For Maine history is everything, the underlying continuity from ancient to modern times is perfect and unbroken, a penetration into the past which covers the broadest possible span of time is the most useful approach to the problems of the present, and rationalistic reform tends to be reactionary. Sidgwick was neither so sceptical of reform, nor so confident of the lessons learned from history. For him society does change in substance, if somewhat slowly and with the retention of many residues from the past. The study of history is useful as a means of understanding the conditions under which the end of the society may be realized, and will not afford insight into both the ends and means of society. Consequently, a study of recent history is more likely to be of value than longer-range studies.[15] But the thesis of gradualism and empiricism is common to both writers and is a source of their philosophical conservatism. Sidgwick never indulged in the kind of "technical political conservatism" that characterizes parts of Maine's criticism of democracy in his *Popular Government*, however.

141

On the whole, Sidgwick's conservatism is directed far more toward determining the conditions under which change directed toward a particular end is likely to be most effective than to proposing insuperable barriers against any change whatever.

Perhaps the most important concept for assessing Sidgwick's idea of history is his distinction between the a priori and historical methods in political theory. This separation is obviously an extension to the history of ideas of his usual differentiation between deductive and empirical methodology. The main source of the opposition between the two methods may be found in the works of Montesquieu and Rousseau. The place that Montesquieu occupies "lies largely in the fact that he represents the first great systematic introduction of the historical method into modern jurisprudence and politics: and the historical method, we think, is as hostile to the *a priori* method of Rousseau, and his assumption of universally applicable principles of political construction, as water is to fire."[16]

The results of the practical application of the a priori method may be witnessed in the French Revolution. Although Montesquieu had a hand in arousing revolutionary ardor, "still, in the movement of thought finally summed up in the Declaration of Rights . . . his influence is quite subordinate to Rousseau's."[17] The revolutionary doctrine was an "attempt to determine the structure and powers of government on principles of abstract justice based on natural law."[18]

It is possible that change could have been effected without the violence of the Revolution if it had been properly introduced and carried with a consideration for the satisfaction of habits long established. Instead, the Revolution was dominated by "the tendency under the influence of Rousseau to seek national prosperity by a renovation of the structure of government, instead of a limitation of its functions."[19]

In Sidgwick's less striking language we seem to hear echoes of Burke when he wrote that "the science of constructing a commonwealth, or renovating it, or reforming it, is, like every other experimental science, not to be taught *a priori*." But Sidgwick would have been more wary of Burke's continuing remarks to the effect that it is not "a short experience that can instruct us in that practical science; because the real effects of moral causes are not always immediate; but that which in the first instance is prejudicial may be excellent in its remoter operation; and its excellence may arise even from the ill effects it produces in the beginning."[20] The reverse, as

Burke is careful to note, is also true; and in no historical event truer, perhaps, than in the French Revolution.

In one sense the least conservative element in the ideas of the early utilitarians was their optimism regarding the rationality of man. It was only necessary for the reformer to release the individual from the restrictions imposed on the pursuit of his interest, and from that time he would calculate his true happiness and live in harmony with others. On the other hand, psychological egoistic hedonism is a deterministic conception of man's moral nature which gives no place to the idea of free choice of good or evil. Egoism is regarded in most dichotomic ethical theories, and especially in the Christian, as predominantly bad. In early utilitarianism it is not only an adequate, but often is regarded as the sole, motivation of behavior. Consequently, Benthamism presupposes an institutional determination of the problem of man in society. If the institutions are framed in accordance with principles deduced from the Benthamic view of human nature, the moral problem is solved.

For Sidgwick the problem does not solve itself so simply. To some extent he shares the Benthamic faith in the reasonableness of man. But his dualistic ethics takes cognizance of the moral problem of egoism. Sidgwick does not repudiate rational egoistic motivation as predominantly evil. Like Butler, he feels that the antithesis between self-love and benevolence has been too stringently drawn. Nevertheless, the danger from overemphasis of self-love is one of the pressing problems of practical ethics.[21] There is a strong psychological tendency to act irrationally on the basis of egoism. This tendency is not to be overcome by a mere change in institutions. Ethics for Sidgwick forms an implicit foundation to politics; politics, while it may make certain moral obligations explicit through the law, cannot regenerate the moral nature of man.[22]

This conception of the primacy of man, not institutions, in the study of ethics and politics is the basis for Sidgwick's emphasis on the usefulness of common-sense moral precepts in ordinary moral reasoning. These precepts, as has been shown in the chapter on the reconstruction of the utilitarian ethic, are part of the traditional expectancy of the community and are therefore sources of order. They can be altered and in some circumstances their alteration may be highly desirable, but there is always the danger that if their authority is undermined, a moral vacuum may be left which could produce results more undesirable than the displaced customary principle. Sidgwick's understanding of the character and importance of such inherent moral traditions is regarded by W. R. Sorley as one of his most important philosophical attainments. Sorley notes that Sidgwick's "powers are seen at their highest when he analyzed and described the moral opinions of ordinary men, not as they are reflectively set down in philosophical books, but as they are expressed in life, compact of reason and tradition, fused by emotion and desire. The third book of his *Methods of Ethics* consists, in large part, of an examination of the morality of common sense. It is an elucidation and sifting of the ideas under which men act, often without consciousness of them; and it shows the sympathetic apprehension of a mind which shares the thoughts it describes and can yet see them in perspective and sum up their significance."[23]

While Sidgwick's attitude can hardly be described as "distrustful of human nature," it does indicate an introspective and observational understanding of the nonrational aspect of man. It further indicates the necessity for an application of these principles of human nature to ethics and politics. Revolutionary changes in established traditions and institutions are unlikely to alter (except for worse) the moral basis of society which subsists in the unconscious habits and expectancies of individuals. However much he may have desired that it be taken, Sidgwick, like Spinoza, found the road from human bondage to human freedom a difficult one.

The Philosophical Radicals were possessed of a faith of their own, and from that faith derives a conception of an ordered world. However, the order which is envisaged is primarily mechanistic. On a theory of egoistic psychological hedonism they have superimposed a universalistic moral theory, and the reconciliation between the two is made in some cases by an assumption of a completely naturalistic moral order and in others by an optimism about the deterministic effects of institutional reforms in turning a community of psychological egoists into a society in which the utilitarian end is fully realized.

Sidgwick's position is quite different. His hedonism is not psychologically determined, but is the result of free choice. He feels that true moral order can result only from a close rational calculation of the results of action. At the same time there is a manifest obligation resting on the individual to accept a universalistic end. Although in order to be completely realized, this moral end may ultimately depend on a transcendental moral order in the universe, the responsibility for realizing it insofar as possible in the finite world belongs to man as a moral being. Since, in Sidgwick's estimation, the worldly moral order is largely a product of man's will, it is far from a perfect order. And since such mundane order as exists is dependent on human volition, it is not subject to indefinite modification solely through environmental change.

Sidgwick felt that the imperfect world moral order required correction by some apprehensible guarantee that moral action would ultimately be requited justly. In the concluding chapter of *Methods of Ethics*, which became the source of a great deal of controversy,[24] he examined the possibility of a theological resolution of the contradiction between the performance of moral duty and the failure to secure the requisite happiness which ought to be the reward of a morally good individual. Although he does not discover any clear moral intuition that this transcendental reward will be forthcoming, he has a strong moral sentiment that it will and ought to occur.[25] This does not mean that "if we give up the hope of attaining a practical solution of this fundamental contradiction, through any legitimately obtained conclusion or postulate as to the moral order of the world, it would become reasonable for us to abandon morality altogether; but it would seem necessary to abandon the idea of rationalising it completely."[26]

The latent theism of this point of view is indicative of an acute awareness in Sidgwick of the problem of good and evil. It also bears out his idea of the imperfectibility of the world, which is a conservative counterbalance to the idea of progress which reached its zenith in the Victorian period.

Sidgwick's conception of limited government has already been touched upon and will be treated further in the discussion of his theory of institutional politics. One or two points, however, need to be made respecting the relation between limited government and conservatism. In spite of the recognition of a corporative bond among the members of the state, Sidgwick was still a utilitarian. As a utilitarian he had a firm attachment to the individualism of his predecessors. The self-determined individual had a need for the state, but he also had a personal existence which could not be wholly subordinated to the state. This personal existence was not manifested solely in other voluntaristic groups, either, for Sidgwick did not anticipate the later pluralist development; it was entirely an experience of self-conscious individualism.

Sidgwick had, as we have seen, a typically liberal mistrust of government as the final coercive agency in society. However, like John Stuart Mill, his acute sensitivity to individualism led him to deal with the question of limitation of coercion in a manner differing from the early utilitarians. Instead of James Mill's somewhat crude institutional check, Sidgwick adopted a substantive theory of freedom. The older Mill's argument that majority rule left less than one person to be coerced by each member of the majority gave small consolation to the victim of coercion. "It may be fairly affirmed that a *body* of persons is 'free'—in the ordinary sense—when the only rules restraining them are in accordance with the corporate will of the body: but it is only in a very peculiar sense—liable to collide markedly with the ordinary meaning of the term that 'freedom' can be therefore affirmed of every *member* of the body."[27] When he speaks of freedom in its widest meaning, Sidgwick does "not mean constitutional freedom, but civil freedom . . . absence of physical and moral coercion."[28]

Like John Stuart Mill, too, Sidgwick feared the restrictions on liberty resulting from the actions of private individuals and groups. For this reason his liberal conception of a positive role for government accords well with the conservative idea of a limitation of individual, social, or excessive governmental control of the person. In fact, "it may be fairly said that the end of government is to promote liberty, so far as governmental coercion prevents worse coercion by private individuals."[29]

Sidgwick's ideas on property have already been treated as an aspect of his liberalism. Private property is a valuable institution from the standpoint of utility. He does not contend that private property is a "natural" institution nor that it is absolutely necessary for a sound national economy. He does insist that regardless of the manner in which property was confiscated historically, the social utility and traditional expectancy on which it has come to rest are sufficient grounds for exercising caution in regard to any scheme for a sudden change in its status. He gives credence, too, to sentimental attachment to property and to pride of ownership, both of which add to its social utility; through the universality of their presence, they lend historical constancy to the problem of property.

In his treatment of property Sidgwick is a philosophical, rather than a technically political, conservative.[30] The empirical gradualness, not the absolute rejection, of the extension of social control over private property is a true mark of reflective conservatism. And there is little difference on this point between conservatism and later liberalism.

Sidgwick's use of history would be sufficient to set him apart from the earlier utilitarians. The Philosophical Radicals helped to create a silent revolution with their rationalistic economic and political ideas. Sidgwick accepted many of the results of that revolution, and indeed used it as a starting point for his ideas in much the same manner that Burke had used the Glorious Revolution. Sidgwick was first and foremost a liberal, but he was a liberal in the older English sense of accepting an almost mystical adherence to the traditional customs and liberties of historical society. Of his politics as well as his ethics it might, with some truth, be said that he "called the established moral laws 'a wonderful product of nature,' the 'result of a centuries-old growth,' and hated nothing so much as 'that spirit of revolution' which rebels against and tries to destroy the morality of the settled customs, institutions, and orders of society. He was genuinely conservative, at the furtherest remove from Nietzsche's demand for a 'transvaluation of all values.' In this attachment to the natural products of our historical development and in his reliance on these as important determinants of any reasonable ethical position, Sidgwick embodied the general temper and manners of thinking characteristics of his nation, and takes his place in the long line of British moral philosophers in whose doctrines that way of thinking has again and again been crystallized."[31]

In accepting much of the liberal revolution, however, Sidgwick rejected many of the premises that had previously gone with it. The nature of his liberalism demonstrated his elevation of empiricism over rationalism, of man over institutions, and of the utilitarian end over its supposedly scientific means. Largely because of this, Sidgwick's conservatism was without the rigidity characterizing so much of technical political conservatism and frequently leading to reactionism. With Burke, Sidgwick would have said that "a state without the means of some change is without the means of its conservation."[32] But he made this dictum on change mean much more in his practical politics than it apparently meant to Burke.

CHAPTER SEVEN

Institutional Politics

I N COMPARISON with the work of his contemporaries, such as Green, Bradley, Bosanquet, Dicey, or Bryce, Sidgwick's work has been neglected by twentieth-century scholars. Those who have taken the trouble to read him carefully, however, are prone to use superlatives in describing certain of his writings. In addition to the high rank awarded *Methods of Ethics* by Professor Broad, Max Lerner maintains that "on Greek political institutions Henry Sidgwick's *Development of European Polity* (1903), Chapters V-IX, has not to my mind been supplanted by later books."[1]* The *Elements of Politics* deserves, but has not to my knowledge received, praise equal to that bestowed by Broad and Lerner on the other books. If not the first, it was among the earliest works on the "principles of modern politics," and therefore may be listed among the innovations leading to the current division of political science into several specialized branches. But its claim to recognition does not rest entirely on its originality of approach, for even today it is a valuable index to the institutional problems of the modern state.

In formal method *Elements of Politics* is completely abstract in the best Benthamic tradition. It is divided into two parts, the first dealing with the functions of government and the second with the institutions by which the functions are to be carried out. Sidgwick's

*Notes to this chapter are on page 180.

148

functional theory of government was described in the chapter on liberalism, therefore most of the attention here may be concentrated on the last half of the work. It should be noted, however, that the book is uniform in its treatment of the two main problems, and the interrelation between function and instrument is made quite clear by Sidgwick.

The greatest fault of the study in one way, and its greatest virtue in another, is the method used by Sidgwick. It has been noted that this method is similar to Bentham's; that is, it is deductive and characterized by the thoroughness with which each problem is pursued through every possible ramification. It is a "pure" book inasmuch as the commentary is confined strictly to those problems that the author has intended to deal with from the beginning. There is no extensive discussion of philosophical questions such as the nature of the individual, the state, or of individual or social ends and their relations. The answers to these basic questions are either assumed or are mentioned only where they are necessary to delimit the area of discussion. Nevertheless, the greatest-happiness principle, the dualism of ethical ends, and the primacy of empirical methodology are omnipresent, shading every opinion on a hypothetical case.

The main faults of *Elements of Politics* are its aridity and uniformity. Both of these qualities make for difficulty in reading; and since the same criticisms are true of most of Sidgwick's writing, they help explain the lack of interest in his works, even where his intrinsic worth is greater than many authors who are more widely read. D. G. Ritchie appraises this aspect of the book very well when he says, "Some effort, it must be confessed, is requisite; not that anything is obscure, but that everything is smooth and uniform. And the difficulty of keeping the attention fixed is due, in great measure, to the abstract and general form in which the discussion is carried on, the conspicuous scarcity of proper names, the deliberate refusal to adopt the historical and inductive method."[2]

One apparent reason for Sidgwick's use of suppositional rather than actual institutions was his intention to write a separate treatise on comparative government.[3] Had his death not prevented this projected study, Sidgwick would have completed a tripartite treatment of politics with each part standing alone, yet relying for completeness on the other two. Thus the analytically comparative work would have complemented both the historically empirical

Development of European Polity and the more deductive *Elements of Politics*.

In spite of the noticeable similarity to Bentham's method, the very real differences between Sidgwick and Bentham are equally clear to the careful reader. In the first place, many of the ostensibly hypothetical institutions set up by Sidgwick are clearly drawn from existing arrangements and are, therefore, experiential and empirical. Ritchie seems to recognize this underlying empiricism, even when he criticizes Sidgwick for excessive abstraction.[4] Secondly, Sidgwick's dialectical method is much more balanced than Bentham's. Bentham never appears to be arguing with himself on equal terms. The reader knows from the beginning that no matter how many alternatives are set up by Bentham, only one really amounts to much. For Bentham the true deduction is always clear and manifestly superior to any other possibility. With Sidgwick one is on a different level of abstraction. He may prefer one arrangement to another, but that preference only makes him more diligent in presenting a complete case for the other side. Sidgwick had true respect for, and insight into, opposing views; Bentham had a self-confident scorn for ideas which competed with his. As a result, Sidgwick's preference for one idea or institution over others is never more than tentative; Bentham's conclusion, on the other hand, is always clear and undoubted in the best Cartesian tradition. Finally, Sidgwick's latent conservatism contrasts strongly with Bentham's pronounced radicalism. Not only does Sidgwick frequently point out specifically that a state's historical development will have a pronounced effect on its existing institutions, but his abstract conclusions about the best devices of government rest on a broad experiential basis. Even though the method is purportedly Bentham's, "there is none of Bentham's strong critical antagonism to the institutions of his time, and the mode of thought is much more what we might expect from an end of the nineteenth-century Blackstone, or from an English Hegel, showing the rationality of the existing order of things, with only a few modest proposals of reform. If this is Benthamism, it is Benthamism grown tame and sleek."[5]

It is doubtful whether a work like *Elements of Politics* could have been written before the end of the nineteenth century. The nineteenth century was what Sidgwick has identified as the "constitution-making century." In other words, that era was the time in which the modern liberal state was completely rationalized. And it was only at the close of the nineteenth century that this work of rationalization was completed sufficiently to allow an extensive consideration of the complexities of structure of a modern technological state. While it may have been immediately true that the discussion in the *Elements* was "distinctly of today, not of yesterday, and with just a slight regard for tomorrow morning early,"[6] in perspective this statement is not correct at all. For the institutional problems of the present rational liberal state are virtually the same as those with which Sidgwick dealt in 1891. The limitation of government, the relation of the governed to government, bureaucracy, the constitutional position of the branches of government, and the problem of corporative private organizations in the state were the late nineteenth century's problems in much the same manner as they are ours. If they are more complex today, and if we have added to them the serious consideration of the defense against totalitarianism, the shadow of complexity and even the shadow of totalitarianism are dimly discernible in Victorian times. Of course, many of the questions with which Sidgwick was concerned are treated less extensively than they would be now, largely because they were just beginning to be recognized as problems. On the other hand, time has settled irrevocably several of the most pressing issues of late Victorianism. Few would dispute today at any length over the Australian versus the open ballot, but much more space would be given to political parties than Sidgwick devotes to them. On the whole, though, the reader is struck by the number of institutional developments revealed as probabilities in Sidgwick's searching analysis long before they came into practice.

In stating that this work could hardly have been produced before the end of the nineteenth century, we must take cognizance of the sources from which Sidgwick drew much of his material. He had access to unsurpassed empirical studies of the state of constitutional development in England and the United States, the two diverse examples on which he relies most heavily for his generalizations. He had read Bryce's *American Commonwealth* in manuscript[7] and had had the benefit of long acquaintance with Bagehot's *English Constitution*. In addition, he draws to some extent on Dicey's *Law of the Constitution* and Story's *Commentaries on the Constitution of the United States*.

Sidgwick owes his greatest debt, however, to John Stuart Mill's *Representative Government*. Many of the conclusions reached on details are those of Mill. But in spite of this apparent proximity, Mill and Sidgwick are not handling quite the same set of problems. Mill is still involved primarily with arguing the case in favor of representative government, and only secondarily with the structure of the representative institutions. In addition, Mill is concerned with the conditions (in particular the stage of historical development) under which a society can operate a representative system effectively. Sidgwick assumes the representative form all the way through; for him the liberal state can be taken for granted as the basic type of modern political organization, at least in Western Europe and the United States, with which he is most concerned. Mill's institutionalism, too, rests mainly on the English pattern and is less broadly comparative than Sidgwick's. The great similarity, however, and one which shows how far utilitarianism had moved from its early doctrinaire form, is the extent to which both men make explicit the fact that the behavior of man has more effect than institutions in producing a good society. If anything, Mill goes out of his way to assert this point as a basic premise. He says that the one cause of good government, transcending all others, "is the qualities of the human beings composing the society over which government is exercised";[8] and an examination of the framework of individual ethics in which Sidgwick's discussion is set leaves little doubt as to his wholehearted concurrence in this view.

It seems desirable, in discussing Sidgwick's main institutional theories, to invert the order in which he deals with the various problems. Instead of analyzing the branches of the government first, as he has done, it is feasible to discuss first the relation of governed to government in modern society.

Sidgwick recognized in the nineteenth century what has too often been forgotten today—the fact that even where representative government exists, people are still governed. He learned early from his foremost instructor in politics, John Stuart Mill, that the cure for the ills of democracy is not necessarily more democracy. His fundamental concern, therefore, is the avoidance of either mass or minority tyranny. And since the tendency of representative government is toward absolute majority rule, the main checks must be against this danger.

Politics, especially at the highest level, requires wisdom and experience. Although the specialized technician has his place in administration, the knowledge of the representative should be more widely based; his concern must be with broad principles of the national interest. The role that can be recommended for the enfranchised populace of the political society, then, is that of carefully choosing those persons of superior quality who can be entrusted with the governing authority. When that choice has been made (with certain exceptions to be noted later), the majority "will" should thenceforth be dependent on the counsel of these qualified persons, at least until the legal arrangements call for another expression from the citizenship. Sidgwick is staunchly opposed to most devices for direct popular interference in the legislative process. He thinks that the historical development of European government precludes the extensive use of the referendum there, and he regards the instructed mandate as a perversion of the representative idea. He favors long parliaments in order that the electorate may have ample opportunity to judge the merits of the representative; however, they should not be so long that the sense of responsibility to the constituents is lost. His attitude on these questions is summed up in the remark that "the periodical election of legislators should aim at being as far as possible a selection of persons believed to possess superior political capacity; and it seems reasonable to assume that the responsibilities and experience of such persons must tend materially to increase their original advantage in political insight."[9]

This theory of the necessity for a political elite is further borne out in Sidgwick's chapter on the classification of governments. He disagrees with the classical division of government according to the number participating. It is not true to say that democratic government is the only form which governs on behalf of the people or that where democratic government exists there can be no interest opposed to the general interest.[10]

The realization of the end of government, which is the general happiness of the whole society, can be promoted by the one, the few, or the many. Government resting on consent is generally preferable to other forms not because it is sure to be better conducted, but because it is more likely to be obeyed and consequently better avoids the danger of revolution.[11]

Limited government, however, cannot take the form of pure democracy, since in pure democracy the absolute rule of majority will is implied, and absolute rule of any sort entails instability.[12] It is only when there is a constitutionally limited government with the major functions confided to those best equipped to carry them out that representative government achieves a true order. Therefore, "the representative system in its best form will realize to a substantial extent the principle of aristocracy in combination with the principle of democracy."[13]

Although he clearly recognizes the importance of a natural aristocracy for evading the danger of the purely political type, Sidgwick gives no indication of the source from which this aristocracy is to be drawn in the liberal state. He apparently does not have the unlimited confidence of James Mill in the acquisitive middle class, even when he rejects the Jacksonian democratic idea that any man is fit to rule. He is forced to rely, therefore, on what he admits is a "vaguely understood" conception of the aristocratic element in modern society. This indefinite theory of aristocracy envisages a combination of wealth—presumably for leisure and not for its own sake—and "a cultivation of mind above that of the 'masses' and also certain valuable traditions of political experience: so that its claim to a share in government disproportionate to its members is based on a belief in its superior intellectual qualifications."[14]

Trends in institutions indicate shifts away from the mixture of aristocracy and democracy toward unlimited democracy. Included among these tendencies are an increase in the use of initiative and referendum, a shortening of the time for which the assembly is elected, the demand for election pledges, popular mandates, and appointment of officials for reasons other than qualification. To offset these developments the nonpayment of legislators is recommended in order to afford protection to the minority and give independence to the members of the deliberative body.[15]

Sidgwick does indicate two important occasions on which the "direct intervention of the people in legislation appears ... on the whole advantageous." In both instances there is a recognition of the latent political supremacy of the electorate in what (since Woodrow Wilson made the term acceptable) we would now call a constitutional democracy. In the first place, if the two houses of a bicameral legislature deadlock on badly needed legislation, the decision might be made by referendum. By this means neither house would lose dignity; at the same time an expression of popular will on a single definite issue is preferable to a general election in which pledges are likely to be demanded of candidates. The second case is one in which the society uses a written constitution. A single documentary fundamental law must be legally alterable in some way, yet changes in it should be beyond the scope of the ordinary legislative process. As a result of this combination of circumstances, it seems reasonable to amend the constitution by reference to the electorate, but the requirement of an extraordinary popular majority of some sort is probably in order.[16]

It may readily be seen from the above that the location of effective political power in a modern liberal state is a complex matter. Sidgwick contests Austin's theory of sovereignty at some length. The sovereign, in Austin's view, is a determinate, common superior who is habitually obeyed by the bulk of a given independent society. It is impossible legally to limit the sovereign's power or to divide sovereignty.[17] John Stuart Mill acquiesces in Austin's theory when he says that "the power of final control is as essentially single, in a mixed and balanced government, as in a pure monarchy or democracy."[18]

Sidgwick feels that this view is an oversimplification of the problem in the modern constitutional state. The balance of political forces in a complex liberal state is likely to shift in actual practice at almost any time. Any number of factors might enter into the determination of existing sovereignty. A body of the electorate may, for example, have the right to dismiss the legal governing body of the society at any time, yet through fear or for other reasons be unable to do so. Or again, the corporate body politic may have the force necessary to withdraw its obedience from governing authority, but an absence of consciousness of that power may prevent such action.[19] The question of order also enters into the problem. Order includes not only obedience of the bulk of the citizens, "but observance of assigned limits on the part of the organs" of government.[20] This consideration means that there is a tacit limitation of any legally "unlimited sovereign" in the interest of order, thereby running afoul of another of Austin's basic conceptions. All the complexities of constitutional usages, therefore, prevent an exact location of the indivisible sovereign. And when we add to these matters the complications of a federal system with its calculated division of powers, or a written constitution under which it is necessary to accept some agency as the interpreter of the basic law, the idea of a single, easily located sovereign is even more questionable.

Ritchie holds that Sidgwick's failure to distinguish between *Staatsrecht* and *Politik* in his discussion of sovereignty prevents his complete escape from Austin's confusion.[21] In the second edition of the *Elements*, however, Sidgwick adds an appendix on Austin's theory. In the closing paragraph of that discussion he approves Dicey's conception[22] of dualistic sovereignty, which apparently overcomes Ritchie's objection. He feels that Dicey's separation of the "legal sovereignty" of parliament from the "political sovereignty" of the electorate is as satisfactory as any devisable means for making it possible to retain the conception of sovereignty. "But it must be observed that this new view of a double sovereign differs essentially from the traditional doctrine, handed down to Austin from Bodin and Hobbes—since it was a cardinal point in that doctrine that there could be only one sovereign in a State."[23]

If under constitutional government actual political power is distributed in some complex manner among the branches of government and the public, and if in one sense ordered society always requires some element of consent on the part of the governed, it is especially important to know the manner in which the public exercises its power in a representative system. The treatment of political parties is basic to this knowledge. It is unfortunate that the study of political parties as institutions of popular government was developed after Sidgwick's time.[24] On the whole, the handling of parties is the weakest part of *Elements of Politics*. There is little of a positive nature in the entire chapter, even though the usual attempt at objectivity and thoroughness is made.

Sidgwick feels that in the modern state the tendency is toward a multiple rather than what he calls a "dual" system.[25] About the only factors contributing to the two-party form are the value of combination for election purposes and the ability to gain undivided organizational control over spoils. As far as advantages are concerned, a dual organization is perhaps more stable than a multiple arrangement, and there is some merit in the opposition idea.[26] The disadvantages, on the other hand, are grave. Party spirit in a dual system may be less narrow and fanatical, but is nonetheless "more comprehensive and absorbing."[27] Other faults result from this comprehension and absorption: the selection of unqualified executives is promoted, the desire to retain a majority leads to the elevation of minority interests over national welfare, and party discipline produces a demoralizing loss of independence on the part of legislators.

It could almost go without saying that Sidgwick has missed the main contributions of the two-party system to orderly democratic society. There is no consideration of the value of parties in channeling public opinion into a practicable force for influencing the conduct of government, of their usefulness in compromising narrow interests into broad national ones, or of their educative effect. And only slight recognition is given to the clarification of political questions produced by the separation of government and opposition, and of the ordering element of party discipline in reaching decisions in the two-party state. Sidgwick's individualistic idea about the independence both of the voter in his choice of representatives and of the legislator in his governing role account for this omission. In his view it is the duty of those seriously concerned with politics to stand firm in their reasoned convictions. "And probably the country would gain from an increase in the number of persons taking a serious interest in politics who keep out of party ties altogether."[28]

The discussion of the relation of the state to voluntary associations contains many more ideas germane to liberal politics than the section on parties. In fact, Sidgwick's handling of political parties places them mainly in the class of private associations rather than public representative institutions. The basic difference between the state and voluntary associations lies in the possession by the state of legitimate coercive authority and the force necessary to carry it out. Sidgwick is naturally opposed, however, to the idea that there is a necessary conjunction between this force of the state and the moral absolutism of nationalism. Great care should be exercised, therefore, in suppressing voluntary associations even when they conflict ideologically with the state. But there is a point at which action in concert, even where individual action of the same type is legal, becomes a threat to the state and may have to be suppressed.[29]

It is clear that all voluntary associations must accept the minimum basis for agreement generally recognized in the state in order to be tolerated. Combination for applying social, political, and economic pressure was already partially characteristic of England in the late nineteenth century; the transition from individual to corporate interest was a problem which had to be faced. In keeping with his functional theory, Sidgwick wanted the state to act as court of final appeal against indirectly coercive collective action, such as monopolization or boycott, but he preferred moral to political sanctions where they could be applied.[30]

In treating churches as voluntary associations, Sidgwick treads a wary path. The extent of state control will nearly always depend upon the historical background of the society. By and large he approves separation of church and state, in typical liberal fashion, but feels that a quasi-government position would afford a suitable compromise. The church might be allowed to validate some contracts, such as marriage; it might also be permitted special opportunities for religious instruction in public schools; and the clergy could be exempt from such civil functions as jury duty and military service. The state may go so far as to endow the church indirectly through tax exemption or even directly for some purposes, so long as the clergy was not converted into salaried governmental servants. But there is no recognition of the superior moral claim of any church; in case of conflicts, where actual disorder threatens, the church is apparently on the same basis as any other voluntary association.[31]

It was Sidgwick's opinion that a proper understanding of the fundamental governmental arrangements of the modern state is essential to its proper operation. He is obviously in full agreement with Bagehot's statement that the characteristic danger of great nations is that they may fail from not comprehending the institutions they have created. One approach to making the fundamental legal arrangements of society as clear as possible had started, in Sidgwick's view, over a century before with the adoption of the practice of written constitutions. But even when a constitutional structure was "flexible"—that is, created entirely by usage, unwritten, and changeable by the ordinary legislative method—it should still be rationalized into an orderly, understandable process. Although it is true that institutions "hastily introduced without due regard to the special characteristics and previous history of the people for whom they are designed, are apt to have no stability," even the state with an "organic" historical constitution may subject its institutions to the test of certain carefully drawn principles.[32] And since the movement of opinion in representative government is a major factor in organic constitutional change, it is desirable that opinion be educated as to actual governmental arrangements as well as to theoretically ideal ones.

Sidgwick's presentation of the alternative structural arrangements of government and the arguments for and against each type is extensive enough to furnish almost unlimited topics for debate. Each problem is carried to its remotest possible consequences, so that only by reading the whole of *Elements of Politics* can one appreciate the subtlety, the scholarship, and the deductive power of the author.

The scope and intention of the present work preclude anything more than an outline of his major conclusions and their relation to the social philosophy of which they are a part. In order to systematize as much as possible, the first part of the discussion will be confined to the technical organization of the branches of government favored by Sidgwick, followed by a consideration of the functions and power arrangement of the branches.

The legislature, as the agency truly representative of the whole body politic, should be selected by direct vote on the basis of universal suffrage, subject only to such normally recognized restrictions as being of age, sane, and not convicted of crime. Questions may also be raised as to the right of suffrage of paupers supported by public funds, illiterates where state education is available, the military and other coercive administrative agents such as police, and married women. Sidgwick theoretically favors weighted voting in order to implement his idea of governmental elites; but he recognizes the difficulty of establishing satisfactory criteria, and ends by pointing out that wealth and intellect will always exercise political influence even when denied special legal status.[33]

The single-member constituency is the most desirable division of the country for electoral purposes. Sidgwick rejects proportional or any other form of class representation as tending to elevate special interests over national ones.[34] He does note that localism might be fostered by the single-member district, but he feels that so long as there is no residence restriction for candidates, men of national reputation and interests will be successful in their bid for election. Frequent reapportionment is essential to avoid the American practice of gerrymandering.

The legislator himself should be the prototype of the politically educated minority. Although formal qualifications are only briefly discussed, Sidgwick's standards are optimistically high. The ideal legislator should know law as well as the lawyer, but he should also know much more. "He must have an insight... into the actual relation of the laws to the social life of the community regulated; the manner in which they modify the conduct of the individuals whom they affect; the consequences, proximate and remote, that are likely to result from any change in them."[35] These criteria could only be advanced by one who had lived in the shadow of a long aristocratic tradition and who had more than the usual faith in the good common sense of the average voter, especially when reliance for

159

fulfillment of the qualifications is based almost entirely on the principle of noncompensation of the legislature.

The idea of expertness is carried over into the organization of the assembly for deliberation. Sidgwick holds, with John Stuart Mill, that a large representative assembly is not equipped for the technical process of making laws.[36] The representative assembly, instead, acts as a sounding board and furnishes the will for effecting the statutes produced by a small, technically competent body of experts, possibly in the form of a legislative council. However, Sidgwick would not go as far as Mill did in holding that the assembly should never alter proposed legislation, but should adopt or reject it outright.[37] This rationalization of the legislative process through expert clarification and systematization requires, in addition, a house large enough to be truly representative, yet small enough to be workable, a division of labor through the use of the committee system, and a comparatively small quorum so that the representative may properly allocate his time.[38]

Sidgwick devotes a separate chapter to the discussion of bicameralism versus unicameralism.[39] In the parliamentary form of government a second chamber seems superfluous when it loses its co-ordinate powers through the extension of the power of the lower house. Additionally there is the disadvantage of conflict between the two houses, which may only be settled by the reduction of power of the one or the other. But a second chamber might still be a means of securing the advice of that intellectually superior group favored by Sidgwick if the requirements for membership and method of selection are put on a sound basis. In a federal government the necessity for a second chamber is manifest—some form of separate representation should be given the member states even where it is not feasible to make the representation equal.

The systematic problems of executive organization receive similar treatment.[40] The functions of the executive branch, however, necessitate a unity of control in order that harmonious relations may exist among the various line departments and responsibility, particularly fiscal responsibility, may be clearly vested. There are really two classes of administrators, the decision-making or directing group and the routinized technician. The latter class, because of the limited and measurable scope of its competence, should be selected and promoted by a merit system and ruled out of any extensive political activity.

Insofar as the chief executive is concerned, Sidgwick favors as a general type what seems to be a combination of the English and American practices. He prefers unification of the hierarchy of administration under one head, but he dislikes the monarchial form which characterizes the American executive, with its exaggerated independence of the legislature. The reasons for this preference and a more detailed outline of its operation will be presented later in the discussion of the relations of the branches.

Although there are drawbacks to legislative selection of the highest executive, it is likely to be better than popular election. The electorate is not especially equipped to judge the qualifications of a chief executive, and direct election makes him too independent for harmonious relations with the assembly. For those immediately subordinate to the chief executive, appointment by the head is probably the most satisfactory means of retaining an integrated, responsible administrative organization. It should be mentioned, however, that Sidgwick recognized the advantages of the use in some cases of plural decision-making boards or councils with a single subordinate administrator to enforce the decisions of the plural executive agency.

Sidgwick's treatment of the judiciary is mainly functional with only an occasional interspersion on organization.[41] Two points are worth stressing in illustration of the utilitarian desire for systematization of political institutions. The first is that a state needs a supreme court, not only as a final seat of adjudication, but also in order to administer the judicial system in a consistent manner. Secondly, a legal revision agency—or Law Council— should be set up to "remove inconsistencies and ambiguities in the recognized authoritative statement of the law . . ." and to serve as a "channel for bringing judicial experience to bear on legislation whenever this experience clearly pointed to the expediency of material changes in civil and criminal law."[42]

The selection of judges may be made by the executive, but the independence of the judiciary in its review of administrative acts should be protected by appointment during good behavior. Right of dismissal of judges from the higher courts could be placed in the hands of a high judicial tribunal for further protection.

In his exposition of the relations of the branches of government, Sidgwick develops a limited separation of powers theory. The motivation for this stand is not so much the fear of concentration of power as the idea that there are three distinct functions of government, calling for three entirely different attitudes on the part of the officials who comprise them and for entirely different types of organization. Thus the rational allocation of function in modern government demands a certain measure of independence in the exercise of the particular skills of lawmaking, law enforcement, and adjudication. At the same time, the separation can never be complete because each branch will occasionally perform functions related to those of the other branches; and, since the legislature is the representative agency vested with the power of making law, it always exercises an implicit supremacy.

The legislature is vested with the primary duty of modifying the law. It is also charged with the responsibility for controlling the purse and for the critical supervision of the executive in carrying out the law, especially those branches of the administration vested with the rights to coerce private citizens. A separate legislature, therefore, "is continually needed, in a modern State, to secure the best possible definition even of the individualistic minimum of legal duty."[43] The conception of rational lawmaking instead of law declaration which exists in the modern state calls for the elimination of judge-made law except where ambiguities in statutes require clarification for decisions on individual cases or where the facts of a case are not covered by legislation. In a rationalized state an exact knowledge of the existing law should be apprehensible, and this is possible only when the law is laid down by a competent governmental agency. Even when the judiciary does exercise a narrow function of legislation, the use of precedent is preferable to an a priori ruling for cognitive puposes.[44] Where a written constitution exists, the question of judicial review will arise relative to the legislative process. Sidgwick dislikes this usage in spite of the fact that interpretation of the law is a judicial function. There is always the danger of thrusting the judiciary too much into the political arena, thereby threatening its impartiality. He would prefer, therefore, some limitation of absolute judicial review, possibly by general constitutional definition of the matters subject to interpretation.

The executive as well as the judiciary exercises functions which take it to the fringe of the legislative process. The delegation of legislative power to the administration is expediential "on matters requiring regulations that vary from time to time according to circumstances"; but for the protection of the citizens at large "such powers should be ordinarily exercised for certain strictly defined ends, within limits fixed by the legislature."[45] In rare emergency cases, where executive orders are issued on matters for which there is no statutory delegation, "such ordinances are to be communicated as soon as possible to the legislature, and ... cease to be valid if disapproved by that body."[46]

The executive, while in some ways subordinate to the legislature, would have a measure of independence in Sidgwick's conception of a governmental division of labor. While greater harmony is produced by a straightforward parliamentary system, serious drawbacks result from the merger of the executive and legislature. A merger of functions is likely to follow the union of offices, since ministers will be distracted from administrative functions by the duty of preparing bills and superintending their passage. Contrariwise, the assembly will be tempted to interfere excessively in current administrative problems and especially in foreign affairs, a field in which executive prerogative should be paramount. In a combined form, too, the executive is likely to steer the easiest course in the house rather than risk an overthrow in defending a better, but more provocative, policy. A parliamentary executive form is more unstable owing to the power of dismissal; consequently, it is less likely than an independent executive to follow a consistent and far-sighted policy. Finally, the limitation of personnel from which executives may be selected, combined with the strict party usage in this respect, makes it likely that men will be selected as ministers for reasons other than administrative experience.[47] Sidgwick apparently favors something resembling a combination of the executive independence of the American Presidency and the harmonious relationship of the English cabinet system. In order to realize this, a fixed tenure with a permanent budget could be set up for the executive and the right to appear in the house and recommend legislation retained.

The judiciary, likewise, should exercise its functions independently of the other two branches. The necessity for immediate judicial remedy of arbitrary administrative actions makes its protection against executive influence mandatory. As we have seen, this separation may be partially achieved by long tenure and careful selection of judges on the basis of qualification.

Sidgwick's conclusions on the institutional structure of the modern state seem, in retrospect, prosaically orthodox. The unique quality of *Elements of Politics* lies in the originality of its approach to the study of institutions and in the thoroughness with which each problem is treated. Beneath the surface of this work, however, the disturbing problems of the liberal state are always present.

The constant theme of the treatise is the demand for quality in governmental personnel and the consequent fear of the deterioration of politics into a mass of corporate interests, controlled by self-seekers. This characteristic is evidenced in the theory of the political elite, in the fear of parties, and in the separation of governmental functions. The exponent of the liberal state always appears to be waging a losing battle, his forces seem too weak and too visionary to halt the hordes of problems that he faces. How, when the values of the liberal state are grounded in self-interest, does one secure sanctions for the ethics of universal welfare? Or again, how is fitness to rule passed to the mass along with the legal right to rule, when their only example of a "natural aristocracy" is the middle class whose blind materialism led to the lower-class demands for political activism in the first place? Where does one secure the political aristocrat for whom rulership is an onerous responsibility, under taken as a traditional duty only to protect himself and society against the power politician?

Sidgwick's solutions to institutional problems are defensible as forms; it is the human substance which is necessary to support them that is weak. The dilemma of the liberal state is that no artificial separation of the governed from the government or of the branches of the government from one another can keep the grubby fingers of the electorate out of the governmental pie, and there seems to be no hope of educating our masters to better political manners. And this indictment was as true of the negativistic liberal state as it is of the existing positive one.

Sidgwick's case for the liberal state is ideally suited to the political aristocrat. A source of values rooted in a humanistic ethical dualism, a functional theory which started from the premise of the individualistic minimum, yet justified extensive collectivist change, and an institutional arrangement combining checks against abuses of individual liberty and efficiency in carrying out the functions of the state are the best materials that liberalism can offer. Unfortunately it would take a nation of political aristocrats to make these things work. And equally unfortunately for the modern problem of the tension between freedom and authority, there is a dearth of political aristocrats.

CHAPTER EIGHT

Utilitarianism Transformed & Absorbed

IN HIS STUDY of *The Metaphysical Society* Alan Willard
Brown has identified Henry Martin, the fictionalized professor
in G. Lowes Dickinson's *Modern Symposium,* as Henry Sidgwick.[1]* Although he devoted only a few pages to each speaker
in the symposium, Dickinson demonstrated his artistry as a dialogist
almost to perfection in that little book. In it he dealt with the complex of political ideas which dominated the Victorian scene, and he
used for this purpose a succession of speakers who are thinly dis-
guised, prominent representatives of the various ideas in vogue
during the period. In the case of Sidgwick, as is apparently true
also of the other speakers, Dickinson not only conveyed in a brief
sketch the striking attributes of the man's personality and the
essence of his manner of thinking about politics, but he also managed
to place him remarkably well in terms of the overall structure of
the complicated picture being painted.[2]

With characteristic care Dickinson made the order in which his
participants speak reflect both the chronological development of
political ideas in nineteenth-century England and the logical relations in which these ideas stood to one another. In this respect it
is altogether appropriate that Sidgwick should have been the last
speaker among those "who were primarily interested in politics."

*Notes to this chapter are on page 180.

This structural position afforded Dickinson the artistic opportunity to set Sidgwick's specific remarks in the context of his fundamental function as critic and eclectic, and to insert the detached academic between the preceding speakers, who were more actively engaged in politics, and the succeeding ones, including a biologist, whose dominating ideas, while not political, impinged so heavily on the political ideas of the period.

Sidgwick, in the fictional character of Martin, explains at the outset of his remarks that his role is that of the critic, but holds that his aim is to be fruitful through criticism rather than barren. He then proceeds to apply his criticism and to demonstrate through it that unphilosophical political convictions, which vary in a number of degrees between the extremes of collectivism and anarchy (pursuing as ends order and liberty respectively), all contain useful truths, but that they require correction by the critical faculties. When criticism is applied it becomes apparent that a wide measure of agreement on fundamentals exists even between the two extreme convictions, and neither of them is totally satisfactory unless it partakes in some measure of the truths contained in the other.

Dickinson, of course, allowed Sidgwick to say much more than this and to say it in a manner which is so subtly contrived that it defies successful quotation of excerpts. The main point is that Sidgwick's characteristic tendency as a philosopher—that of beginning as a critic and allowing criticism to lead him gradually into eclecticism—stands fully revealed. Further, Sidgwick's method of examining critically the views held by ordinary men about politics for the purpose of abstracting relevant factors from them clearly emerges.

As a critic Sidgwick was in no instance more effective than when he reviewed the theories which had been developed by the utilitarians, whose fundamental principle, the greatest happiness of the greatest number, he adopted as the central doctrine of his own moral and political theories. He found, as did so many others in the nineteenth century, that the doctrine was very plausible indeed.[3] More than this, it had proved itself capable of providing a practically satisfactory manner of looking at morals and politics and a standard of judgment by which institutions could be examined and, where found to be wanting, reformed. Tested pragmatically, utilitarianism worked. Whether it worked, as some might argue, because the clumsier attempts to justify the system philosophically were almost completely overshadowed by the concentration on specific reform projects, the fact is nonetheless striking that at few periods in English history is it possible to trace, over such a long period of time and on so many political issues, the direct influence of a moral doctrine upon practical politics as it is in the case of utilitarianism. It would have been strange if a man whose interest in the ordinary ideas of mankind and in practical problems of morals and politics was so overriding as Sidgwick's had not found much to commend itself to him in this system. It would have been equally strange, however, had a mind of such subtlety and such acute philosophical penetration not felt it necessary to examine, clarify, and restate the philosophical doctrines which sustained the utilitarian reform movement.

Sidgwick's criticisms of the philosophical methods and doctrines of earlier utilitarianism are, despite his adherence to the school, as thorough as any examination made by philosophical opponents of the system. In contrast to the gifted polemics of a Macaulay, Sidgwick's criticism is painstakingly detached and thorough. Consequently he exposed with unrivaled clarity and precision the logical inconsistencies and the methodological difficulties of Benthamic utilitarianism, and the practical problems which result from them.

The main philosophical problems of early utilitarianism—the analytic-synthetic method and the conflict between its psychological and ethical doctrines—were thoroughly examined by Sidgwick. In both instances he found the position of the early utilitarians untenable. He was in agreement with John Stuart Mill's judgment that the Benthamic method was effective only to the extent that its original analysis took account of all the relevant facts, but he went beyond Mill, or at least beyond Mill's essay on utilitarianism, in bringing into question the larger problem of the coherence of empiricism itself. Not only were many of the relevant facts missing from Bentham's and James Mill's analyses of experience into its component parts; but some matters of concern to the moral philosopher, and among these the most important, could neither be directly apprehended by the empirical method nor deduced from the psychological hedonism which their method yielded for the Benthamites. Thus the cornerstone of utilitarian reform—the greatest happiness of the greatest number, which was the criterion of right action both in individual conduct and in the organization and activities of government—could not be sustained on the philosophical basis provided for it by the early utilitarians.

Sidgwick did not content himself, however, merely with criticizing the doctrines of his predecessors in preparation for a restatement of the utilitarian position. What gives greater range to his work is the fact that his formulation of a later utilitarian theory owes about as much to a critical review of the schools of thought other than utilitarianism as it does to utilitarianism itself. There are few representatives of nineteenth-century political ideas whose works demonstrate so sure a knowledge of the diverse strains of thought of that period as Sidgwick's. Fewer still are as dispassionate as he in their treatment of opposing ideas, especially in conceding the validity of arguments directed against his own position and in assimilating ideas from so many different sources. It was no easy task to resolve many of the contradictions of early utilitarianism, to purge it of its naturalistic implications, and to provide a satisfactory philosophical basis for its main doctrine; it was harder still, perhaps, to preserve this doctrine against absorption by the positivists and the evolutionists, who in many respects can claim descent from early utilitarianism, and against annihilation at the hands of others.

It is his ability to criticize without destroying that equips Sidgwick so well for the role of an eclectic. But if he may be termed an eclectic, it is only in the best sense that the designation is applicable, for the extractions that he made from various schools of thought were so refined by criticism and so carefully merged into his own thinking that the final product displays the unique qualities of creative thought. "He was the very last man to select principles indiscriminately from here and there in order somehow to build up a system which would please all parties. If, so far as he was a constructive philosopher, he was an eclectic, he was certainly not a shallow one."[4]

It was Sidgwick's task to demonstrate again the debt which nearly all contemporary systems of thought implicitly owed to utilitarianism, and how pliable, yet how durable, were its fundamental tenets. It would appear in retrospect that this could only be done after the utilitarian reform movement had run its practical course and the tendency to dogmatism which characterizes reformist zeal could be dispensed with. Bentham's belief that all philosophies were reducible to utilitarianism when stripped of their paraphernalia was inverted by Sidgwick. Nobody could make his actions conform invariably to the demands of the felicific calculus. In Sidgwick's view it was only when the "paraphernalia" of other systems of thought were added that man could be observed in the fullness of his being; and it was only in this state that it could be seen that many of the trappings of ordinary behavior either owed their origin to utility or were latently utilitarian in their effect. Furthermore, it could only then be fully seen that despite the fact that traditionalistic modes of behavior guided the actions of men in most circumstances, it was necessary at times to judge an act and its consequences in the light of a rational moral principle and that utilitarianism provided on the whole the most suitable standard for this purpose. In this respect Sidgwick merged the disparate utilitarian teachings of Hume and Bentham. He revived the traditionalism of Hume without the naturalistic limitations which prevented the judgment of morals and politics by the standard supplied by the utilitarian doctrine of the greatest happiness.

Sidgwick's contribution to the development of utilitarian thought was twofold. In the first place he took the diverse and often directly conflicting doctrines which had developed out of Benthamic reform (and had been dealt a near-fatal blow by John Stuart Mill's defense of them) and remolded them into a consistent body of thought. This required the pruning of much that was characteristic of earlier utilitarianism, especially its mechanistic theory of knowledge, its affinity for psychological hedonism, its extreme individualism, and some of the more sweeping deductions concerning morals and politics which had been made from extremely narrow premises about human nature. If much was cut out of earlier utilitarianism in the course of Sidgwick's restatement, however, much that was new to utilitarianism was brought in, including a tentative dualistic metaphysics which derived from common-sense philosophy, the acceptance of the independent nature of moral experience by the recognition that ethical ends are apprehended intuitively, the expanded use of the historical method and an explanation of morals and politics that incorporated far more of the complexities of actual human experience in both its rational and nonrational forms than had earlier utilitarianism. In many respects Sidgwick accomplished, without the emotional appeal or the unfortunate logical consequences, what John Stuart Mill attempted when he tried to supplement Bentham with Coleridge and to adjust his utilitarian heritage to the Comtian system.

Sidgwick's second contribution to utilitarian thought follows directly from this reformulation of utilitarian theory. By his criticism and corrections he demonstrated that the system was still viable and that it was not sufficient simply to attack the glaring weaknesses in the logical structure of Benthamic utilitarianism in order to destroy the entire theory. The careful way in which Sidgwick extracted the essence of the system from its oversimplified and often carelessly expressed philosophical context and gave it logical coherence within a framework that did not overlook the extreme difficulties of reducing the complexities of man and society to any simple set of generalities forced the opponents of utilitarianism to attack the substance of its doctrines rather than the form. After Sidgwick it is hedonism itself, as a satisfactory end by which to order behavior, which must be attacked if utilitarianism is to be rendered untenable, rather than a logical confusion between certain forms of hedonism. And it is humanistic individualism in a moral and social setting that takes account of the vast "unanalyzed experience" of mankind and not an uncompromising egoism based on a mechanistic psychology which has to be criticized and accounted for in some other way if utilitarianism is to be rejected.

Even if the opponents of hedonism are correct in their most telling criticism—that hedonism abstracts one quality, pleasure, from the complex content of actual experience and erects it into an explanation of the whole—the amount of practical moral and political experience which is explained by Sidgwick's exposition of the utilitarian position remains striking. As Sidgwick himself was among the first to admit, men actually make use of widely varying and often inconsistent methods of ethics in ordering their moral and political actions. It still seems plausible, however, to suggest that there are many instances in which moral decisions are made which appear to require the use of a rational standard of conduct, and very often that standard seems to be hedonic. And if this is true of moral judgments, it is much more true in the case of political action in the modern liberal state. The calculations on which a government sustains itself in office must nearly always be primarily directed toward the effect that an action is likely to have on the voting public's views of its own welfare, largely measured by a vague hedonistic standard. Conversely, the public makes its periodic decision about the government on the basis of this hedonistic end, the realization of which is sought by the method of rough empirical calculation reflected in the counting of heads. If these practical applications of utilitarianism are dependent on the prior existence of the state as a going concern whose origin and development cannot be explained on utilitarian grounds, that does not destroy utilitarianism as a practical, if philosophically limited, way of looking at many aspects of morals and politics.

If a fair estimate of utilitarianism as a system of political thought is to be made, it needs to be done on two levels. In the practical sense it should take into account the great influence of the Benthamites on the development of liberalism in the nineteenth century. But for a complete appraisal of the content of utilitarianism as a tenable theory of politics, it is not sufficient to stop with Bentham and his associates in the utilitarian reform movement, or even with John Stuart Mill's later writings. For a full appreciation of its theoretical possibilities one needs to turn to the infinitely more subtle form which Sidgwick gave to utilitarian doctrines in their final expression.

Notes

CHAPTER ONE

1. Arthur Sidgwick and Eleanor Mildred Sidgwick, *Henry Sidgwick, a Memoir*, pp. 1-5.

2. Asa Briggs, *Victorian People*, p. 167.   3. *Henry Sidgwick*, p. 8

4. *Ibid.*, p. 10.   5. *Ibid.*, p. 11.   6. *Ibid.*, p. 366.

7. *Ibid.*, p. 32.

8. See, for example, the two poems published in *Macmillan's Magazine* in 1860 and 1861 and reprinted in *Henry Sidgwick*, pp. 51, 64. Also two lectures on Shakespeare are reprinted in Henry Sidgwick, *Miscellaneous Essays and Addresses*, pp. 91, 120. Lord Bryce emphasizes this aspect of Sidgwick's scholarship in the chapter on Sidgwick in *Studies in Contemporary Biography*, p. 338.

9. *Henry Sidgwick*, p. 28.

10. D. A. Winstanley, *Early Victorian Cambridge*, p. 175.

11. *Ibid.*, p. 404.   12. *Ibid.*, pp. 397 ff.

13. G. M. Young (ed.), *Early Victorian England*, II, 495-496.

14. *Henry Sidgwick*, p. 28.

15. Ethel Sidgwick, *Mrs. Henry Sidgwick, a Memoir by her Niece*, p. 198.

16. Quoted in *Henry Sidgwick*, p. 136.

17. *Ibid.* The statement is Dr. Venn's.

18. *Ibid.*, p. 36. The quotation is from a biographical fragment dictated by Sidgwick shortly before his death.

19. *Ibid.*, pp. 39-40. This quotation is also from Sidgwick's autobiographical fragment.

20. *Ibid.*, p. 90.   21. *Ibid.*, p. 151.

22. Bryce, *Studies*, p. 335.

23. D. A. Winstanley, *Later Victorian Cambridge*, p. 237.

24. *Ibid.*, Chapter 5.   25. *Henry Sidgwick*, p. 159.

26. Winstanley, *Later Victorian Cambridge*, pp. 242-243.

27. *Henry Sidgwick,* p. 198.
28. Winstanley, *Later Victorian Cambridge,* pp. 67 ff.
29. Bryce, *Studies,* p. 329.
30. Alan Willard Brown, *The Metaphysical Society,* p. 32.
31. C. D. Broad, *Religion, Philosophy and Psychical Research,* p. 108.
32. *Henry Sidgwick,* p. 347.   33. Broad, *Religion,* pp. 109-110.
34. Brown, p. 196.   35. *Henry Sidgwick,* pp. 205-206.
36. Winstanley, *Early Victorian Cambridge,* p. 189; *Henry Sidgwick,* p. 153 ff.
37. *Henry Sidgwick,* pp. 223-224.
38. C. D. Broad, *Five Types of Ethical Theory,* p. 143.
39. Bryce, *Studies,* pp. 332-333.
40. Robert S. Rait (ed.), *Memorials of Albert Venn Dicey,* Letter to Mrs. Dicey, dated 31 August and 1 September, 1900, p. 187.
41. *Henry Sidgwick,* pp. 300 ff.   42. *Ibid.,* pp. 371-373.
43. *Ibid.,* p. 210.   44. *Ibid.,* pp. 349-351.
45. *Mrs. Henry Sidgwick,* p. 94.
46. *Proceedings of the Society for Psychical Research,* I (1882-3), 3-6.
47. *Ibid.,* X (1894), 25-422.   48. See *Mrs. Henry Sidgwick,* p. 106.
49. *Henry Sidgwick,* p. 400.   50. Cited *ibid.,* p. 305.
51. *Ibid.,* p. 311.   52. *Ibid.,* p. 313.
53. *Ibid.,* p. 456. The quotation is from Sidgwick's *Journal,* August 13, 1886.
54. In his inaugural lecture a short while later Alfred Marshall set this change in the manner of looking at economic questions in a very broad philosophical context. Writing in 1885, he pointed out that in large part, "It is due to the discovery that man himself is in a great measure a creature of circumstances and changes with them." In the early nineteenth century, when classical economics was consolidating its position, the "mathematics-physical group of sciences was in the ascendant," with the result that man was viewed as rather a "constant quantity" and Ricardo and his followers neglected a large group of facts and a method of studying them which was later seen to be of primary importance. See A. C. Pigou (ed.), *Memorials of Alfred Marshall,* pp. 153-155.
55. *Henry Sidgwick,* p. 456.   56. *Ibid.,* pp. 497 ff.
57. *Ibid.,* p. 448.   58. *Mrs. Henry Sidgwick,* pp. 127-129, 144.
59. *Society for Psychical Research,* V (1887-8-9), 271-278.
60. *Henry Sidgwick,* p. 458.   61. *Ibid.,* pp. 509-511.
62. *Ibid.,* p. 518.
63. "On the Nature of the Evidence for Theism," February 25, 1898; and "Authority, Scientific and Theological," February 24, 1899. Reprinted in *Henry Sidgwick,* Appendix I.
64. *Henry Sidgwick,* pp. 584 ff.   65. Bryce, *Studies,* p. 337.
66. *Ibid.,* p. 329.   67. Cited in *Mrs. Henry Sidgwick,* p. 58.
68. *Henry Sidgwick,* p. 407.   69. Bryce, *Studies,* p. 334.
70. *Henry Sidgwick,* p. 373; H. A. L. Fisher, *Frederic William Maitland,* pp. 29-30.
71. *Mrs. Henry Sidgwick,* p. 185.
72. Cited in H. A. L. Fisher, *James Bryce,* II, 275.
73. Bryce, *Studies,* p. 328.   74. *Mrs. Henry Sidgwick,* p. 153.

CHAPTER TWO

1. John Plamenatz, *The English Utilitarians*, p. 2.   2. *Ibid.*, p. 22.
3. Leslie Stephen, *The English Utilitarians*, III, 77.   4. *Ibid.*, II, 90.
5. G. M. Trevelyan, *British History in the Nineteenth Century and After*, p. xiii.
6. Albert Venn Dicey, *Law and Opinion in England*, pp. 188-204.
7. *Ibid.*, p. 126.
8. Elie Halévy, *The Growth of Philosophical Radicalism*, p. 514.
9. Guido de Ruggiero, *The History of European Liberalism*, p. 13.
10. Halévy, p. 6.
11. N. Kemp Smith, *The Philosophy of David Hume*, p. 56.
12. *Ibid.*, p. 3.   13. *Ibid.*, p. 197.   14. *Ibid.*, p. 11.
15. *Ibid.*, p. 143.   16. *Ibid.*, pp. 11-12.   17. *Ibid.*, p. 147.
18. *Ibid.*, pp. 539-540.   19. Halévy, p. 11.
20. Wilfred Harrison, Introduction to Jeremy Bentham, *A Fragment of Government and An Introduction to the Principles of Morals and Legislation*, p. xxiv.
21. Smith, p. 201.   22. Halévy, p. 12.   23. Plamenatz, p. 23.
24. Bentham, pp. 125 ff.   25. *Ibid.*, p. 125.
26. *Ibid.* Although the book was first printed in 1780, the footnote was not added until 1822.   27. *Ibid.*, fn. 1.   28. Plamenatz, p. 18.
29. Henry Sidgwick, *The Methods of Ethics*, p. 41.
30. On this point see Halévy, pp. 15 ff.
31. Sidgwick, *Methods of Ethics*, p. 88.   32. Plamenatz, p. 72.
33. J. S. Mill, *Utilitarianism*, reprinted in Plamenatz (pp. 163-228), at p. 198.
34. *Ibid.*, p. 169.   35. *Ibid.*, p. 166. Italics supplied.   36. *Ibid.*
37. *Ibid.*, p. 198.   38. G. E. Moore, *Principia Ethica*, p. 67.
39. Plamenatz, p. 135.
40. Smith, p. 169. For Smith's comments on Hume's nonhedonistic position see pp. 163-69.   41. J. S. Mill, *Utilitarianism*, p. 198.
42. On this point see Moore, pp. 68 ff., for a full discussion of the form in which Mill makes this assumption.   43. *Methods of Ethics*, pp. 387-388.
44. C. D. Broad, pp. 183 ff.   45. J. S. Mill, *Utilitarianism*, p. 170.
46. Moore, p. 78.   47. Moore, p. 78.   48. Moore, pp. 78-79.
49. Plamenatz, p. 134.
50. John Stuart Mill, *Dissertations and Discussions*, I, 359.
51. *Ibid.*, p. 360.   52. Plamenatz, p. 144.
53. James Mill, *An Essay on Government*, p. 2.   54. *Ibid.*, p. 17.
55. *Ibid.*, p. 6.   56. *Ibid.*, p. 34.   57. *Ibid.*, p. 10.
58. *Ibid.*, p. 49.   59. *Ibid.*, p. 50.   60. Stephen, II, 75.
61. James Mill, p. 17.   62. *Ibid.*, p. 65.   63. Cf. Stephen, II, 83.
64. Plamenatz, p. 84.
65. Lewis H. Haney, *History of Economic Thought*, p. 218.
66. Eric Roll, *A History of Economic Thought*, p. 173.
67. John Stuart Mill, *Autobiography*, p. 19.   68. Roll, p. 146.
69. *Ibid.*   70. Roll, pp. 146-147.   71. Cf. Haney, pp. 215 ff.
72. Haney, p. 224.   73. Haney, p. 150.   74. Roll, p. 173.
75. Haney, p. 275.   76. Haney, pp. 276 ff.
77. W. Stark, "Liberty and Equality, or: Jeremy Bentham as an Economist," *Economic Journal*, LI (1941), 56-79; and "Bentham as an Economist," *Economic Journal*, LVI (1946), 583-608.

78. Stark, "Liberty and Equality," p. 57. 79. *Ibid.*, p. 58.
80. *Ibid.* 81. Quoted *ibid.*, p. 63.
82. *Ibid.*, p. 72. 83. *Ibid.*, p. 73. 84. Quoted *ibid.*, p. 74.
85. *Ibid.* 86. *Ibid.* 87. Quoted *ibid.*, p. 75.
88. Lionel Robbins, *The Theory of Economic Policy, passim.*
89. Pigou, *Memorials of Alfred Marshall*, p. 156.
90. Haney, p. 429. 91. Haney, p. 431. 92. Haney, p. 432.

CHAPTER THREE

1. Henry Sidgwick, *The Methods of Ethics*, 1st ed. (1874), Preface, p. v.
2. *The Methods of Ethics*, p. 65. 3. *Henry Sidgwick*, p. 472.
4. *Ibid.*, pp. 472-473.
5. Ernst Cassirer, *The Problem of Knowledge*, pp. 153 ff; see also R. G. Collingwood, *The Idea of History*, p. 129.
6. Henry Sidgwick, *Lectures on the Philosophy of Kant and Other Philosophical Lectures and Essays*, p. 416.
7. Henry Sidgwick, *Philosophy, Its Scope and Relations*, pp. 42-43.
8. These biographical notes are from Dugald Stewart, "Account of the Life and Writings of Thomas Reid, D.D., F.R.S.E.," Introduction to Sir William Hamilton's edition of Reid's Works: *The Philosophical Works of Thomas Reid*, hereafter cited as Reid, *Works.*
9. Reid, *Works*, I, 7. 10. *Ibid.*, I, 100 ff. 11. *Ibid.*, I, 102.
12. *Ibid.*, I, 184-185. 13. *Ibid.*, I, 102.
14. Stewart, Introduction to Reid, *Works*, I, 17.
15. J. B. Bury, *The Idea of Progress*, p. 278; see also Carl L. Becker, *The Heavenly City of the Eighteenth Century Philosophers*, p. 48.
16. David Easton, *The Political System*, p. 13.
17. G. P. Gooch, *History and Historians in the Nineteenth Century*, p. 13.
18. *Philosophy, Its Scope and Relations*, p. 123.
19. D. C. Somerville, *English Thought in the Nineteenth Century*, p. 125.
20. Collingwood, p. 128. 21. Cassirer, p. 243.
22. Helen Merrell Lynd, *England in the Eighteen-Eighties*, p. 82.
23. *The Positive Philosophy of Auguste Comte*, pp. 25-30.
24. *Ibid.*, pp. 339 ff.
25. See especially Ernest Albee, *A History of English Utilitarianism*, Chapters 13, 14, 15; Sir Ernest Barker, *Political Thought in England, 1848-1914*, Chapter 4; Crane Brinton, *English Political Thought in the Nineteenth Century*, Chapter 4; and Harald Höffding, *A History of Modern Philosophy*, II, 452 ff.
26. Barker, pp. 73-74. 27. Herbert Spencer, *First Principles*, p. 359.
28. Barker, p. 77. 29. Brinton, p. 274.
30. A number of essays preceded Sidgwick's general lectures on metaphysics and philosophical fundamentals included in *The Philosophy of Kant* and *Philosophy, Its Scope and Relations*. These early essays indicate no basic change in Sidgwick's attitude toward positivism from the beginning. The most noteworthy were: "The Theory of Evolution in its Application to Practice," *Mind*, I (1876), 52-67; "On Historical Psychology," *The Nineteenth Century*, VII (February, 1880), 353-360; and "The Historical Method," *Mind*, XI (1886), 203-219.
31. *Philosophy, Its Scope and Relations*, pp. 126-127.
32. *Ibid.*, p. 143. 33. *Ibid.*, p. 144. 34. *Ibid.*, p. 146.
35. *Ibid.*, p. 147. 36. *Ibid.*, p. 149. 37. *Ibid.*, p. 150.

38. Henry Sidgwick, *Miscellaneous Essays and Addresses*, p. 420.
39. *Philosophy, Its Scope and Relations*, p. 151.
40. *Ibid.*, p. 166.   41. *Ibid.*, p. 163.   42. *Ibid.*, p. 167.
43. *Ibid.*, pp. 176-177.   44. *Ibid.*, p. 185.   45. *Ibid.*, p. 189.
46. *Ibid.*, p. 193.   47. *Ibid.*, p. 218.   48. *Ibid.*, p. 220.
49. *Ibid.*, p. 228.   50. *Ibid.*
51. Eric Voegelin, "The Origins of Scientism," *Social Research*, XV (December, 1948), 488.
52. Barker, pp. 6-7.
53. Thomas Hill Green, *Prolegomena to Ethics*, pp. 75 ff.
54. Robert Magill, *Der rationale Utilitarismus Sidgwicks oder seine Vereinigung des Intuitionismus und des Utilitarismus*, p. 73.
55. Collingwood, p. 125.
56. John Stuart Mill, *A System of Logic*, pp. 597 ff.
57. John Stuart Mill, *Auguste Comte and Positivism*, pp. 76, 77, 79.
58. In *Utilitarianism* Mill actually praises the religion of humanity as a generator of obligation to promote the general happiness, even though he indicates his objection to the political and moral aspects of the later Comtian development. See, J. S. Mill, *Utilitarianism*, reprinted in Plamenatz, p. 196.
59. See especially Henry Sidgwick, "Incoherence of Empirical Philosophy," *Mind*, III (October, 1894), reprinted in *The Philosophy of Kant*, pp. 372-391.

CHAPTER FOUR

1. *The Methods of Ethics*, p. xv.   2. *Ibid.*, p. 32.
3. See C. D. Broad, *Ethical Theory*, pp. 145-146.
4. *Methods of Ethics*, p. 34.   5. *Ibid.*, p. 40.
6. *Ibid.*, p. 35.   7. *Ibid.*, p. 9; also p. 78.
8. *Ibid.*, Book I, Chapter 6. Sidgwick discusses egoism, intuitionism, and utilitarianism in that order. Broad's criticism to the effect that the two varieties of hedonism belong together is accepted as valid, and the present work follows his organization rather than Sidgwick's.
9. Sidgwick denies the validity of other forms of egoism, such as "self-realization," on the grounds of indefiniteness. *Ibid.*, p. 91.
10. *Ibid.*, Book III. The citation is to the main discussion. The general problem is outlined in Book I, Chapter 8.
11. *Ibid.*, p. 98.   12. Broad, *Ethical Theory*, p. 216.
13. *Methods of Ethics*, p. 379.   14. *Ibid.*, p. 127.
15. *Ibid.* The main sections on egoistic hedonism are in Book I, Chapter 7, and in Book II; on universal ethical hedonism, Book IV.
16. *Ibid.*, p. 411.   17. *Ibid.*, p. xix.
18. Broad, *Ethical Theory*, p. 159.
19. "Desirable" is used here, as it is always used by Sidgwick, in the sense of "worthy of being desired," rather than in the psychological meaning of "actually desired." John Stuart Mill frequently equates the psychological fact that an object is desired with the ethical conclusion that it is desirable. See *Utilitarianism; Methods of Ethics*, Book I, Chapter 4.
20. Emphasis on this means of reconciling interest and duty is important in John Stuart Mill; cf., *Utilitarianism*, pp. 195 ff.
21. *Methods of Ethics*, p. 423.   22. *Ibid.*, p. xxi.   23. *Ibid.*, pp. xix, 86.
24. *Outlines of the History of Ethics for English Readers*, p. 173.
25. *Methods of Ethics*, p. 96.   26. *Ibid.*, p. 422.   27. *Ibid.*, p. 427.

28. *Ibid.*, p. 438.   29. *Ibid.*, p. 461.   30. *Ibid.*, p. xx.
31. Broad, *Ethical Theory*, p. 157.
32. Robert Magill, *Der rationale Utilitarismus Sidgwicks*, p. 67.
33. *Henry Sidgwick*, p. 158.   34. *Methods of Ethics*, pp. xvii-xix.
35. *Henry Sidgwick*, pp. 506-507. 36. *Methods of Ethics*, p. xix.
37. *Philosophy, Its Scope and Relations*, p. 47.
38. Thomas Babington Macaulay, "Mill's Essay on Government," *Edinburgh Review*, XLIV (March, 1829), pp. 159 ff.
39. Henry Sidgwick, "Bentham and Benthamism in Politics and Ethics," *Miscellaneous Essays and Addresses*, p. 145.
40. For the main source of this analysis see F. S. C. Northrup, *The Logic of the Sciences and the Humanities*, pp. 255 ff.
41. Professor A. D. Lindsay, in *The Modern Democratic State*, I, 84, points out what has been emphasized here; that is, that Hobbes' invention of the man of self-interest actually constitutes a denial of the independent existence of ethics.   42. "Bentham and Benthamism," p. 163.
43. *Ibid.*, p. 151.   44. *Ibid.*, p. 164.

CHAPTER FIVE

1. A. V. Dicey, *Law and Opinion in England*, p. 125.
2. *Ibid.*, p. 146; Dicey's italics.
3. See, e.g., Eric Roll, *Economic Thought*, Chapter 4; and D. H. MacGregor, *Economic Thought and Policy*, Chapter 3.
4. Dicey, *Law and Opinion*, p. 126.   5. *Ibid.*, p. 177.
6. *Ibid.*, pp. 179-180.   7. *Ibid.*, pp. 303 ff.
8. See John Duffy, "Early Factory Legislation: A Neglected Aspect of British Humanitarianism," in *British Humanitarianism*, ed. by Samuel Clyde McCulloch, p. 70; and Guido de Ruggiero, *The History of European Liberalism*, p. 48.
9. Dicey, *Law and Opinion*, p. 217.
10. *Ibid.*, pp. 219 ff.   11. *Ibid.*, p. 260.
12. Harry K. Girvetz, *From Wealth to Welfare*, pp. 146-147.
13. Guido de Ruggiero, "Liberalism," *Encyclopaedia of the Social Sciences*, IX, 437.
14. Dicey, *Law and Opinion*, p. 39.
15. Henry Sidgwick, *The Principles of Political Economy*, p. 499.
16. Sidgwick, *Methods of Ethics*, p. 274.
17. *Ibid.*, pp. 288-289.   18. *Ibid.*, p. 275.
19. *Ibid.*, p. 276.   20. *Ibid.*, p. 294.   21. *Ibid.*, p. 278.
22. Sidgwick, *The Elements of Politics*, p. 44.
23. *The Principles of Political Economy*, 1st ed. (1883), p. 1. The quotation is from the first edition for convenience in dating; in both subsequent editions the wording remained the same except for a change in time in the second sentence. Other references to the *Political Economy* in this chapter are to the third edition unless otherwise noted.
24. *Political Economy*, p. 6.   25. Dicey, *Law and Opinion*, p. 182.
26. Robbins, p. 5.   27. Robbins, p. 46.   28. Robbins, p. 47.
29. Roll, *Economic Thought*, p. 144.
30. *Ibid.*, p. 300.   31. *Ibid.*, p. 301.   32. *Ibid.*
33. *Political Economy*, p. 13.
34. *Ibid.*, p. 14   35. *Ibid.*, p. 15.   36. *Ibid.*, p. 19.

37. *Ibid.*, p. 18.   38. *Ibid.*, p. 19.   39. *Ibid.*
40. Quoted in Helen Merrell Lynd, *England in the Eighteen-Eighties*, p. 69.
41. *Political Economy*, p. 23.   42. *Ibid.*, pp. 35-36.
43. *Ibid.*, p. 36.   44. *Ibid.*, p. 40.   45. *Ibid.*, p. 41.
46. *Ibid.*, p. 46.   47. *Ibid.*, p. 51.   48. *Ibid.*, pp. 51-52.
49. John Maynard Keynes, *The End of Laissez-Faire*, pp. 32-33.
50. *Elements of Politics*, pp. 144-145.
51. *Ibid.*, p. 136.   52. *Ibid.*, p. 137.   53. *Political Economy*, p. 581.
54. *Ibid.*, pp. 402 ff.   55. *Ibid.*, p. 515.   56. *Ibid.*, pp. 419 ff.
57. *Ibid.* The full quotation is from the first edition, p. 503; in later additions it was shortened, but the substance of the argument remained the same. See 3rd ed., pp. 499 ff.
58. *Ibid.*, pp. 475 ff.   59. *Ibid.*, p. 519.
60. The repeated use of Sidgwick as an example of the adamant liberal opponent of land nationalization may be traced to George Bernard Shaw. See E. R. Pease, *History of the Fabian Society*, Appendix I (by Shaw), pp. 273-274.   61. *Political Economy*, p. 511.
62. *Elements of Politics*, p. 147. Italics supplied.
63. *Political Economy*, pp. 464 ff.
64. *Ibid.*, pp. 434-435, 579-580.
65. *Ibid.*, pp. 417-418.   66. *Ibid.*, p. 529.

CHAPTER SIX

1. Roberto Michels, "Conservatism," *Encyclopaedia of the Social Sciences*, IV, 230.
2. *Ibid.*   3. Francis Graham Wilson, *The Case for Conservatism*, p. 12.
4. Henry Sidgwick, *The Development of European Polity*, pp. 4-5.
5. See *Henry Sidgwick, a Memoir*, pp. 140, 170, 179; see also *European Polity*, editor's preface, p. v.
6. *Henry Sidgwick, a Memoir*, pp. 436-437.
7. *European Polity*, p. 26.   8. *Ibid.*, p. 235.   9. *Ibid.*, p. 223.
10. The terms "open" and "closed" are used here in the sense in which they were used by Henri Bergson, *Two Sources of Morality and Religion;* an "open society" being one whose moral and religious "essence" stresses the commonality of all humanity and is not restricted to more parochial forms of social organization in which the members of a given local society are "closed" against other groups in the sense that outside groups are not regarded as participating in the substance of the particular community and so no moral obligation is felt toward them.
11. *European Polity*, p. 439; see also Sidgwick, *Elements of Politics*, Chapter 26.
12. *European Polity*, p. 210.   13. *Ibid.*, p. 346.
14. *Ibid.*, p. 21.   15. *Ibid.*, p. 5.   16. *Ibid.*, p. 372.
17. *Ibid.*, p. 377   18. *Ibid.*, p. 390.   19. *Ibid.*, p. 294.
20. Edmund Burke, *Reflections on the French Revolution*, p. 58.
21. Sidgwick, *Methods of Ethics*, p. 501.   22. *Ibid.*, p. 16.
23. W. R. Sorley, *A History of English Philosophy*, p. 281.
24. F. H. Hayward, *The Ethical Philosophy of Sidgwick*, p. 267.
25. *Methods of Ethics*, pp. 507-508.   26. *Ibid.*, p. 508.
27. *Elements of Politics*, p. 46.   28. *Ibid.*, p. 47.   29. *Ibid.*, p. 46.
30. See the distinction, based on Michels, between these forms of conservatism in the introduction to this chapter.

31. Rudolf Metz, *A Hundred Years of British Philosophy*, p. 89.
32. Burke, *French Revolution*, pp. 19-20.

CHAPTER SEVEN

1. Max Lerner, Introduction to Aristotle, *Politics*, p. 29.
2. D. G. Ritchie, Review of "Sidgwick's 'Elements of Politics,'" *International Journal of Ethics*, II (1891), 256.
3. Sidgwick, *European Polity*, Editor's Preface, p. v.
4. Ritchie, p. 255.   5. *Ibid.*   6. *Ibid.*
7. James Bryce, *The American Commonwealth*, p. viii.
8. John Stuart Mill, *Representative Government*, p. 11.
9. Sidgwick, *Elements of Politics*, p. 556; cf. Mill, *Representative Government*, p. 96.
10. *Elements of Politics*, pp. 609, 615.
11. *Ibid.*, p. 616.   12. *Ibid.*, p. 612.   13. *Ibid.*, pp. 618-619.
14. *Ibid.*, p. 608.   15. *Ibid.*, pp. 617-618.   16. *Ibid.*, pp. 559-560.
17. John Austin, *Lectures on Jurisprudence*, pp. 220 ff.
18. J. S. Mill, *Representative Government*, p. 35.
19. *Elements of Politics*, pp. 629-631.
20. *Ibid.*, p. 634.   21. Ritchie, p. 257.
22. Albert Venn Dicey, *The Law of the Constitution*, Chapter 1.
23. *Elements of Politics*, p. 658.
24. Although concerned only with the American aspect, Austin Ranney, "The Reception of Political Parties into American Political Science," *Southwestern Social Science Quarterly*, XXXII (December, 1951), 183-191, gives a general insight into the slowness of this development. It should be remembered that Ostrogorski did not complete his great study until 1902.
25. *Elements of Politics*, p. 591.   26. *Ibid.*, p. 596.   27. *Ibid.*, p. 598.
28. *Ibid.*, p. 603.   29. *Ibid.*, p. 576.   30. *Ibid.*, pp. 580-582.
31. *Ibid.*, p. 584.   32. *Ibid.*, p. 366.   33. *Ibid.*, pp. 383-394.
34. *Ibid.*, pp. 394-400; cf. Mill, *Representative Government*, Chapter 8.
35. *Elements of Politics*, p. 371.
36. *Ibid.*, pp. 368 ff.; see also Mill, *Representative Government*, pp. 39 ff.
37. *Elements of Politics*, p. 368 n.   38. *Ibid.*, pp. 406-407.
39. *Ibid.*, Chapter 23.   40. *Ibid.*, Chapter 21.   41. *Ibid.*, Chapter 24.
42. *Ibid.*, p. 483.   43. *Ibid.*, p. 343.   44. *Ibid.*, pp. 483-484.
45. *Ibid.*, p. 455.   46. *Ibid.*, p. 456.   47. *Ibid.*, pp. 444-446.

CHAPTER EIGHT

1. Alan Willard Brown, *The Metaphysical Society*, p. 299.
2. Martin's comments appear on pp. 74-91.
3. As Plamenatz notes, "Whether the utilitarian theory is true or false, it is at least plausible." John Plamenatz, *The English Utilitarians*, p. 1.
4. F. H. Hayward, *The Ethical Philosophy of Sidgwick*, p. 10.

Bibliography

BOOks

ALBEE, Ernest, A History of English Utilitarianism. London: Swan Sonnen-schein & Co., Ltd., 1902.

ARISTOTLE. Politics. ("The Modern Library," No. 228.) Introduction by Max Lerner. New York: Random House, Inc., 1943.

ARNOLD, Matthew, Culture and Anarchy. ("Modern Readers' Series.") New York: The Macmillan Co., 1925.

AUSTIN, John. Lectures on Jurisprudence (5th ed.). 2 vols. London: John Murray, 1885.

BARKER, Sir Ernest. Political Thought in England, 1848-1914 (2nd ed.). ("Home University Library.") London: Oxford University Press, 1947.

BECKER, Carl L. The Heavenly City of the Eighteenth Century Philosophers. New Haven: Yale University Press, 1932.

BENTHAM, Jeremy. A Fragment on Government and An Introduction to the Principles of Morals and Legislation. Introduction by Wilfred Harrison. Oxford: Basil Blackwell, 1948.

BERGSON, Henri. The Two Sources of Morality and Religion. Translated by R. A. Audra and C. Brereton. Garden City, N. Y.: Doubleday Anchor Books, 1954.

BRADLEY, F. H. Collected Essays. 2 vols. Oxford: Clarendon Press, 1935.

BRIGGS, Asa. Victorian People. London: Odhams Press, 1954.

BRINTON, Crane. English Political Thought in the Nineteenth Century. London: E. Benn, Ltd., 1933.

BROAD, C. D. Five Types of Ethical Theory. London: Kegan Paul, Trench, Trubner & Co., Ltd., 1930.

————. Religion, Philosophy and Psychical Research. London: Routledge & Kegan Paul, Ltd., 1953.

181

Bibliography

BROOKFIELD, Frances M. *The Cambridge Apostles.* New York: Charles Scribner's Sons, 1906.

BROWN, Alan Willard. *The Metaphysical Society.* New York: Columbia University Press, 1947.

BRYCE, James. *The American Commonwealth* (2nd ed.). 2 vols. London: Macmillan & Co., Ltd., 1891.

————. *Studies in Contemporary Biography.* London: Macmillan & Co., Ltd., 1903.

BURKE, Edmund. *Reflections on the French Revolution.* ("Everyman's Library.") London: J. M. Dent & Sons, Ltd., 1910.

————. *Speech on Conciliation with the American Colonies.* New York: American Book Co., 1895.

BURY, J. B. *The Idea of Progress.* London: Macmillan & Co., Ltd., 1928.

CASSIRER, Ernst. *The Problem of Knowledge.* Translated by William H. Woglom and Charles W. Hendel. New Haven: Yale University Press, 1950.

COLLINGWOOD, R. G. *The Idea of History.* London: Oxford University Press, 1946.

COMTE, Auguste. *The Positive Philosophy of Auguste Comte.* Translated and edited by Harriet Martineau. Chicago: Bedford, Clark and Co., n.d.

DICEY, Albert Venn. *Law and Opinion in England* (2nd ed.). London: Macmillan & Co., Ltd., 1914.

————. *The Law of the Constitution* (9th ed.). London: Macmillan & Co., Ltd., 1948.

DICKINSON, G. Lowes. *A Modern Symposium.* London: George Allen & Unwin, Ltd., 1905.

EASTON, David. *The Political System.* New York: Alfred A. Knopf, 1953.

FISHER, H. A. L. *Frederic William Maitland.* Cambridge: Cambridge University Press, 1910.

————. *James Bryce.* 2 vols. London: Macmillan & Co., Ltd., 1927.

GIRVETZ, Harry K. *From Wealth to Welfare.* Stanford, Calif.: Stanford University Press, 1950.

GOOCH, G. P. *History and Historians in the Nineteenth Century* (2nd ed.). London: Longmans, Green & Co., 1952.

GREEN, Thomas Hill. *Prolegomena to Ethics* (5th ed.). Oxford: Clarendon Press, 1906.

HALÉVY, Elie. *The Growth of Philosophic Radicalism.* Translated by Mary Morris. London: Faber & Faber, Ltd., 1928.

HANEY, Lewis H. *History of Economic Thought* (rev. ed.). New York: The Macmillan Co., 1933.

HAYWARD, F. H. *The Ethical Philosophy of Sidgwick.* London: Swan Sonnenschein & Co., Ltd., 1901.

HOBBES, Thomas. *Leviathan.* Introduction by Michael Oakeshott. Oxford: Basil Blackwell, n.d.

HOBHOUSE, L. T. *Liberalism.* ("Home University Library.") London: Oxford University Press, 1911.

HÖFFDING, Harald. *A History of Modern Philosophy.* 2 vols. Translated by B. E. Myer. London: Macmillan & Co., Ltd., 1900.

KEYNES, John Maynard. *The End of Laissez-Faire.* London: The Hogarth Press, 1926.

LASKI, Harold J. *The Rise of European Liberalism.* London: George Allen & Unwin, Ltd., 1936.

Bibliography

LINDSAY, A. D. *The Modern Democratic State*. London: Oxford University Press, 1943.

LYND, Helen Merrell. *England in the Eighteen-Eighties*. New York: Oxford University Press, 1945.

MCCULLOCH, Samuel Clyde (ed.). *British Humanitarianism*. Philadelphia: The Church Historical Society, 1950.

MACGREGOR, D. H. *Economic Thought and Policy*. ("Home University Library.") London: Oxford University Press, 1949.

MAGILL, Robert. *Der rationale Utilitarismus Sidgwicks oder seine Vereiningung des Intuitionismus und des Utilitarismus*. Jena: Druck Von Ant. Kämpfe, 1899.

MAINE, Henry Sumner. *Ancient Law* (3rd American, from 5th London ed.). New York: Henry Holt & Co., n.d.

————. *Popular Government*. London: John Murray, 1885.

METZ, Rudolf. *A Hundred Years of British Philosophy*. Translated by J. N. Harvey, T. E. Jessop, and Henry Sturt. New York: The Macmillan Co., 1938.

MILL, James. *An Essay on Government*. Cambridge: Cambridge University Press, 1937.

MILL, John Stuart. *Auguste Comte and Positivism* (5th ed.). London: Kegan Paul, Trench, Trubner & Co., Ltd., 1907.

————. *Autobiography*. New York: Columbia University Press, 1924.

————. *Dissertations and Discussions* (3rd ed.). 4 vols. London: Longmans, Green, Reader & Dyer, 1875.

————. *Principles of Political Economy* (People's ed.). London: Longmans, Green, Reader & Dyer, 1871.

————. *Representative Government* (People's ed.). London: Longmans, Green & Co., 1886.

————. *A System of Logic* (8th ed.). London: Longmans, Green & Co., 1947.

MOORE, G. E. *Principia Ethica*. Cambridge: Cambridge University Press, 1903.

MORLEY, John. *Edmund Burke*. New York: Harper and Brothers, n.d.

MUIRHEAD, John H. *The Platonic Tradition in Anglo-Saxon Philosophy*. New York: The Macmillan Co., 1931.

NORTHROP, F. S. C. *The Logic of the Sciences and the Humanities*. New York: The Macmillan Co., 1948.

PEASE, E. R. *History of the Fabian Society* (2nd ed.). London: Fabian Society and George Allen & Unwin, Ltd., 1925.

PIGOU, A. C. (ed.). *Memorials of Alfred Marshall*. London: Macmillan & Co., Ltd., 1925.

PLAMENATZ, John. *The English Utilitarians* (with a reprint of John Stuart Mill, *Utilitarianism*). Oxford: Basil Blackwell, 1949.

Proceedings of the Society for Psychical Research. 15 vols. London: Trubner & Co., 1882-1889; Kegan Paul, Trench, Trubner & Co., Ltd., 1890-1900.

RAIT, Robert S. (ed.). *Memorials of Albert Venn Dicey*. London: Macmillan & Co., Ltd., 1925.

REID, Thomas. *The Philosophical Works of Thomas Reid* (8th ed.). Edited by Sir William Hamilton. Introduction by Dugald Stewart. Edinburgh: James Thin, 1895.

ROBBINS, Lionel. *The Theory of Economic Policy*. London: Macmillan & Co., Ltd., 1952.

Bibliography

ROLL, Eric. *A History of Economic Thought* (3rd ed.). London: Faber & Faber, Ltd., 1954.

RUGGIERO, Guido de. *The History of European Liberalism.* Translated by R. G. Collingwood. London: Oxford University Press, 1927.

SEELEY, J. R. *Introduction to Political Science.* London: Macmillan & Co., Ltd., 1896.

SIDGWICK, Arthur, and Sidgwick, Eleanor Mildred. *Henry Sidgwick, a Memoir.* London: Macmillan & Co., Ltd., 1906.

SIDGWICK, Ethel. *Mrs. Henry Sidgwick, a Memoir by her Niece.* London: Sidgwick & Jackson, Ltd., 1938.

SIDGWICK, Henry. *The Development of European Polity* (3rd ed.). London: Macmillan & Co., Ltd., 1920.

————. *The Elements of Politics* (2nd ed.). London: Macmillan & Co., Ltd., 1897.

————. *Lectures on the Ethics of T. H. Green, H. Spencer and J. Martineau.* London: Macmillan & Co., Ltd., 1902.

————. *Lectures on the Philosophy of Kant and other Philosophical Lectures and Essays.* London: Macmillan & Co., Ltd., 1902.

————. *The Methods of Ethics* (7th ed.). London: Macmillan & Co., Ltd., 1907.

————. *Miscellaneous Essays and Addresses.* London: Macmillan & Co., Ltd., 1904.

————. *Outlines of the History of Ethics for English Readers* (2nd ed.). London: Macmillan & Co., Ltd., 1888.

————. *Philosophy, Its Scope and Relations.* London: Macmillan & Co., Ltd., 1902.

————. *Practical Ethics: A Collection of Addresses and Essays.* London: Swan Sonnenschein & Co., 1898.

————. *The Principles of Political Economy* (3rd ed.). London: Macmillan & Co., Ltd., 1924.

SMELLIE, K. B. *A Hundred Years of English Government* (2nd ed.). London: Gerald Duckworth & Co., Ltd., 1950.

SMITH, N. Kemp. *The Philosophy of David Hume.* London: Macmillan & Co., Ltd., 1941.

SOMERVILLE, D. C. *English Thought in the Nineteenth Century* (5th ed.). London: Methuen & Co., Ltd., 1947.

SORLEY, W. R. *A History of English Philosophy.* Cambridge: Cambridge University Press, 1920.

SPENCER, Herbert. *First Principles* ("Thinker's Library.") London: Watts & Co., 1937.

STEPHEN, Leslie. *The English Utilitarians.* 3 vols. London School of Economics Reprint, 1950.

TREVELYAN, G. M. *British History in the Nineteenth Century and After* (2nd ed.). London: Longmans, Green & Co., 1947.

WILLEY, Basil. *The Eighteenth Century Background.* London: Chatto & Windus, 1940.

————. *Nineteenth Century Studies: Coleridge to Matthew Arnold.* New York: Columbia University Press, 1949.

WILSON, Francis Graham. *The Case for Conservatism.* Seattle: University of Washington Press, 1951.

WINSTANLEY, D. A. *Early Victorian Cambridge.* Cambridge: Cambridge University Press, 1940.

Bibliography

WINSTANLEY, D. A. *Later Victorian Cambridge.* Cambridge: Cambridge University Press, 1947.

YOUNG, G. M. (ed.). *Early Victorian England.* 2 vols. London: Oxford University Press, 1934.

ARTICLES

MACAULAY, Thomas Babington. "Mill's Essay on Government," *Edinburgh Review,* XLIV (March, 1829), 159-189.

MICHELS, Roberto. "Conservatism," *Encyclopaedia of the Social Sciences,* IV, 230-232.

RANNEY, Austin. "The Reception of Political Parties into American Political Science," *The Southwestern Social Science Quarterly,* XXXII (December, 1951), 183-191.

RITCHIE, D. G. Review of "Sidgwick's 'Elements of Politics,'" *International Journal of Ethics,* II (1891), 254-257.

RUGGIERO, Guido de. "Liberalism," *Encyclopaedia of the Social Sciences,* IX, 435-441.

STARK, W. "Bentham as an Economist," *Economic Journal,* LVI (1946), 583-608.

————. "Liberty and Equality or: Jeremy Bentham as an Economist," *Economic Journal,* LI (1941), 56-79.

VOEGELIN, Eric. "The Origins of Scientism," *Social Research,* XV (December, 1948), 462-494.

The following article bibliography does not contain a definitive list of Sidgwick's periodical writings. It includes only those items which are of importance to the present work; and, in addition, it omits articles reprinted in the various collections listed in the book bibliography. A complete periodical list may be found in Appendix II to *Henry Sidgwick, a Memoir.*

SIDGWICK, Henry. "Barzelotti's La Morale nella Filosofia Positiva,"*Academy,* July 1, 1872.

————. "Beale's Life Theories and Their Influence on Religious Thought," *Academy,* October 15, 1871.

————. "Bikker's and Hatton's Ethics for Undenominational Schools," *Athenaeum,* July 27, 1872.

————. "Bluntschli's Theory of the State," *English Historical Review,* April, 1886.

————. "Bradley's Ethical Studies," *Mind,* I (1876).

————. "Conjectures on the Constitutional History of Athens," *Classical Review,* October, 1894.

————. "A Criticism of the Critical Philosophy" (in two parts), *Mind,* VIII (1883).

————. "Critique of Professor Fraser's Edition of Berkeley," *Athenaeum,* June 17 and 24, 1871.

————. "D. G. Ritchie's Natural Rights," *Mind,* IV, N.S. (1895).

————. "Dr. Bree's Exposition of Fallacies in the Hypothesis of Mr. Darwin," *Athenaeum,* July 20, 1872.

————. "Dr. Martineau's Defence of Types of Ethical Theory," *Mind,* XI (1886).

185

Bibliography

Sɪᴅɢᴡɪᴄᴋ, Henry. "Dr. Tuke's Effect of the Mind upon the Body," *Athenaeum*, July 12, 1873.

———. "Economic Method," *Fortnightly Review*, February, 1879.

———. "The Establishment of Ethical First Principles," *Mind*, IV (1879).

———. "The Feeling-Tone of Desire and Aversion," *Mind*, I, N.S. (1892).

———. "Fouillée's L'Idée Moderne du Droit en Allemagne, en Angleterre et en France," *Mind*, V (1880).

———. "Fowler's Progressive Morality," *Mind*, X (1885).

———. "G. H. Lewes' History of Philosophy," *Academy*, November 15, 1871.

———. "Green and Grose's Edition of Hume's Essays," *Academy*, August 7, 1875.

———. "Green and Grose's Edition of Hume's Treatise," *Academy*, May 30, 1875.

———. "Green and Grose's Hume," *Spectator*, March 27, 1875.

———. "Green's Ethics," *Mind*, IX (1884).

———. "Guyau's La Morale d'Epicure et ses Rapports avec les Doctrines Contemporaines," *Mind*, IV (1879).

———. "Hedonism and Ultimate Good," *Mind*, II (1877).

———. "The Historical Method," *Mind*, XI (1886).

———. "H. Spencer's Justice," *Mind*, I, N.S. (1892).

———. "Hutton's Essays, Theological and Literary," *Academy*, July 1, 1871.

———. "Idiopsychological Ethics," *Mind*, XII (1887).

———. "J. Grote's Examination of the Utilitarian Philosophy," *Academy*, April 1, 1871.

———. "J. Grote's Examination of the Utilitarian Philosophy," *Cambridge University Reporter*, February 8, 1871.

———. "J. Grote's Treatise on Moral Ideals," *Mind*, II (1877).

———. "J. F. Stephen's Liberty, Equality, Fraternity," *Academy*, August 1, 1873.

———. "J. Martineau's Types of Ethical Theories," *Mind*, X (1885).

———. "Jodl's Leben und Philosophie David Humes," *Academy*, October 15, 1872.

———. "John Stuart Mill," *Academy*, May 15, 1873.

———. "Kant's Refutation of Idealism," *Mind*, V (1880).

———. "Leifchild's Higher Ministry of Nature Viewed in the Light of Modern Science," *Athenaeum*, April 6, 1872.

———. "Liberal Education," *Macmillan's Magazine*, April, 1867.

———. "L. Stephen's The Science of Ethics," *Mind*, VII (1882).

———. "Maguire's Essays on the Platonic Ethics," *Academy*, September 15, 1871.

———. "Maguire's Essays on the Platonic Ethics," *Cambridge University Reporter*, March, 1871.

———. "Mahaffy's Kant's Critical Philosophy for English Readers," *Academy*, September 15, 1872.

———. "Mansel's Letters, Lectures, and Reviews," *Academy*, July 15, 1873.

———. "Miss Cobbe's Darwinism in Morals and Other Essays," *Academy*, June 15, 1872.

———. "Mr. Spencer's Ethical System," *Mind*, V (1880).

———. "Note in Reply to Dr. Bree's Vindication of his Book," *Athenaeum*, August 3, 1872.

———. "On the Fundamental Doctrines of Descartes," *Mind*, VII (1882).

Bibliography

———. "On a Passage in Plato's Republic," *Journal of Philology*, V, No. 10 (1874).

———. "On Historical Psychology," *Nineteenth Century*, February, 1880.

———. "Philosophy at Cambridge," *Mind*, I (1876).

———. "Plato's Utilitarianism: A Dialogue by John Grote and Henry Sidgwick," *Classical Review*, March, 1889.

———. "Pleasure and Desire," *Contemporary Review*, April, 1872.

———. "Professor Cairne's Political Essays," *Spectator*, November 8, 1873.

———. "Professor Calderwood on Intuitionism in Morals," *Mind*, I (1876).

———. "Prof. Gidding's Elements of Sociology," *Economic Journal*, September, 1899.

———. "Prof. Gidding's Principles of Sociology," *Economic Journal*, September, 1896.

———. "Pulszky's Theory of Law and Civil Society," *English Historical Review*, October, 1888.

———. "Ranke's History of England," *Macmillan's Magazine*, May 1, 1861.

———. "Rejoinder to Bradley's Reply to Notice of his Book," *Mind*, II (1877).

———. "Reply to Mr. Barrett on 'The Suppression of Egoism,'" *Mind*, II (1877).

———. "The So-Called Idealism of Kant," *Mind*, IV (1879).

———. "Some Fundamental Ethical Controversies," *Mind*, XIV (1889).

———. "Spencer's Principles of Psychology," *Academy*, April 1, 1873.

———. "Spencer's Principles of Psychology," *Spectator*, June 21, 1873.

———. "Spicker's Die Philosophie des Grafen von Shaftesbury," *Academy*, August 15, 1872.

———. "The Theory of Evolution in its Application to Practice," *Mind*, I (1876).

———. "Theory and Practice," *Mind*, IV, N.S. (1895).

———. "Verification of Beliefs," *Contemporary Review*, July, 1871.

———. "The Wages Fund Theory," *Fortnightly Review*, September, 1879.

———. "What is Money?" *Fortnightly Review*, April, 1879.

Index

189

Index